BECOMING AN

Unstoppable

WOMAN IN FAITH

EMBRACE FAITH, EMPOWER LIVES, INSPIRE CHANGE

Hanna Olivas & Nicole Curtis

WITH 19 INSPIRING WOMEN AUTHORS

TABLE OF CONTENTS

INTRODUCTION

Welcome to *"Becoming An Unstoppable Woman in Faith: Embrace Faith, Empower Lives, Inspire Change."* Within these pages, you will embark on a transformative journey that celebrates the profound strength and resilience of women who have harnessed their faith to navigate life's challenges and achieve their dreams.

This anthology is a vibrant mosaic of stories from women across various walks of life, each united by a common thread: their unwavering faith. Through personal triumphs, moments of deep reflection, and spiritual revelations, these narratives reveal how faith can serve as a beacon of light, guiding us through darkness and empowering us to live with purpose and passion.

Each chapter is a testament to the remarkable power of faith to overcome obstacles and catalyze change. These stories are not just about surviving; they are about thriving—about how faith transforms trials into triumphs and ordinary moments into extraordinary experiences. As you read, you'll find yourself inspired by the courage and conviction of these women, who show us that faith is not just a passive belief but an active force that shapes our lives and the world around us.

"Becoming An Unstoppable Woman in Faith" is more than a collection of inspiring stories; it is a call to action. It invites you to embrace your own faith, to seek strength in adversity, and to become a beacon of hope and transformation in your community. Whether you are looking for motivation, spiritual growth, or practical wisdom, this book is here to uplift and encourage you.

As you turn these pages, may you find renewed inspiration to walk boldly in your faith, empowered to make a difference and inspire change. Your journey toward becoming an unstoppable woman in faith begins now.

Hanna Olivas

Founder and CEO of She Rises Studios

https://www.linkedin.com/company/she-rises-studios/
https://www.facebook.com/sherisesstudios
https://www.instagram.com/sherisesstudios_llc/
www.SheRisesStudios.com

Author, Speaker, and Founder. Hanna was born and raised in Las Vegas, Nevada, and has paved her way to becoming one of the most influential women of 2022. Hanna is the co-founder of She Rises Studios and the founder of the Brave & Beautiful Blood Cancer Foundation. Her journey started in 2017 when she was first diagnosed with Multiple Myeloma, an incurable blood cancer. Now more than ever, her focus is to empower other women to become leaders because The Future is Female. She is currently traveling and speaking publicly to women to educate them on entrepreneurship, leadership, and owning the female power within.

Fall In Love With Faith

By Hanna Olivas

In a world filled with uncertainties, faith stands as the invisible thread that binds hope to reality. To me, faith means believing in things that I know are real, even when I cannot see them. It's about trusting the process and holding onto hope, love, trust, and perseverance. Faith has been a divine connection that has shaped my identity, especially during the hardest and darkest times. It's the assurance that, no matter what, things will work out. Through faith, I've learned the importance of surrender—acknowledging that I cannot control everything and sometimes, I must simply let go and trust the journey.

Throughout my life, I have faced countless tests of faith, whether through ongoing health challenges, family struggles, or my business endeavors. One of the most pivotal moments came during a time when I was trapped in a toxic and abusive relationship. After enduring physical and emotional abuse, I reached a breaking point and prayed fervently for God's help. The answer came swiftly, as if my prayer unlocked the path I needed to take. With only $40 to my name and my two youngest children by my side, I got into the car and drove through the night to another state, leaving that relationship behind forever. I never looked back, nor did I speak to him again. This was just one of many moments where my faith was tested, but it also marked a defining moment where faith shaped my decisions and ultimately saved me.

Faith has been the driving force behind my journey toward becoming an unstoppable woman. It is the source of hope that fuels my resilience, continuously whispering to me to keep going, even when the road is difficult. Without hope, there is nothing to strive for, and faith and hope are inseparable companions. Together, they have been my guiding light, helping me push forward in the face of adversity.

My faith journey has not been without its challenges, and there have been moments when doubt overwhelmed me. One of the most difficult times was when I was diagnosed with multiple myeloma; I couldn't help but ask, "Why me?" I faced similar doubts when I lost my baby boy and during the struggles in my marriage. In those moments, I questioned whether God truly loved me—if He did, why wouldn't He save me from these painful experiences? At those times, it was nearly impossible to see any good, and the weight of my circumstances felt unbearable. Yet, even though my faith was as small as a mustard seed, it moved mountains and carried me through those dark days, eventually leading me to where I am today. These experiences, though challenging, have molded my perspective on life, teaching me that even in the midst of doubt, faith has the power to bring about transformation.

Maintaining my faith during difficult times requires intentional practices and habits that keep me grounded. Daily prayer is essential, as I stay in constant communication with God, seeking guidance and strength. I also make it a point to surround myself with people who have stronger faith than I do, drawing inspiration and support from them. Being honest with myself about the challenges I'm facing is crucial, as is sharing my fears with others. Journaling daily about my mood, gratitude, health, and wellness helps me process my emotions and maintain perspective.

To create a peaceful environment, I often light candles around the house and listen to worship music, which calms my mind and allows me to think clearly. When I need to truly disconnect from the outside world, I immerse myself in worship music and find solace in reading my favorite scripture, Jeremiah 29:11. Early mornings are my sacred time for reflection, a time when I can deeply connect with my faith in the quiet hours before the world awakens.

Overcoming obstacles has consistently strengthened my faith and resilience. Each time, I've found that things worked out better than I could have ever imagined. Despite the fears that once seemed overwhelming, they never materialized in the ways I had dreaded. Instead, my faith proved true, guiding me through challenges and reinforcing my belief that, no matter how difficult the journey, there is always a way forward. Each experience has deepened my trust in the power of faith and built an unshakeable resilience within me.

Faith has played a pivotal role in my personal growth and development as a woman, instilling in me a profound sense of confidence. I am unafraid to speak openly about my faith and spirituality, and this confidence has empowered me to believe that anything is possible. Through my faith, I've been aligned with incredible people, opportunities, and experiences that have further shaped my journey. This unwavering belief has allowed me to embrace challenges and pursue my dreams with determination and courage.

Faith has also empowered me to take several bold steps in both my life and career, including the decision to open my nonprofit organization and launch the FENIX TV streaming platform. However, perhaps the most significant step I've taken was seeking help for my mental health, particularly for my anxiety. Learning to trust others and build meaningful relationships was a challenge, but my faith gave me the strength to move forward. Faith has a way of eliminating fear, as the two cannot coexist. This belief has been instrumental in helping me take these courageous steps and continue growing personally and professionally.

Balancing faith with the demands of everyday life and the pursuit of my goals requires intentionality. I dedicate time each day for devotion, gratitude, and prayer. Every morning, I start my day at 5 a.m. with what I call "My Holy Hour," a sacred time when I focus on these practices. I believe that faith, even as small as a mustard seed, can blossom into a garden of opportunities, but it requires daily nurturing, watering, and growth. By prioritizing this time each day, I ensure that my faith remains at the forefront, guiding me through the challenges and ambitions of life.

Faith has profoundly influenced my relationships with others, whether with family, friends, or within the broader community. It has shaped these relationships by teaching me the importance of growth, understanding, and authenticity. Through faith, I've learned the values of hope, love, kindness, and the power of being genuine. It has allowed me to embrace who I am without placing unrealistic expectations on myself or others. As a result, my connections with people have become more transparent and meaningful, built on a foundation of trust and mutual respect.

One of the most rewarding aspects of my faith has been the ability to guide and support my family in their own spiritual journeys. By nurturing my own faith, I was able to bring my youngest daughter to faith as well. She now actively participates in church, attends church camp, and frequently says, "Let's pray about it." This same influence has extended to my grandson, who once asked me to teach him how to pray. He often says, "Grandma, Jesus is good, the devil is bad, and we love Jesus." Witnessing how my faith has positively impacted the lives of my children and grandchildren has been incredibly fulfilling, and it reinforces the importance of leading by example.

Faith plays a crucial role in fostering a sense of community and connection with others. It often brings together like-minded individuals who believe in the power of the unseen and the possibilities that lie ahead. You find yourself either in a group of believers who uplift and inspire, or in a room with doubters who can drain your spirit. Choosing your environment is pivotal. As the saying goes, you can either pray or panic, but you cannot do both. To find the answers and support you need, you must have faith and align yourself with those who share that belief. This shared faith creates strong bonds and a deeper sense of community.

To other women seeking to become unstoppable in their own faith journeys, my advice is to take the biggest leap of faith you've ever imagined. Dive deeply into your spirituality, and trust the process, even when the path ahead is unclear. Do not let fear of the unknown hold you back; instead, embrace faith wholeheartedly. Faith is a beautiful, fearless, and peaceful force—it is the very thread that holds the world together. By trusting in your faith, you'll find the strength to overcome any obstacle and become truly unstoppable.

Looking ahead, I envision faith continuing to play a pivotal role in my future growth and empowerment by leading me into new levels of spiritual understanding and trust. As I enter what I consider "season 2" of my life, I recognize the importance of deepening my faith even further. This phase is about exploring more of what faith can offer and continuing to trust the process and the journey ahead. I believe that as I grow, so too will my faith, guiding me through new challenges and opportunities with greater wisdom and strength.

Cultivating an unstoppable faith requires intentional habits and practices that reinforce and deepen your spiritual connection. For me, daily prayer is foundational, as it keeps me grounded and focused. I also dedicate time to expressing gratitude and engaging in prayer together with others, which strengthens both my faith and my relationships. Journaling is another key habit; it allows me to reflect on my thoughts, emotions, and progress in my faith journey. Building deep connections with people who have even more faith than I do has been incredibly impactful, as their strength inspires and uplifts me. Finally, I regularly take time to reflect on where I was compared to where I am now, recognizing that almost everything I have achieved is a result of having faith.

The message I want readers to take away is that faith is both a powerful and transformative process. When you embrace faith, you'll be amazed at how it can change your life—how it can make everything look and feel different. Faith has the power to guide you through challenges, open doors to new opportunities, and empower you to become truly unstoppable. So take that leap, trust in the unseen, and watch as faith transforms your life in ways you never thought possible.

Nicole Curtis

She Rises Studios
Intl. Bestselling Author, Speaker, Crazy Chicken Lady

https://www.linkedin.com/in/nicole-curtis-sherisesstudios
https://www.facebook.com/nicolecurtiscrazychickenlady
https://www.instagram.com/nicolecurtiscrazychickenlady
https://www.sherisesstudios.com
https://www.facebook.com/groups/sherisesstudioscommunity

Nicole Curtis, an International Bestselling Author, Speaker, and self-proclaimed Crazy Chicken Lady, is a revered figure in women's leadership. With over 17 years of experience in personal growth and self-leadership development, Nicole is a sought-after expert who exudes a unique blend of personality and empowerment.

Nicole's mission is to empower women to embrace growth, elevate their lives, and expand their horizons in both personal and professional aspects. Through her engaging writing and compelling speeches, she resonates with women worldwide, encouraging them to unlock their natural leadership potential and navigate life and business authentically. With her guidance, women are inspired to step into their true selves, leading with confidence and purpose on their journey towards self-discovery and success.

Faith-Fueled Resilience:
Embrace, Endure, Empower

By Nicole Curtis

Hello, beautiful soul! I'm thrilled you've joined me on this journey toward becoming an Unstoppable Woman In Faith. Before diving into this chapter, I celebrate your decision to invest in yourself and embrace transformative knowledge. Today isn't just another day—it's an opportunity for a fresh start, a journey that promises personal empowerment and a profound impact on your life.

For years, I lived to please others, sacrificing my own happiness and identity. Every day felt like a struggle until one pivotal moment changed everything. Kneeling in my bedroom, tears streaming, I heard God's voice urging me:

"Stop living in the dirt, child. Get up! Take my sword and shield! I have never left you. Rise and fight for yourself, your life, and your future. You were made for more. Get up and slay your demons!"

From then on, I chose to rely on Him and embraced my inner power. I picked up His armor and haven't stopped since. Every day, I wake up as an Unstoppable Woman, empowered by spiritual faith and self-belief.

Are you ready to join me? Ready to rise, embrace your strength, and become the Unstoppable Woman In Faith you were meant to be?

This chapter testifies to the transformative power of faith—in God's unwavering presence and the resilience it ignites within oneself. Through personal anecdotes and reflections, I illuminate how these forces have shaped my journey, empowering me to overcome challenges and embrace life's uncertainties.

Faith has anchored me amidst stormy seas of doubt and adversity. It's more than belief; it's deep trust in God's guidance, sustaining and propelling me forward. It's given me the courage to confront fears, stand firm, and find meaning in chaos.

Faith isn't just external; it's an inner journey of self-discovery and empowerment. Growing in faith, I discovered inner resilience—a strength to face challenges with purpose and determination. It freed me from limitations, embraced my identity, and pursued my dreams boldly.

Through stories and reflections, I inspire others to journey—lean into God's promises and discover inner strength. Join me as we explore how faith transforms hardships into opportunities, doubts into certainty, and fear into action.

First, I dive into early challenges testing faith, sparking discovery—doubts, setbacks, questions of purpose and identity. These challenges shaped faith as dynamic, evolving through adversity.

Next, I explore moments deepening faith in God, intertwined with self-discovery—encounters in need, guidance in whispers, nudges, reassurances in uncertainty. Each wove faith, personal, transformative.

Then, faith in myself—cornerstone of empowerment—journey of self-belief, overcoming doubt, confronting fears, and discovering strengths Trust instincts, embrace gifts, and navigate with resilience.

Lastly, reflection on beliefs—impact, growth, resilience—insights on empowerment. Share strategies, reflections, and insights—guide through adversity, embrace uncertainty with faith and courage.

Together, inspire and empower—cultivate faith in God, intrinsic worth, and transformative belief in oneself.

Early Challenges and Discoveries

My faith journey began amidst significant challenges that tested my beliefs and resilience from an early age. Childhood trauma, uncertainty, and the weight of societal expectations shaped my path, leading me through turbulent waters where self-worth and peace seemed elusive.

As a child, I faced deep emotional challenges stemming from the trauma I endured. These experiences left me questioning my own worth and struggling to find peace and forgiveness. The pressure of societal expectations only added to my internal turmoil, creating a sense of inadequacy and uncertainty about my future.

In my teenage years, my family encountered a severe financial crisis that shook our stability to its core. Nights were filled with anxious prayers, desperately seeking solace and reassurance in God's promise of provision. These moments of uncertainty deepened my reliance on faith as a source of hope and perseverance. It was through these adversities that I began to understand the profound strength found in trusting God's guidance and provision.

One pivotal moment in my faith journey occurred during my late thirties, a period marked by intense personal struggle in both my career and personal life. Facing setbacks and uncertainty about the future, I turned to prayer and sought guidance from scripture.

During a particularly challenging week, overwhelmed with fear and doubt, I found a moment of quiet reflection. In that moment, a deep sense of peace washed over me—a reassuring presence that I recognized as God's comfort. It was then that I made a conscious decision to surrender my fears and uncertainties to God, trusting that He had a plan for my life, even if it was unclear to me at the time.

This experience marked a turning point, deepening my daily spiritual practices. Prayer, meditation on scripture, and fellowship with others of faith became integral to strengthening my personal relationship with God. It instilled in me a lasting sense of peace and resilience in the face of life's challenges.

These early challenges profoundly shaped my understanding of myself and my capabilities. Confronting deep-seated insecurities and doubts forced me to search for inner strength and resilience I didn't know I possessed. Growing up amidst childhood trauma and societal pressures, feelings of inadequacy and self-doubt often clouded my thoughts. Through prayer, introspection, and support from mentors and friends, I began to recognize my inherent resilience and determination.

A significant moment of self-discovery came when I chose to leave behind a corporate career and pursue entrepreneurship. Despite uncertainties and financial risks, I committed to a path aligned with my passions and aspirations. This decision deepened my trust in God's guidance and empowered me to navigate challenges with resilience and determination.

Leaving the stability of corporate life was daunting, considering financial risks and potential failure yet, I knew I needed to integrate my faith more fully into daily life and work. This shift represented more than a career change; it was a profound leap of faith, trusting that God would provide and guide me through uncertainties.

My entrepreneurial journey presented numerous obstacles that tested my resolve and faith. Each challenge became an opportunity to rely more deeply on God's guidance and discover new aspects of my strength and perseverance. Embracing uncertainties and risks inherent in entrepreneurship, I found purpose and fulfillment beyond my previous career.

This journey taught me invaluable lessons about resilience, adaptability, and staying true to faith. It strengthened my conviction that God's plan for my life surpasses personal envisioning. As I continue growing on this path, God's grace sustains and leads me forward, even amidst adversity.

Deepening Faith in God

Throughout my life, my faith in God has been a steadfast anchor, sustaining me through some of the most challenging times. One profound example of this occurred during a period of intense personal struggle in my early twenties. At that time, I faced a series of setbacks in both my career and personal life. The weight of uncertainty and disappointment felt overwhelming, leaving me unsure of how to move forward.

Amidst this turmoil, I turned to prayer and sought solace in scripture. I remember one particularly difficult week when fear and doubt clouded my thoughts. In a moment of quiet reflection, I felt a deep sense of peace wash over me—an unmistakable presence that I recognized as God's comfort and assurance. It was in that moment of surrendering my fears and uncertainties to Him that I experienced profound clarity and peace. This encounter strengthened my resolve to trust in God's plan for my life, even when circumstances seemed bleak.

Another significant testament to God's faithfulness in my life was during a health crisis that threatened my well-being. During this time, I leaned heavily on God's promises of healing and restoration, finding strength in prayer and the reassurance found in scripture. Despite the physical and emotional challenges, I witnessed God's grace and provision in unexpected ways, reinforcing my belief in His steadfast presence.

Reflecting on these experiences, I've come to understand that faith isn't just about belief—it's about active trust and surrender to God's will. Each trial I faced deepened my spiritual resilience and taught me valuable lessons about perseverance and humility. Through adversity,

I learned the importance of patience and persistence in prayer, knowing that God hears and answers according to His perfect timing.

One of the most profound lessons I've learned is the power of surrender. In moments of uncertainty and doubt, surrendering my fears and anxieties to God has brought peace and clarity that surpasses understanding. It's a continual journey of letting go of control and trusting in His wisdom and provision, even when the path forward is unclear.

These experiences have taught me the transformative power of gratitude. In the midst of trials, cultivating a grateful heart has helped me to see God's blessings amidst challenges. It's a perspective shift that has allowed me to find joy and hope in all circumstances, knowing that God works all things together for good for those who love Him.

Integrating scripture into my journey has been instrumental in deepening my faith and understanding of God's character. One scripture that resonates deeply with me is Isaiah 41:10, which says, "So do not fear, for I am with you; do not be dismayed, for I am your God. I will strengthen you and help you; I will uphold you with my righteous right hand." This verse has been a constant source of comfort and assurance during times of fear and uncertainty, reminding me of God's steadfast presence and promise to sustain me.

Another scripture that has guided my faith journey is Romans 8:28, which declares, "And we know that in all things God works for the good of those who love Him, who have been called according to his purpose." This verse has been a reminder that even in the midst of trials and hardships, God is working behind the scenes for my ultimate good and His glory.

Additionally, the story of Job has been a profound example of faithfulness and endurance in the face of suffering. Job's unwavering trust in God despite losing everything serves as a powerful reminder that our faith is tested in the fires of adversity, yet God remains faithful through it all.

Deepening faith in God has been marked by personal testimonies of His faithfulness, lessons learned through trials, and the transformative power of scripture. Each experience has strengthened my relationship with God and deepened my understanding of His unconditional love and grace. As I continue to walk in faith, I am reminded that God's promises are steadfast, His presence is constant, and His plans for me are good.

In the midst of life's struggles and uncertainties, I have often found myself wrestling with questions of purpose and direction. Yet, through it all, God has consistently shown His faithfulness and guidance. One of the most poignant lessons I've learned is that God's timing is perfect, even when it doesn't align with my own desires or expectations. There have been moments when I've felt impatient or discouraged, wondering why certain prayers seem unanswered or why trials persisted. However, looking back, I can see how each season of waiting or difficulty has been a crucial part of my spiritual growth.

For instance, during a period of career instability, I struggled with feelings of inadequacy and fear of the future. Despite my best efforts to secure stability through my own abilities, doors seemed to close and opportunities felt out of reach. It was during this time that I turned to Psalm 46:10, which says, "Be still, and know that I am God." This verse became a mantra of sorts, reminding me to surrender my anxieties and trust in God's sovereignty.

The journey of trusting God's timing has not been easy. There were moments of frustration and doubt, wondering if I had misunderstood God's will or if I was simply not doing enough. Yet, as I persisted in prayer and sought guidance through scripture, God revealed His faithfulness in unexpected ways. Doors began to open, not according to my timeline, but in His perfect timing.

One such instance was when a job opportunity aligned perfectly with my skills and passions, despite initial setbacks and rejections. It was a clear reminder that God's plans are far greater than my own, and His timing ensures that His purposes are fulfilled. Through this experience, I learned the importance of patience and trust in God's provision, even when circumstances appear bleak.

Navigating personal relationships has also been a testing ground for my faith. There were seasons of heartache and disappointment, where I questioned God's plan for my relational journey. In these moments, scriptures like Jeremiah 29:11, "For I know the plans I have for you, plans to prosper you and not to harm you, plans to give you hope and a future," provided comfort and reassurance. They reminded me that God's love for me is unwavering, regardless of temporary setbacks or relational challenges.

One of the most profound examples of God's faithfulness in my relational life came during a period of deep emotional healing. I had experienced betrayal and broken trust, which left me questioning my worth and ability to trust again. It was through prayer and surrendering my pain to God that I began to experience healing and restoration. God's love became a balm to my wounded heart, teaching me the power of forgiveness and the importance of extending grace to others.

As I reflect on these experiences, I see how each trial and triumph has shaped my faith journey. They have taught me to rely not on my own understanding but to lean on God's wisdom and guidance. Proverbs 3:5-6 became a foundational scripture for me, "Trust in the Lord with all your heart and lean not on your own understanding; in all your ways submit to him, and he will make your paths straight." This verse encapsulates the essence of trusting God's plan and seeking His will above my own desires.

My journey of deepening faith in God has been a tapestry of personal testimonies, spiritual growth through trials, and the transformative power of scripture. Each experience has contributed to a deeper understanding of God's love, grace, and sovereignty in my life. As I continue to walk in faith, I am reminded that God's promises are true, His presence is constant, and His plans for me are good. Through it all, I have learned to surrender my fears, trust in His timing, and embrace His unfailing love that sustains me through every season of life.

Cultivating Faith in Yourself

Cultivating faith in yourself begins with the vital step of embracing your worth. In a world where external achievements and societal expectations often dictate our sense of value, it's essential to recognize that your true worth is inherent and unchanging. Embracing your worth means acknowledging that you are wonderfully and fearfully made, as the scriptures affirm, and understanding that your value is intrinsic, not reliant on external validation. This recognition forms the foundation for developing a deep-seated faith in yourself.

By embracing your worth, you cultivate self-compassion, acceptance, and love, creating a nurturing environment for personal growth and empowerment. This journey involves silencing the inner critic, celebrating your unique strengths, and believing in your potential to make a positive impact. As you internalize this sense of worth, you build the confidence and resilience needed to face life's challenges with grace and determination. Embracing your worth is not just an act of self-love; it is an act of faith, affirming that you are capable, valuable, and deeply loved, just as you are.

Embracing Your Worth

At the core of personal empowerment and growth lies the journey of embracing one's worth. Self-love transcends fleeting emotions; it's a profound belief in our inherent value. Recognizing that we deserve love, respect, and kindness sets the stage for building a resilient and positive relationship with ourselves. This foundational realization isn't just about self-esteem but about acknowledging our fundamental right to happiness and fulfillment.

Acknowledging Your Unique Qualities and Strengths

To start on the path of self-worth, it's crucial to celebrate our unique qualities and strengths. These attributes are not mere surface-level characteristics but integral parts of our identity. Whether it's creativity, kindness, resilience, or humor, these qualities define our essence. Embracing them wholeheartedly allows us to recognize their significant contribution to our individuality and worth.

Reflecting on moments of overcoming challenges or demonstrating resilience is essential. These experiences serve as powerful testaments to our inner strength and capabilities. Celebrating our achievements, both big and small, becomes a way to highlight our growth and perseverance. By consciously acknowledging these aspects of ourselves, we affirm our worth and lay a stronger foundation for self-love.

Overcoming Doubt

Self-doubt and insecurity often cloud our perception of self-worth. Confronting and overcoming these internal obstacles is a crucial step in cultivating faith in ourselves. It requires introspection and courage to challenge negative self-talk and replace it with affirmations of our capabilities and potential. Each moment of doubt conquered is a victory that strengthens our belief in ourselves.

Practicing Self-Compassion

Central to nurturing self-worth is the practice of self-compassion. It involves treating ourselves with the same kindness and understanding that we would extend to a close friend facing a difficult situation. During setbacks or moments of self-doubt, practicing self-compassion means offering ourselves gentle encouragement and support. It's about recognizing that experiencing setbacks or making mistakes is a natural part of being human and responding to ourselves with empathy rather than harsh criticism.

Setting Boundaries

Protecting our emotional and physical well-being is essential in affirming our worth. Setting boundaries that honor our needs and preserve our sense of self-worth is crucial. Learning to say no to obligations or relationships that drain our energy or compromise our values isn't about building walls but about creating space for healthy, fulfilling connections. Respecting our boundaries communicates our self-worth to others and fosters relationships based on mutual respect and consideration.

Cultivating Gratitude

Gratitude serves as a powerful tool in shifting our focus from what we lack to the abundance in our lives. Cultivating gratitude for who we are and what we have achieved reinforces our sense of worthiness. Regularly taking time to acknowledge and appreciate the positive aspects of our journey fosters a positive mindset. Consider keeping a gratitude journal where you can jot down things you appreciate about yourself and your life, regardless of how small they may seem. This practice helps us build a foundation rooted in self-appreciation and contentment.

Building a Foundation for Self-Love

By embracing our inherent worth through acknowledging our strengths, practicing self-compassion, setting boundaries, and cultivating gratitude, we lay a solid foundation for practicing self-love. This journey isn't about striving for perfection but about recognizing and honoring the inherent value we possess. It's a process of growth and discovery that begins with embracing our worth and nurturing a compassionate relationship with ourselves.

Reflection

Empowering Personal Growth and Resilience Through Faith

My journey of integrating faith in God with self-empowerment practices has profoundly empowered my personal growth and resilience. During a challenging career transition, my faith enabled me to trust in God's timing and plan, which gave me the courage to pursue new opportunities despite uncertainties. This pivotal period in my professional life was marked by moments of doubt and apprehension. I faced the daunting prospect of change and the unsettling reality of stepping into the unknown. Yet, amidst these uncertainties, my faith provided a steadfast anchor.

Through prayer and reflection, I learned to silence the voices of self-doubt and embrace God's promises. Each morning, as I turned to scripture and sought guidance through prayer, I felt a profound sense of peace. It was in these quiet moments of communion with God that I found clarity and reassurance. His presence, palpable and reassuring, emboldened me to take decisive steps forward, trusting that His plan for my life transcended my immediate circumstances.

This alignment of actions with beliefs—practicing forgiveness, compassion, and perseverance—became the cornerstone of my personal growth. I discovered that faith isn't passive but a dynamic force that shapes attitudes and actions. As I navigated professional setbacks and personal adversities, I drew strength from these principles, fostering emotional stability and profound personal growth.

Furthermore, a significant health crisis underscored the transformative power of faith in my life. This period of illness tested my resolve and faith like never before. Yet, in the depths of uncertainty and pain, my faith provided a steadfast foundation of hope and perseverance. Embracing spiritual disciplines—meditation, scripture study, and prayer—deepened my inner strength and resilience.

Through these practices, I discovered that faith is not merely a source of comfort but a catalyst for personal transformation. It enabled me to navigate life's challenges with grace and confidence, demonstrating how faith can be a profound force in overcoming adversity and fostering personal growth.

Impact on Others: Sharing Faith and Authenticity Online

My journey of sharing faith and being authentically myself online has resonated deeply with many, both locally and globally. Through my social media posts, podcasts, interviews, and speaking engagements I have created a space where individuals can find solace, hope, and inspiration. By openly discussing my personal struggles, triumphs, and the role of faith in my life, I've connected with a diverse audience, many of whom have reached out to share how my story has impacted them.

For instance, I've received messages from individuals who were struggling with their own faith and found renewed strength through my posts. One person shared that my story of overcoming adversity through faith gave them the courage to face their own challenges with a new perspective. Another follower mentioned that my vulnerability and honesty about my journey helped them feel less alone in their struggles, prompting them to start their own faith journey.

The comments and messages I receive are a testament to the power of authentic storytelling and the impact it can have on others. By being genuine and open about my faith, I've been able to foster a community of individuals who support and uplift one another, creating a ripple effect of positivity and encouragement.

Future Outlook: Growing in Faith and Empowerment

Looking ahead, I am committed to continuing this journey of sharing my faith authentically online and empowering others. My aspirations include deepening my understanding of scripture and spiritual practices, investing in my own spiritual development to lead by example, and demonstrating the ongoing journey of faith and empowerment.

Ultimately, my future is shaped by a commitment to authenticity, faith, and empowerment. By consistently showing up online as my true self, I hope to inspire others to embrace their own faith journeys with courage and conviction.

As you reflect on your journey, embrace the transformative power of faith. Whether you navigate uncertainty, face setbacks, or celebrate victories, your faith can be a wellspring of strength and resilience. Trust in God's timing, believe in His promises, and allow His love to guide you through every season of life.

Personal growth unfolds through both challenges and triumphs, shaping our character and deepening our faith. Embrace this journey, cultivate gratitude amidst difficulties, and find joy in knowing that God's plan for you is good and purposeful.

Take a moment to consider your faith in God and yourself. Integrating faith practices—like prayer, scripture study, and acts of kindness—empowers you to navigate life's uncertainties with resilience and hope Embrace your unique path, be confident in your ability to overcome obstacles, and inspire others through faith-filled actions.

Together, encourage one another to authentically embrace our faith journeys, knowing each step forward aligns us more closely with who God created us to be.

May your journey overflow with grace, courage, and a profound sense of purpose. Trust in God's guidance, believe in your potential, and embrace the empowerment that comes from boldly living out your faith in Him and within yourself.

Xx Nicole Curtis,
Crazy Chicken Lady

Carrie Wehunt

Teacher/Coach

My name is Carrie Sokolowski Wehunt. I am a mother of three beautiful children - Dalton, Hayden Claire, and Grayson. I have been a teacher for 24 years - first grade, science, library, PE, and sign language. During my career as a teacher, I coached many sports for middle and high school students along with the Battle of the Books teams. I played three sports at Juniata College and was inducted into the Sports Hall of Fame in October 2013 for Softball, Field Hockey, and Women's basketball. I was a trainer for years empowering women to become stronger mentally and physically so they may enjoy their lives to the fullest. I have a background in sports conditioning for varsity sports and different aged kids. I love spending time with my kids coaching, assisting, and cheering them on. I owe all my accomplishments and life achievements to GOD, my family, and my friends. My FAITH is what moves through this journey of life - "So, whether you eat or drink, or whatever you do, do everything for the glory of God." (1 Corinthians 10:31)

Serenity, Courage, and Wisdom

By Carrie Wehunt

God grant me the **Serenity**
To accept the things I cannot change;
Courage to change the things I can;
And **Wisdom** to know the difference.

Imagine a place where all chaos fades into silence. Your soul finds solace in the gentle embrace of serenity - a sense of tranquility and inner peace. Picture a sunrise over the calm ocean. The still water reflects the soft hues of the awakening dawn with only the sound of waves gently lapping against the shore. Imagine lying on a blanket under the stars, with the cool night air admiring the beauty above stargazing on a clear quiet night - mesmerized with awe and wonder. Or sitting all snuggled up with a warm blanket listening to a crackling fire and watching the flames dance and flicker in complete silence.

Serenity can be experienced in many different ways throughout life. Unfortunately, the world around us is full of neverending noise, commotion, and movement making it difficult for people to truly encounter moments of serenity. Oftentimes we need to cultivate practices and instill habits to create our inner peace and tranquility. For example, the practice of gratitude. Gratitude is being thankful for things in your life each and every day. It shifts your focus to the positive aspects of your life and helps foster a sense of contentment and peace within.

How can gratitude make our lives peaceful and calm?

Gratitude promotes positive mindsets. We shift away from negative thoughts and gain an appreciation for the present moments in our lives.

Expressing gratitude towards others helps to strengthen relationships and allows deeper connections. Gratitude for others cultivates feelings of warmth, trust, and mutual respect.

Gratitude helps to redefine challenges as opportunities for growth. When we are faced with adversity, it's important to focus on what we're grateful for so we can overcome obstacles.

When we practice gratitude, we appreciate the positive aspects of ourselves and our lives, and develop a greater sense of confidence and empowerment.

Gratitude is a powerful tool in which we focus on the abundance in our lives rather than dwelling on what we don't have and then we can cultivate a sense of contentment and happiness.

Philippians 4: 6-7

"Do not be anxious about anything, but in every situation, by prayer and petition, with thanksgiving, present your requests to God. And the peace of God, which transcends all understanding, will guard your hearts and your minds in Christ Jesus."

Psalm 100:4

"Enter his gates with thanksgiving and his courts with praise; give thanks to him and praise his name."

Colossians 3:17

"And whatever you do, whether in word or deed, do it all in the name of the Lord Jesus, giving thanks to God the Father through him."

Throughout the Bible many scriptures emphasize the importance of gratitude in our lives, teaching us to always approach God with thanksgiving, regardless of our circumstances, and to cultivate a spirit of gratitude in all aspects of our lives. In Luke 17:11-19, Jesus encounters ten lepers. They cry out for mercy to Jesus. Jesus encounters them and instructs them to go to the priests, and as they go, they are healed. Afterwards one of the lepers returns to Jesus, praising God and expressing unending gratitude for his healing. Jesus commends him for his faith and gratitude. Jesus said, "Rise and go; your faith has made you well." This story displays the connection between gratitude and serenity - the former leper's expression of thankfulness led him to both physical healing and spiritual peace within.

What a beautiful example of how gratitude can create a sense of serenity in our lives; and how important it is to have serenity for us to feel God's love.

Three years ago my life took an unexpected turn. My former husband decided he didn't want to be married to me anymore - 19 years, 3 kids, 3 dogs, 3 moves, and 4 houses suddenly didn't seem to matter in his heart. He had found happiness somewhere else. I will never forget the moment he expressed his decision to leave the family dynamic. I was sitting at the kitchen table creating the family Christmas card. He was pacing back and forth giving off a sense of anxiousness and uncomfortableness. The words he spoke will forever be ingrained in my mind. "I don't want to be married anymore. I hope you find someone who will love you the way you deserve to be loved." Not fully comprehending what was happening at that exact moment, I closed my laptop and said,"I guess we won't be needing a family Christmas card this year." My heart sank and I got an awful pain in my stomach. I couldn't breathe. I just kept saying "No! I don't want this. We have a family." Nothing seemed to phase him nor break his stride as he went into our kid's rooms and let them know their parents were getting a divorce. I was in complete shock and denial. I just kept thinking to myself 'This can't be real. This can't really be happening.' After asking thousands and thousands of questions seeking answers and following him around begging only to receive complete silence, I walked into my bedroom, shut the door and dropped to my knees. Crying deeply, I begged God for help - help to change his heart; to help him see the beautiful family we created; help him with whatever pain or unhappiness he was feeling. I knew at that moment I was surrendering the entire situation over to God. Surrendering my thoughts, my feelings and emotions, my complete TRUST and FAITH in God that He will handle what happens from that moment.

The next morning I got up and went about my typical morning routine of waking the kids for school, making breakfast, and preparing for my day of teaching. I smiled around the kids and went to my teaching job sharing in the excitement of Christmas among teachers, parents, and students. Every time I felt a moment that was not distracted with the fun and craziness of festivities, I prayed. I asked God to give me the strength to navigate everything around me with grace. My outside looked the same as any other day, but inside I was dying of a broken heart, consumed by a deep feeling of sadness and hurt. My family was in shock, but encouraged me to stay strong in my FAITH - it will all work out the way it's supposed to - God has a plan. Every morning that followed, as soon as my feet touched the floor I recited the **Serenity Prayer** and thanked God for the air in my lungs and my beating broken heart.

God grant me the **<u>SERENITY</u>** to accept the
things I cannot change.

Music became like air to me - I couldn't live without it. When someone you love says "I hope you find someone to love you the way you deserve" you immediately feel unloved and empty inside. You begin to question your worth and what happened to become unloved. I filled moments with songs that reminded me of the one I can always count on for unconditional love - God's love. One song in particular that gave me a feeling of comfort and peace was;

Who said that you weren't beautiful
And that you didn't belong in your own skin?
Who said that you were all alone
And that you're never gonna find love again?
So many little words, so many little lies
That have followed you all of your life
Looking for the truth, look into your eyes
And you'll see it's been there the whole time
even when you were running
Even when you were hiding
Never been a moment that you were not perfectly loved
When you barely believed it
When your eyes couldn't see it
Every single moment, you've always been perfectly loved

Perfectly Loved is a Christian song celebrating God's unconditional love. Despite our flaws and imperfections, we are deeply cherished and accepted by our Creator. It is a message of redemption and grace, teaching us that God's love is constant and unwavering. It encourages us to find peace knowing we are loved exactly for who we are, without needing to prove ourselves or beg for God's affection.

1 John 4:18

"There is no fear in love. But perfect love drives out fear, because fear has to do with punishment. The one who fears is not made perfect in love."

One of my favorite movies growing up was The **Wizard of Oz**. Every character was fun and enjoyable to watch. They brought humor and people could relate to their personalities and imperfections. My favorite character was the cowardly lion. No matter how hard he tried to be courageous, he just couldn't find it within himself. He openly admits his fear and reluctance to face dangerous situations. I loved the way the lion's journey was one of self-discovery and personal growth. The lion taught us that courage is not the absence of fear, but rather the ability to act in spite of your fear. He started out cowardly but then he realized he had courage all along, he just needed to believe in himself.

Having courage is defined by the strength and willingness to face fear, pain, danger, uncertainty, or intimidation. Courage can come in all different forms within everyday living - speaking up for others, facing fears, making tough decisions, admitting wrongdoings, and standing up for beliefs.

Franklin D. Roosevelt said "First of all, let me assert my firm belief that the only thing we have to fear is fear itself - nameless, unreasoning, unjustified terror which paralyzes needed efforts to convert retreat into advance."

There were many moments in my life where I had to look deep inside to find the courage to advance forward. One situation that stands out in my mind was in middle school. The summer before sixth grade I went to an overnight basketball camp with a good friend. We were going to be roommates in the college dorms of Mount St. Mary's College in Emmitsburg, Md. I couldn't wait to eat, sleep, and play basketball for an entire week - nothing could contain my excitement as I counted the days until drop off. The time had approached quickly and after the final goodbyes to my family, I felt excited, nervous, happy, grateful, and lucky to have the opportunity to experience this particular camp. The first day was filled with meeting new friends, new coaches, team assignments, new skills, and a new form of independence with eating in a cafeteria and having the freedom to come and go to our rooms with no parental permission. The first night was a new sense of anxiousness being in a different environment, but I had my roommate to rely on for laughter, strength, and encouragement.

The next day was filled with an early breakfast, skills and drills, team meetings, lunch, mini-games, review sessions, and then a walk to the dining hall for dinner. I was exhausted. . It was refreshing to spend time with my roommate during meal times. We shared our experiences, funny moments, and moments of frustration. We also talked about the new friends we found in our teammates. It was the comfort of home in a foreign place. Later that night after our evening competition games, I got word my roommate was not feeling good. She was going home. What? She can't go home. Who was I going to eat and talk with at meals? Who was I going to stay up late with laughing about the day? Who was I going to rely on for strength and encouragement during moments I felt completely weak and nervous? I gave my roommate a hug goodbye and watched her drive away leaving me alone.

As I stood in the parking lot ready to cry, I immediately went to my dorm room and called my parents. I explained what had happened and how I wasn't sure I could continue the week on my own. As always, I was reminded that I can do anything I put my mind to. I was told to pray, **look up** and ask God for courage. Courage to face the loneliness of the dorm room, courage to sit at tables with other girls, courage to step out of my comfort zone with evening downtime activities, and most importantly, the courage to put everything into becoming a better basketball player.

Upon reflection, my mind immediately went to the Bible story of Joseph and His Colored Coat. Joseph demonstrated courage during his time in Egypt, especially in the face of adversity. He experienced resiliency in slavery, temptation, forgiveness, and reconciliation. What I admire most about Joseph was his integrity, his faithfulness to God's principles, but most importantly, his moral courage. The courage to follow God's plan and know that God works through the most challenging and difficult situations always creating something good. When I think of this story it reminds me "God is good all the time, and all the time God is good".

This statement will always be my "go-to" reminder in everything I do, so after I collected my thoughts and said my prayers, I progressed on throughout the week. I showed up at every workout ready to play with a smile on my face and I found my voice of encouragement for others which in turn created a sense of peace and empowerment within myself. I stayed after lessons to ask what I could do to become stronger and better in my basketball skills. I talked with teammates on and off the court developing a shared bond, and I practiced my skills during time set aside for downtime. I put all my energy, focus, thankfulness, and courage into my purpose on and off the courts.

The last day of camp was a tournament among all the teams. My family came to watch and support my basketball playing. My team came in second place in the tournament and we received medals during the awards ceremony. This ceremony encompassed all parents, coaches, staff, and players. To receive a medal was so exciting because I knew my hard work had paid off stepping up my game and skills. As the director of the camp was wrapping up with thank yous to all that were present, he had one final trophy to give out - the Most Outstanding Player. This trophy was given to one camper who demonstrated exceptional skills, performance, attitude, and impacted others to become better teammates, players, and coaches. At that moment my team coach said a few words " this trophy goes to someone who stands out from all other athletes due to their performance, leadership qualities, and overall influence on the game of basketball. It's my pleasure to give this trophy to Carrie Sokolowski." Who? It's almost as if my mind went blank and I didn't hear the player's name because I sat there clapping and looking around to see who it was. My friend and teammate nudged me and said "It's you! They called your name!" Me?

I stood up on the stadium bleachers and made my way down to the court. My coach gave me a big smile, a huge hug, and placed the trophy in my hands. I was beyond surprised and extremely grateful for the recognition. I knew at that moment that I would never allow fear to keep me from accomplishing my potential and would always seek God for **COURAGE** to keep moving forward no matter what obstacles and challenges come my way.

<u>**COURAGE**</u> to change the things I can

Mother Theresa said "We can do no great things, only small things with great love." Wow! This is one of the most humbling statements from one of the most courageous women to ever grace this world. Small, regular moments can sparkle with significance if we put our time, energy, and desire to be better into everything we do. Courageous moments that are seen or unseen can encourage those whose hearts are broken, those whose spirits are floundering, and those whose doubts and anger are raging to never give up hope. Hope in God's promises of blessings, restoration, grace, and redemption in every aspect of our lives. People are not born courageous, but instead provided opportunities to exemplify courage - It's a perfectly thrown spiral that we do everything we can to catch it and then run as fast and hard to get to the moment we can stand and rejoice in the blessings and success.

1 Corinthians 16:13 - 14

"Keep alert; stand firm in the faith; be courageous; be strong. Everything you do should be done in love."

And the **WISDOM** to know the difference.

Serenity is calmness, peace, and acceptance among things we cannot control. We search daily for serenity and inner peace among moments of adversity, obstacles and challenges that allow us to live without fear and uncertainty. Courage is the actions we take to change things that are within our control. Courage is the strength, persistence, and determination to confront adversity, to overcome our fears, and make positive changes in everything we do. So where does wisdom fall among these two? Wisdom is knowing when to call on surrender and acceptance in situations, and when to rely on courage to jump into action using perseverance, taking risks and stepping out of our comfort zones.

The book, **The Shack,** is a story about devastating grief, questioning faith, and seeking redemption. When I read this book, I was filled with different thoughts, questions, and emotions all swirling around in my heart and my mind. This is a very powerful example of "wisdom to know the difference between serenity and courage". The main character Mack experienced wisdom in so many different ways emotionally and spiritually.

Wisdom of Forgiveness - Mack struggled with forgiving the man who killed his daughter. He needed to realize that the true act of forgiveness is not making excuses for the wrongdoing but it is the freeing of himself from the anger and hatred felt deep within his heart.

Wisdom of Acceptance - Mack knew he couldn't go back and change the chain of events that occurred in his family, especially to his daughter. He needed to accept what happened and find a way to let go in order to move forward. By accepting the painful events in his life, he was able to gain a better understanding of himself and his faith.

Wisdom of Unconditional Love - Mack lost his faith in God, but throughout the story Mack is reminded of God's unconditional love for him through his pain and his suffering.

Wisdom of Surrendering - Mack realizes through his deep pain and suffering there is meaning and purpose. By trusting God and surrendering all control, Mack experienced true healing and freedom within himself. Mack became the person he was in the end because he laid it at God's feet.

The overall message and meaning is powerful and unforgettable. All of us are faced with tragedies, mistakes, challenges, obstacles, doubt, and fear at different points in our lives. It is how we choose to overcome all of these that defines our journey and who we become. Without suffering there is no compassion.

Eddie Pinero said it best - It's not about what happens to you. No one escapes adversity. No one lives free of discomfort or misfortune or struggle. It will always be about what you do with what happens to you. In other words it's not the event, it's the response. Not the obstacle but the ability to navigate around it. Not the wave but the ability to ride its momentum to something greater. It is not what happens to you. It's about what you do to what happens to you.

Motherhood requires patience and the ability to understand as well as empathize with children's perspectives. Wisdom allows mothers to approach challenging moments with grace and compassion, recognizing that each one of her children is unique and requires different approaches.

On December 22, 2021, my oldest son became ill while visiting family. He has severe food allergies and at first, it seemed like a typical allergy response to something he may have eaten. His stomach began to ache and nauseousness set in creating a feeling of uneasiness. We gave him Benadryl and patiently waited to see if the symptoms would fade away. After some time, he wanted to lie down so we went to my brother's house and put him on the couch to rest. Thirty minutes later my son approached me and showed me a large mass protruding out of his lower abdomen. Immediately I went into mother survival mode where I smiled and reassured him we were going to get things looked at and he would be ok. My sister-in-law drove us to the nearest hospital and waited in the car until we were checked in. Unfortunately, COVID was still predominant and rules limited the number of family members allowed into the ER. My son sat in a wheelchair wrapped in a blanket for 5 hours. I sat next to him constantly shielding him from the unusual situations visiting the ER throughout the evening. Throughout this time, I kept asking for my son to be seen and how much longer the wait was going to be until finally, his number was called. Thankfully we were called to go back and begin the process with the triage nurse after 5 hours of waiting. The triage nurse took one look at my son's abdomen and immediately rushed my son back to one of the beds in the ER. Then it became even scarier.

Doctors and nurses were surrounding him taking vitals and asking tons of questions. I answered the best I could while I myself was in and out of disbelief at what was happening. My son went through a slew of tests including an MRI and I was precautioned with the possibility of multiple myeloma - what?? Multiple myeloma? My father has been diagnosed and battling multiple myeloma for several years. Anxiously waiting for results, I prayed and prayed for answers. It didn't matter what the answers would be, just answers. The doctors finally informed me that he was suffering from a Bowel Blockage Hernia. He was going to need surgery immediately by a "specialist". In disbelief, I signed all the paperwork to begin the process. My son was given an immediate tube placed up his nasal passage to begin draining his stomach. Because this was happening so quickly, they couldn't put him under and had to do it while he was awake and alert. My heart - it was awful watching and holding his hand - the pain. Oh, how I wished I could have changed places with him. Anything to take all pain away from him, but the best I could do was hold his hand tight reassuring him I would never leave him and how much I loved him.

As I held his hand I prayed and I thought about **Footprints in the Sand**

"I dreamed I was walking along the beach with the Lord, and Across the sky flashed scenes from my life. For each scene I noticed two sets of footprints in the sand; One belonged to me, and the other to the

Lord. When the last scene of my life flashed before us, I looked back at the footprints in the sand. I noticed that many times along the path of my life, There was only one set of footprints.

I also noticed that it happened at the very lowest and saddest times in my life. This really bothered me, and I questioned the Lord about it. "Lord, you said that once I decided to follow you, You would walk with me all the way; But I have noticed that during the most troublesome times in my life, There is only one set of footprints. I don't understand why in times when I needed you the most, you should leave me.

The Lord replied, "My precious, precious child. I love you, and I would never, never leave you during your times of trial and suffering. When you saw only one set of footprints, **It was then that I carried you."**

All prep work was completed quickly and efficiently and all we were doing was waiting for the specialist to be brought in - yep, a special surgeon had to be called in to perform the procedure. When he arrived, he reassured me my son was in good hands, but I must prepare myself for the possibility my son could lose part of his intestines and in the worst-case scenario, he could end up with a bowel bag depending on how damaged the intestines were and the amount that may need to be removed - Oh my heart!! I gave my son final hugs and kisses and slowly my hand pulled apart from his.

Jesus, protect my son. Hold him tight. He is in Your hands, Jesus. Take care of him.

I was taken to a private waiting room at 2:30 am where I laid on a couch, closed my eyes, and prayed relentlessly. Feeling God's love, a sense of peace fell upon me and I fell asleep until I was awakened by a smiling nurse. She asked me to follow her into the recovery room where my son was sleeping soundly and peacefully. I sat down next to him and the surgeon came and sat next to me. I was surprised to see him and he reassured me he was going to be fine. There was no permanent damage and he should be healthy and strong moving forward. I thanked him over and over and he sat with me. No words, just sat next to me waiting for my son to wake up. After some time, slowly my son began to open his eyes. He turned his head and smiled at us. I reached for his hand and held it tight, smiling at him with deep love. The surgeon got up and moved closer to my son, grabbed his hand, smiled, and told him "You are going to be ok. You did great. You are one strong young man". Wow!! A wave of pure peace and serenity came over me.

My son and I were moved to another recovery room where he rested until he was ready to move to the 5th floor to finish his recovery at the hospital. The nurses were bubbly, friendly, supportive, and efficient in their love and care for both of us. They gave me a bed and meals throughout my stay. There were many moments when they came in and talked with my son, told jokes, brought him special treats, and took him on adventure walks throughout the floor and other places. During this time in the hospital I spent much time praying and reflecting while my son was resting - so much to be thankful for.

Moments of gratitude:

- The unconditional love from God, my family and friends
- The unwavering care from the doctors, nurses, and staff at the hospital
- The physical, emotional, and spiritual support from my family
- The unending strength from my other two children - showing strength for their brother at a time they were terrified and scared

This is an example of how I pray for WISDOM - wisdom to know the difference between moments of serenity and courage. Trusting God because He is in control of the situation; trusting the doctors who perform the procedure; and trusting the nurses for the care before and after. Surrendering everything and laying it at the feet of Jesus but also having the courage to push for my son's situation to be seen, the courage to make decisions by myself under pressure and time restraints, and the courage to remain strong for my son and my other two children before, during, and the weeks to follow with care and attention.

I'm often asked "How did you do it? How do you stay smiling and thankful for everything?" My response is easy - my **Faith.**

For King and Country's song <u>Shoulders</u> reminds me to always draw my courage from God

> "I look up to the mountains
> Does my strength come from the mountains?
> No, my strength comes from God
> Who made heaven and earth, and the mountains"

And Rebecca St. James song <u>You make Everything Beautiful</u> encompasses every part of me

> Grant me serenity to accept things
> These things I cannot change
> Grant me the courage, Lord, to change what I can
> Wisdom to know the difference
> In my weakness, You can shine
> In Your strength, I can fly
> And You make everything, everything beautiful
> You make everything, everything new
> You make everything, everything beautiful
> In its time, in Your time, it's beautiful

God can take the broken pieces of our lives and transform them into something beautiful and amazing. We need to trust the hope and redemption found in God's love and grace, even in the midst of pain, struggles, and challenges. Never lose FAITH.

Donna J Thomas

Mountainside Gals!!!
CEO, Entrepreneur, Influencer, Podcaster, Speaker & Author

https://www.linkedin.com/in/donnacthomas/
https://www.facebook.com/SurvivoroftheStorms/
https://www.instagram.com/mommadonnafromthemountainside/
https://linktr.ee/MountainsideGals
https://www.mountainsidegals.com/

Donna J. Thomas, CEO of Mountainside Gals is an influencer among LuLaRoe retailers and has sustained sales among the top 10% of the company. Donna coaches and mentors her team and when she has free time, she appears as a guest on podcasts, is a podcaster, is a speaker, and is an international best seller author. She has built a sizeable active community of women who engage and uplift each other, and all share the love fashion. Career wise, Donna has had progressive leadership advancement and built programs for women to be mentored/coached and advanced through the ranks. Her leadership as well as mothering styles are strongly inspired by her life's faith journey. Donna challenges herself to go the extra mile in all that she does, and she aims to bless lives daily. She lives with her husband, son and nephew in mountains of southern Frederick County, Maryland.

My Unwavering Anchor – A Faith Journey on the Wings of His Love

By Donna J Thomas

BACKGROUND

From my earliest memories, I never felt alone; I always sensed God's presence beside me, likely due to my mother teaching me Bible verses and stories. Raised in a Lutheran household, I was christened at three and enjoyed church activities with my dad—Sunday school, vacation Bible school, and Wednesday classes. However, my childhood abruptly changed when my dad announced the divorce, thrusting me into maturity.

My mother battled an undiagnosed sleeping illness, likely diabetes, leaving her bedridden for most of my early years. Compounding her challenges, she carried deep resentment from her father's sudden death during her childbirth hospitalization in the 1950s. My grandmother's decision not to inform her until after the funeral intensified her anguish, eventually, she was diagnosed with paranoid schizophrenia.

Despite her struggles, my mother shared her faith through Bible verses and stories sporadically. These experiences shaped my understanding of compassion and resilience, fostering a deep spiritual grounding that has guided me through life's adversities.

Growing up was a bit of a hard journey for me. I had to learn things earlier than most kids. You see, when my parents split up, it turned my world upside down. Dad left, and suddenly, I was left to fend for myself a lot of the time. Mom struggled with her own issues, so the usual things parents do for their kids—cooking meals, washing clothes—were things I had to figure out on my own. It was tough, but I adapted quickly. I learned to sort laundry, cook simple meals, and take care of myself.

Dad's departure was a shock. He didn't stick around to help Mom through her difficulties. Instead, he left us to cope on our own. It made me question the meaning of commitments and vows, especially when he vowed to stay with us "for better or worse." I didn't see much of him after that.

In those early years, I felt like I had someone watching over me. Maybe it was the Holy Spirit or maybe it was just my own resilience, but somehow, I managed to navigate through those challenging times. Before I even reached the age of reason, I was already taking on responsibilities that most kids my age didn't have to think about. Playing with knives in the kitchen to prepare meals, starting the stove—I was doing things that no child should have to do alone.

Despite the turmoil at home, my faith was a constant source of stability. I didn't have a dramatic conversion story; rather, I grew up in a home where faith was part of everyday life. I sang hymns, attended church, and tried to live according to what I knew was right. Faith became my anchor during those uncertain times.

When my parents divorced, our family's financial situation changed drastically. We moved to Mississippi, where life was very different from what I knew before. I transitioned from a middle-class environment to a poorer part of the country. Yet, amidst these changes, my parents instilled in me a deep respect for all people, regardless of race or background. Growing up colorblind, in a place where racial tensions were palpable, taught me early on about the importance of treating everyone equally. On top of that, about everywhere we lived, there was a church in our backyard or within walking distance. Religion was not a limiting factor—God's house was God's house and so you could find me there on Sunday mornings, evenings, and Wednesday nights. At the age of 8, I dedicated myself to being a Christian; some religions call this being reborn.

SOME CORE FOUNDATIONAL TEACHINGS

MICAH 6:8

In the midst of these experiences, I turned to the Bible for guidance. The stories and scriptures became more than just words; they became my moral compass. One verse in particular, Micah 6:8, resonated deeply with me: "To love mercy, walk humbly, and do justice." These words shaped how I approached life. This verse taught me (and continues to teach me) to be kind and merciful, to remain humble, and to strive for justice in all things.

This is definitely one that my mom taught me, and it has become one of my favorites. This is short and sweet, but boy does it have a punch!

PSALM 23

My mother played a significant role in nurturing my faith. Despite her own challenges, she made sure I knew the Psalms and other passages that spoke of God's love and protection. Psalm 23 became a cornerstone for me, especially during times of uncertainty. Its comforting words reminded me that no matter what challenges I faced, God was with me, guiding me along his path. Today, I believe with all my heart that this is the truth and it is very comforting to know the protection He gives us.

Psalm 23 New International Version

A psalm of David.

[1] The Lord is my shepherd, I lack nothing.
[2] He makes me lie down in green pastures,
he leads me beside quiet waters,
[3] he refreshes my soul.
He guides me along the right paths
for his name's sake.
[4] Even though I walk
through the darkest valley,[a]
I will fear no evil,
for you are with me;
your rod and your staff,
they comfort me.

[5] You prepare a table before me
in the presence of my enemies.
You anoint my head with oil;
my cup overflows.
[6] Surely your goodness and love will follow me
all the days of my life,
and I will dwell in the house of the Lord
forever.

Footnotes

Psalm 23:4 Or *the valley of the shadow of death*

1 CORINTHIANS 13:4-8

A favorite scripture that I've learned to embrace wholeheartedly not only in my life but as an essential element to parenting and role modeling to others in my life is the words from 1 Corinthians 13:4-8. The scripture starts out as "Love is patient, love is kind..." and continues from there. Where you see the word **love**, if you take that word out and you substitute it for a child's name or even your own name, you can certainly begin to firmly understand the meaning of love and what it means to the purpose in God's plan. All of us need to share love just as God loves us. And there's nothing that we can do to make God love us. He already loves us unconditionally, and no matter what we do, He still pours His love out on us. An example He gives us for unconditional love (or sacrificial love is what I'd like to call it) is showing mercy and grace to those around us and that even means our children as well. It can expand to others around us including parents, siblings, cousins, aunts, uncles, friends, acquaintances, and strangers.

This scripture is often read during weddings. When the two become one, this unconditional love needs to be present in the marriage.

1 Corinthians 13:4-8 New International Version

[4] Love is patient, love is kind. It does not envy, it does not boast, it is not proud. [5] It does not dishonor others, it is not self-seeking, it is not easily angered, it keeps no record of wrongs. [6] Love does not delight in evil but rejoices with the truth. [7] It always protects, always trusts, always hopes, always perseveres.

[8] Love never fails. But where there are prophecies, they will cease; where there are tongues, they will be stilled; where there is knowledge, it will pass away

PRAYER LIFE & LORD's PRAYER

As I grew older, I began to understand prayer in a deeper way. My mother's teachings about trusting God's answers to our prayers became clearer to me over time. Despite the hardships and questions that arose from my parents' divorce and our move, my faith remained steadfast.

A prayer that my mom taught me was the Lord's prayer, and when I was little, I memorized the words. I repeat that prayer every day and over the years, "meaning" has arrived in this prayer for me.

Another important thing I learned was the Lord's prayer that I learned early on and I say it every day, I don't miss a day. A key part of that prayer is thanking God for Our Daily Bread and things like that but also reminding us how we need to be kind to other people. Forgiveness is something that we should do not only for other people but we need to forgive ourselves as Jesus enables forgiveness for us. This is often missed when people recite that prayer; they don't stop to think about how important it is if you want somebody to forgive you or you want God to forgive you. You need to be humble and ask for forgiveness from Him. On a larger scale, if someone has upset you and has stirred anger in your heart, the quicker you are to forgive them, the quicker you are ready to receive God's blessings in your life. I have learned to understand that if we harbor bad feelings towards someone and we don't forgive them and we don't show them mercy and grace then we've missed the lesson altogether. God has given us wonderful spiritual gifts and the one that comes into play here is called self-control. Self-control is by far the most challenging out of all of the gifts because it challenges you to temper any hard feelings towards another.

FORGIVENESS

Just a little more expansion on the forgiveness because this is so important. "…Forgive us our sins (trespasses) as we forgive those who sin (have trespassed) against us" has a lot of meaning. When we pray and believe that the prayer was answered, we must ask, "Really?" Asking God to forgive us as we have forgiven others is a very tall order. Have we really forgiven others as God has forgiven us? I said this prayer by memorization for years and the meaning of forgiveness is a powerful request. We must humble ourselves and forgive others – meaning that we need to help them if they are in need (be merciful), edify them (never gossip about them), and gracefully lift them in prayer. God's WORD speaks to us and over our journey, we can learn to listen better and find meaning in His Word. Holding back forgiveness does impact our ability to receive blessings.

REFLECTION

Today, I look back on those early years with gratitude. They shaped who I am—a person who values faith, kindness, and justice. My upbringing taught me resilience and empathy, and it strengthened my belief that God's plan is always unfolding, even when we face adversity. No matter how bad things appear, God has got our backs. Our challenge is to be grateful and thankful, forgive quickly, adopt a positive mindset, be kind and merciful, and dole out grace like there is a never-ending supply. We are expected to choose joy and be patient. Trust God is working through the storm for us, and immeasurable blessings await.

The deeply ingrained principles of faith, resilience, and compassion that defined my upbringing were profoundly shaped by the challenges and adversities my family faced. From an early age, I was immersed in a world where reliance on God's guidance was not just a choice but a necessity for survival.

I was born into a Lutheran household where faith was woven into the fabric of daily life. My mother, despite her own health battles, made sure that I was introduced to the teachings of the Bible from the moment I could comprehend them. Sunday school, vacation Bible school, and weekly church services were regular fixtures of my childhood. These experiences provided me not only with a foundational understanding of Christianity but also with a sense of community and belonging that would prove invaluable in the years to come.

However, my idyllic childhood took an abrupt turn when my parents divorced. I was too young to fully grasp the complexities of adult relationships or the emotional toll it would take on my family. Overnight, the familiar routines of family life were shattered, and I found myself thrust into a new reality where the responsibilities of adulthood seemed to descend prematurely upon my shoulders.

My father's departure left a void that could not be filled by my mother's unwavering strength alone. She, too, was grappling with her own health issues—a mysterious sleeping illness that often left her bedridden for days on end. Looking back, I suspect it was undiagnosed diabetes, exacerbated by the stress of her circumstances. Yet, in the midst of her physical challenges, she remained steadfast in her faith and in her determination to instill those same values in me.

For a child, witnessing a parent's struggle with illness is a sobering experience. It forces you to confront the fragility of life and the unpredictability of circumstances beyond your control. I learned early on the importance of resilience—of finding strength in the midst of adversity. While other children were playing carefree, I was learning how to navigate the intricacies of daily life, from cooking simple meals to managing household chores.

Despite the upheaval in my personal life, my faith became an unwavering anchor. It was not a dramatic conversion moment that defined my journey but rather a gradual deepening of my understanding and reliance on God's presence. The Bible stories and verses that had been imparted to me from a young age took on new meaning as I sought solace and guidance in their timeless wisdom.

CONCLUSION & WORDS OF ENCOURAGEMENT

In conclusion, my faith journey has been a continuous learning experience. It's not defined by a single moment of conversion, but rather by a series of lessons learned through challenges and blessings alike. Through it all, I've come to appreciate the power of faith to sustain and guide us, no matter what life throws our way.

Developing a strong faith can be transformative. Here are some practical steps you can take:

1. **Prayer:** Spend at least 5–10 minutes daily in prayer. This time allows you to connect with God, share your thoughts, and seek guidance.
2. **Bible Reading:** Start with a chapter of Proverbs each day. This book offers wisdom and practical insights that can enrich your understanding of life and faith.
3. **Christian Music:** Listen to Christian music for at least 30 minutes daily. Music has the power to uplift and inspire, reinforcing your faith journey.
4. **Reflection:** Take time to reflect on what you've read and heard. Journaling about your experiences and insights can deepen your understanding and connection with God.
5. **Intercession:** Pray for others regularly. Maintain a journal where you record names and prayer requests. Track answered prayers as a testament to God's faithfulness.

These practices can help nurture and grow your faith. If you have any questions or wish to discuss further, feel free to reach out. Thank you for your interest in my faith journey. May it inspire you to expand your faith beyond perceived limits.

Ginny Hatfield

Virginia Enterprises
Kingdom Speaker , Certified Radiant Leader, Farm Wife & Mom

https://www.facebook.com/vdicehatfield?mibextid=LQQJ4d
https://www.instagram.com/faith_farm_mama
https://beacons.ai/vahatfield

With a heart rooted in farm life, I have cherished being a farm wife, mama, and now a proud farm grandma, sharing both the joys and hardships of this journey to give God the glory. For nearly 36 years, I have embraced the role of a farm wife, and for 33 years, I have been blessed as a farm mama. In 2024, God graced our family with grandchildren, enriching our lives even more. Throughout the years, I have successfully built several network marketing and affiliate online businesses. As a sought-after Kingdom Speaker, I felt compelled to share our transformational story of faith in a book. In 2022, my husband underwent two liver transplants within two weeks. During this challenging time, God spoke to me in a Walmart, asking if I trusted Him enough to surrender my husband's health to Him. Through obedience and surrender, not only was my husband's health restored, but my faith and identity in God were profoundly transformed. This powerful testimony aims to inspire others to know Him and find their home in His Kingdom.

Trust and Obey for There's No Other Way

By Ginny Hatfield

When I sang this along with my new husband and the congregation at our wedding, little did I know how much I was going to have to live this out in my life 34 years later.

Let me share with you a bit about me and the back story to what happened to my husband and me during the Summer of 2022. You see, we had a short whirlwind romance and had married on the seventh date in front of the altar which was November 5, 1988. We met after we had both answered a miscellaneous ad in the Hoards Dairyman, a national farm magazine, back in the Spring of 1988.

God had brought us together through a prayer and wisdom from an elderly lady in my neighborhood. She'd shared with me how God had delivered her and her friend both husbands quickly after they had written down exactly everything they had wanted in a husband, and then both had prayed over each other's list and had trusted God enough for Him to find them husbands. At the time that she helped me make my list and take it to God in prayer, they had already been married 60 plus years. So as a 19-year-old girl, I thought why not?

So when I got my first letter from him on Memorial Day "88, I realized that He was the guy that I had written down in my Prayer request to God. That was the start of my belief that God does answer prayers that are aligned with his will and his path that he is guiding you on if you are only obedient and trust him enough to take that first step.

Each of us had to take that first step of obedience when we read that miscellaneous ad in the Hoards Dairyman. We heard a soft voice telling us to answer this "country singles directory ad" from some lady in Illinois and send $10 to her. She then sent us back a form in the mail to tell a bit more about us and what we were looking for. We mailed the forms back to her and she sent them back to us in a booklet form. We then were able to write to anyone from the booklet and take it from there. So I wrote to my now husband, Dennis, and another guy from Wisconsin, and I figured the first guy that wrote back I would keep writing to, and the other guy I would throw in the trash. Luckily my current hubby wrote back first! Thank goodness because the other guy lived way up in northern Wisconsin!

Life is always interesting when you're married to a farmer and even more so when you become a mom to 4 sons and have to keep them safe as they grow up on a farm around equipment and animals. Trusting and obeying God to guide us through tough farm econom decisions, raising our 4 sons, and keeping a healthy marriage through it all was our focus.

But when you throw sickness into the whole marriage, family and farming equation (especially a life and death situation where you see your husband gradually just keep getting sicker and sicker), you go from trusting and being obedient to God to being mad at God and asking, where are you? Do you even see me, do you even care anymore about me? How do I get you to notice me? To finally, fine! I will do it myself! I will take on trying and do everything on my own! At least I know I can count on myself!

My husband's illness started with salmonella from food poisoning. He ate a bad macaroni deli salad. It usually takes a bad case of flue or like a food poisoning to trigger this disease (Primary Sclerosing Cholangitis-PSC- a liver disease that eventually makes the liver ducts dry up and fall off giving your bile nowhere to go) he had lying in his body at that time. Although we wouldn't know for years what he was officially diagnosed with.

Imagine your farmer hubby goes from being a very healthy strong man to not having any energy and being sick all the time and barely getting through a day of farming, let alone having any energy to go out or having to know where the closest bathroom is always.

I was so mad at God for making this wonderful man suffer. I just did not understand why God would allow this. At the same time my husband was sick, I was wondering what was my purpose in life? I loved being a farmer's wife, and mom to my four sons, but I always had this whisper in the back of my mind. You were made for more. But what did that mean? I would ask myself.

We decided in 2006 to start building our new milking parlor facility and freestall barn because my hips were shot milking cows in a 72-cow milking barn and my farmer hubby's knees were starting to go too. Also, I was told if we built the milking parlor and freestall barn facilities first that would pay for my new house. It was a dream of mine to build a new house.

As soon as we got the new milking facility up and running of course the 2008 recession hit along with the doubling of fuel prices and every other farm expense. I did not understand it because we had done the homework and had worked out all of the things we thought would have gone wrong. We thought we had been good stewards of the money that God had given us and had taken time to make sure we could afford the new facilities. Soon we had to borrow money just to keep afloat every year. My dream of having a new home got smaller and smaller until I eventually just quit dreaming and I just plugged in day by day into the farm. Just surviving but not really thriving on the inside. From the outside, I looked like the mom that had everything, a loving husband, kids that loved me, and I was the mom that never missed a game, or a field trip! But inside I was slowly dying because I had lost hope, and I didn't know what my purpose was anymore. What did God create me for? What was my purpose here on this earth? Certainly, I was designed for more than milking cows and being a farm wife and mom.

Well God was about to answer those questions for me, but they were not the answers that I thought God would give.

After years of milk check price volatility where we felt we were on a roller coaster of milk prices, we finally decided to go all in and start the organic transition of our farm and cows.

So, in 2015 we started the transition from conventional farming, where you can use chemicals for weed control and a penicillin shot to cure anything that was wrong with your livestock, to organic where we had to learn a whole new farming concept of looking for what was causing the weeds and what was causing a cow to get sick. Additionally, we had to treat with more tillage and better soil nutrition and medicate the cows with more natural products like garlic and essential oils.

Well, if you ever want to test a marriage to see if it is strong enough to endure your love for each other, just try taking a farm organic. It's the longest, hardest, hellish 3 years of your life oh, and add in a hubby who keeps getting sicker, conventional milk prices that keep going down, (because remember you have to feed your cows all organic feed the last year the third year of organic transition while getting conventional milk prices), a milking parlor fire in the middle of a blizzard, and you learn that your hubby needs a liver transplant and needs to get on the liver transplant list - all of this within the last year of your organic transition.

Yes, you read that right! We had a milking parlor fire in the middle of one of the worst blizzards to ever hit the area. About 6 weeks before we had started pasturing our cows on pasture to qualify for the organic transition for our final third year so we could be certified organic.

The fire started around 12 noon instead of midnight. Otherwise, we probably would have lost all our cows in the fire and it would have burned down the freestall barn. Our hired man was just putting feed down for the cows when he looked into the milking parlor utility room and saw the smoke and flames shooting through the window.

He was able to run in and grab my farmer husband to call for help and then they were able to run and get the cows out along with neighbors who saw or heard about the fire.

We were able to get enough cattle trucks quickly here because it was on a Monday and all the cattle trucks had been at the local livestock sale when the call came in about our fire. School had just been dismissed because of the weather so we ended up with a lot of help from the high school kids to help us round up cattle outside and bring them up the freestall barn where we could sort them all out to go to the neighbors farm where they could all be kept together instead of getting split up so we could keep our organic transition going instead of having to restart the whole organic transition all over again once we rebuilt our milking parlor facility again.

We got all the cattle safely through the blizzard and over to the neighbor's farm 5 miles away without losing a cow or a truck and trailer!

The community fed us and our employees for 6 weeks every night at the neighbor's milking parlor.

I learned that God does care for me and that he wants to help us when we let him take over when we cannot. Because that night of the fire, I knew I was able to do it on my own and that was the night I started seeking God out to get to know who he was and who I was in Him.

But that was just the start of my journey with God and figuring out what my purpose was for me to do through him.

You see the start of that year, my farmer husband got really sick and ran a high temperature a couple days before the end of the year. On New Years Day of 2018, the doctors came in and told my husband that he was going to have to get on the liver transplant list as his liver was failing and that he was going to need a liver transplant. So the end of

February we had gone down for 2 days and got his testing done with the UW Madison Transplant team. 10 days later, the milking parlor fire started in the middle of a blizzard!

Then started the insurance battles which lasted for close to a month. We were so excited when we finally got that insurance check and handed it over to our bank so that we could start rebuilding so we could get our cows back in time to get them on pasture for 60 days. Normally you have to have your cows on pasture for 120 days but we were given an allowance of only 60 days because of the fire.

We were just dumbstruck with anger when the banker told us that they were not going to allow us to rebuild and for us to go get new jobs. Yes, that would have been great had my farmer husband been healthy enough to have been hired! But no one was going to hire him the way he looked. Also, what were we going to do about the burned-out milking parlor sitting there? Not likely you're going to be able to sell a farm with a burned-out milking parlor sitting there.

I remember after the bankers left that morning, my farmer husband and I just sat there mad, hurt, and stunned. But we did one thing. We stopped, got down on our knees and just asked God to show us what to do next. To give us a plan.

This is when I started learning the power of prayer especially when you take it to church and social media. The power of when you ask others to pray for you and when they do how God shows up and shows off.

I also learned through this experience that when you share your testimony God shows up and he starts showing off how much he loves you. I found out he created me to share my testimony so that others could see the transformation of my faith to see how the darkness that I was sitting in by trusting him and doing what he said by sharing my faith with others in person and online was helping me to grow and shine his light in me outwards so that others could see and be brought to him.

I still remember that night when the bank told us that they were no longer going to let us rebuild, that they were keeping the insurance checks and we should get new careers, how hopeless I felt. I was so lost, hurt, and angry. I wanted to choke those loan officers because they had taken what I thought was our life away from us. Little did I know how God was going to show up and show off. All I had to do was release the hurt and anger and focus on obeying what he told me to do.

That night on the way to milk my cows, I stopped over to return some dishes the neighbors had given us when they had dropped off food for us the night of the milking parlor fire. Now, being a farmer, you keep your emotions and your problems to yourself, you do not tell others what is bothering you. I was always taught to just say I am simply fine when others asked me how I was doing.

But this night was different, when my neighbors asked me how I was doing I heard a whisper - tell them how you are really doing. So, I told them I was hopeless, and I had no more hope left in me that we were going to be farmers. I told them about what the bank loan officers told us that they were not going to let us rebuild because we didn't have the extra $30,000 to rebuild because of the difference of between what it was going to cost to rebuild from what the insurance payout was and that I didn't see any way we could come up with $30,000 in a short amount of time to rebuild.

So, I left to go milk cows. Little did I know how God worked because I had been obedient and told my neighbors what was bothering my heart and mind and was honest that I did not see any hope. That is when God takes over and starts showing up and showing off!

By the next morning, our neighbor came over with an offer of loaning us $30,000 they had sitting in an investment account to help us rebuild our milking parlor. We could repay as we got on our feet after we rebuilt our milking parlor and if we couldn't repay it and lost everything, they would just consider it a gift.

To say the least we were shocked. When we called the bank loan officers they were even more shocked and quickly came up with more hoops for us to jump through in order to rebuild our milking parlor facility. This became about a month-long process. They would make us jump through one more hurdle to start rebuilding. Every Sunday, I would take it to my church and ask them to pray for this hurdle to be answered and the door to be opened for us to rebuild. Not only was I seeing the power of prayer in action, but my church members were seeing the power of prayer and the spark of hope igniting in my life. My light of Jesus' hope was starting to ignite for others to see Jesus shining brightly and to follow the light for themselves.

Finally, one morning while I was feeding a calf down in the barn, the loan officers had given us another hoop to jump through to get the money to rebuild our milking parlor. I was feeling hopeless and just worn out. I was headed out to my company's convention that morning as I had already bought my airplane ticket, paid for the event and the hotel, and honestly, I just needed a mental break to get away from the farm and the whole fire situation. I was so done!

I heard God tell me, go up in front of your burned out miking parlor and do a Facebook live and ask this question "Can anyone tell me why our bank won't let us rebuild our milking parlor even though we have the insurance money and the additional $30,000 needed to rebuild?"

Well, let me tell you once I hit send that post went virtual and God let the right people see that post that took action on our behalf. By that next Monday, when I got back from my trip, the bank was begging us to come in and sign papers to start the rebuilding of our milking parlor.

That was a lesson that I learned but honestly had to keep relearning. When you let go and let God take over, he works supernaturally and multiplies whatever he touches. You just must be still and let him take over.

Pray out your stresses and anxieties and then let God take over and watch in amazement as he shows up and shows off.

We were able to get our milking parlor built in half the time it took our first milking parlor to be built, and by September 7th, 2018, our cows were back home in the pastures grazing and we qualified our last year of organic transition. We got our organic certification on November 30th, 2018.

We were then told it was going to be another year before we were going to be able to get on the organic truck because there was too much milk on the market for us to get picked up. So even though we were organic certified, we were not going to be able to plug into the organic milk price. We were going to have to stay on conventional pricing.

Again, we took this problem to the Lord and asked for his help. He showed up quickly with an answer. He provided a resource within 30 days and we were on the organic milk truck route by January 1st, 2019, we were shipping organic milk and getting paid!

Then fast forward to 2022. Through all of this, my husband, even though he was sick, was still functioning well enough (with some medical procedures, medications and lots of prayers from people) to keep farming. Plus, we had the help of really good employees and the help of our incredible sons along with an awesome community surrounding us with help when we needed some additional help when he was sick and needed help with getting caught up in fieldwork.

With the community's help, we were even able to host our county's dairy breakfast on the farm on June 12th and feed 3,780 people breakfast on the farm a month before my husband got his first liver transplant.

At this point, my husband looked like death walking. He was a lovely shade of yellow green and was so skinny and his eyes were so sunk in when you looked at him you wondered how he was even functioning let alone doing all the demanding work of what needed to be done farming.

But here's where the story of revival and hope really gets interesting.

My husband and I went to his liver transplant doctor's appointment on Monday, July 12th. e arrived late because of issues on the farm, so his blood tests didn't come back in time before we left to go home. The next day he gets the call that his meld score (the score that determines whether you get put on the top of the liver transplant list) was finally 30.

They tell us that we need to have our phone on us because you only got two calls 30 minutes between and if you didn't call back within that time frame, it automatically goes to the next person on the list.

So, I quit sleeping at that point, and I totally went into panic and anxiety mode and worryied that we would not hear the call in time especially where we live as cell phone reliability is not always the most dependable around here.

By Thursday afternoon I was exhausted, sleep deprived, and barely functioning myself. So, when I heard a voice by the dairy case. (yes God does have a sense of humor!) ask me if I would trust him with my husband's health, I really thought I was going crazy. I immediately told that voice no, and shook my head and started walking away from the dairy case.

Then I heard that voice again asking me the question, do you trust me with your husband's health? I again said no, because I am a control freak and try to do everything on my own. By this time, I not only think I am cracking up, I know I am cracking up and losing it.

But then I heard him say it the third time. Do you trust me with your husband's health? That's when I remembered the bible story of Samuel being asked by God three times to be obedient, and that's when I bowed my head in my Walmart cart and cried out and surrendered to God saying, Yes, I trust you with my husband's health no matter what. Whether you take him home to heaven to be with you or whether you find him a liver and heal him here so that he can be here with me and our family, I trust you. No matter what, I will love you and praise you from this point on in my life. As soon as I totally surrendered my husband's health to God, I felt this beautiful peaceful waterfall of a breeze come over me and wash all the anxiety and fear away from me.

I walked out of Walmart that day with Hope and Peace. I knew no matter what, my farmer husband would not be in pain and misery much longer. By that Saturday afternoon, he got the news when we were both together that they had a liver match for him and that he was scheduled for a liver transplant the next day on July 17th.

Due to Covid restrictions, I could only have one other person down there with me during his liver transplant. So my son, Carl was picked as my other person since my other 3 sons were busy working on the farm as we were in the middle of harvesting our second crop of hay at the time.

My husband came through his liver transplant with excellence and was doing good the first 4 days. They had told him that Thursday on the 21st everything looked good and that he might even be able to go home that following Monday. But then the next day, that is when he developed his first high fever and his incision got a tear in it and he started leaking fluids. By that Saturday afternoon, he was back in surgery and had to get his incision repaired. They think that is when his donated liver got a blood clot in it because he never came out of that surgery good again. He started going back yellow again and started itching again (a sign that the liver is not working) and kept getting fevers and his appetite went down. He started sleeping more and just kept getting sicker every day. He went from a mild rejection to a moderate rejection of his liver until the Saturday morning of July 30th.

When I walked into his hospital room, he told me that his liver had quit and that he had been relisted at 7 am that morning and that he was the first one at UW Madison to get a liver that matched him.

I, of course, was in shock and needed to talk to a doctor to explain the whole situation to me as my husband just did not have the strength to explain it all to me.

So, the doctor and I stepped out of his room to talk in the corridor and that is when I asked the doctor, okay, how long does my husband have to live without a functioning liver in his body. She told me he had 24-48 hours to live and that a liver needed to be found within the 24 hours so that he could have the transplant the next day because she did not think he would make it until Monday.

Right at that moment my husband's transplant team of nurses came crashing out with him in his bed and yelling we are taking him to ICU now, hop on the elevator with us. We were quickly put into his ICU room, and I was quickly taken out when all the bells and whistles started going off and taken over to the family visitation room and told to stay there until someone came to get me. I was all by myself.

But you see, that's when I remembered what I had promised God, that I was going to praise him no matter what my husband's health turned out to be. So I got down on my knees and thanked the Lord for giving us this hope liver and told him how grateful I was that he had given us these last few weeks together and that I trusted him no matter what. I would trust him whether he was going to take my hubby home to heaven or find him a liver by the end of today to heal him here. I also reminded him it took him 4 years to get him a liver, but I needed one a bit quicker like today! Like now! I also asked him to bring me people that would pour into me and give me scripture to keep me strong in my faith and to make me bold and confident as my husband's voice for his health and for me to be a bold and confident leader for my family.

After calling my sons, my in-laws, my mom, and my pastor at the time, I got a call from my best friend, Cheryl. She just poured into me scripture and prayed over me. I felt God strengthening me and giving me confidence and power to be a strong leader and step out in faith and obedience to whatever he wanted me to do.

The first thing I remember God telling me to do was put what was going on with my husband's health on Facebook Live so that everyone could pray for us and I also think in hindsight it let them see the power of God showing up and showing off!

The next thing God asked me to do that afternoon was to get up and pray out loud in front of everyone at the busy UW Madison hospital lunch area around 12-noon for God to find my husband a liver that day. Can you just picture how many people are down there eating at that time of day? Now I had never prayed out loud in front of anyone, especially not to a whole cafeteria of strangers. You should have seen the shocked expression on my son, sister in law, and my pastor's face when I stood up and started praying out loud. The entire lunch room immediately got still and listened to my quick prayer of thanksgiving and my request to have God find my husband a liver quickly like now!

When we got back from our lunch around 1 pm we walked into my husband's ICU room where he whispered that they had come in and told him that they had found him a liver.

Of course, at the time, we thought he was in stage 4 of liver failure because before we had gone down to eat lunch, we had met with another doctor, and he had explained the four stages of liver failure and death. He had told us my husband was in stage 2 and that it was not going to be long before he went into stage 3, and that stage 4 was right before a patient would die. In stage 4, they would often be really disillusioned and would hallucinate. SO, when we walked in and heard my husband saying that someone had come in and told him that they had found him a liver, we all looked at each other and thought, oh crap! He is already in stage 4 of liver failure.

Then about 2 minutes later, a nurse tapped me on the shoulder and told me that the organ transplant nurse was on the phone for me. The organ transplant nurse then asked me if my hubby had told me the good news, that they had found him a matching liver and that he was scheduled for a liver transplant the following morning July 31st.

I will never forget going from, oh my goodness he's not going to make it, to the joy of how God came through and he's going to heal him here on earth and make him healthy so that he can see his youngest son get married and see our grandchildren be born and be a grandpa. He is going to restore my husband's health so that he can be strong and a farmer again.

I was able to get both of my youngest sons down to see their dad before surgery the next morning as they had not been able to see him before his first liver transplant because they had been so busy keeping the farm going while their dad was in the hospital.

After coming out of his hospital room with my sons, one of his doctors came in and pulled me to the side and told me to keep the family close as they didn't think he was going to pull through his heart test in order for them to pass him to go through with the liver transplant surgery. They would call me at 9 am and let me know whether he passed the test. If he did not pass the test, the liver would go to someone else immediately, and my husband probably wouldn't make it through the night.

I immediately heard God tell me to stand up, to be bold and courageous in my faith for him, and Boldy say to the doctor that "I am", that isGod personally found this liver for my hubby. In addition, God would give him the strength to pass his heart test and that he needed to have faith in God that he would work everything out in his way and for his purpose. I needed to go into that testing room with my husband in positivity, knowing that God was in charge.

Guess what? At 9:05 am the liver transplant team called me and told me that he had passed his heart test and that he was headed to surgery at that moment and the liver transplant was a go.

Of course, you also get the call when they have physically seen the liver and know for sure it's going to fit and that is when you know for sure there is no turning back. The next call you get is when they call you when the liver transplant is done.

So, we celebrated when we got that call that they were taking out his dead liver and had just put in his new liver.

When we got the call that the liver transplant was done and that his new liver was already functioning and making bile, I jumped into my youngest son's lap and hugged him so hard he thought I was going to hug the stuffing out of him. To hear the triumphant joys and see the tears come out of my sons when they heard that good news will always be a memory I will store in my heart always.

My husband continues to get stronger and stronger every day, and even 2 years later in 2024 as I am writing this, to see his faith grow stronger and to have him at my son's wedding in 2023 walking his son down the aisle with me was a heart desire coming true. I will never forgetseeing him look at and hold our first grandson, Lincoln, this past January the night he was born, this was also a heart memory. I know God loves to give us his daughters their heart's desires when we go before him humbly and seek him out and ask him to take over our worries and give us our heart's desires in his own time and in his own way.

God gives us a future and a hope when we totally trust him and surrender everything to him in prayer and thanksgiving. I know as we are going to be celebrating the birth of our granddaughter Lily Ray here this July and that's been a 9 year seeking and praying to the Lord for that prayer request and heart desire. But that is a whole other story for a whole other book in the future! So, stay tuned in!

Hilary Morris

Hilary Morris Coaching
Christian Life and Health Coach

http://www.linkedin.com/in/hilarymorris/
https://www.facebook.com/hilary.morris/
http://www.instagram.com/HilaryFitandFaithful
http://hilarymorris.net/

Hilary Morris and her husband reside in Texas with their four children, whose ages range over a span of a decade. As a former elementary school teacher for 20 years, she has mastered the art of seeking the Lord amidst a busy life. She believes that when we are at our best, we can focus more on the Lord's work rather than our own challenges, allowing us to better perceive and support those around us. Hilary is the creator and host of the Firestarters Podcast, where she showcases stories of ordinary women accomplishing extraordinary feats through faith. Currently, she plays a vital role as the women's ministry coordinator at Elmont Baptist Church. Her primary dedication lies in her work as a Faith-based life and health coach, guiding women to uncover and conquer limiting beliefs, and helping them take the next steps towards embracing their true selves as designed by God.

Firestarter

By Hilary Morris

"Dad, how do you start a fire?" I asked, eager to learn the secrets of creating a warm blaze in the cool night. As I made my way down the leaf-covered slope toward the firepit at our family cabin, my legs struggled to keep up with my father's brisk pace. I carefully balanced three logs in my arms, determined to impress him. "Well, first we need something dry and catching, like these dried leaves," my father explained, bending down to gather a handful from the ground. He expertly arranged the logs in the firepit while I watched. "Then we'll need something to create heat so the leaves can ignite and start to burn." He reached into his back pocket and pulled out a box of matches, holding it up for me to see. "And that's where these come in," he said with a smile. "Now, it's up to these logs to keep the fire going for as long as we need it tonight." I watched with fascination as my father drew out a match and struck it firmly against the box with a quick flick of his wrist. A sudden flame burst forth, promising the warm blaze we would all enjoy under the starry sky. As the fire grew and the night grew darker, I couldn't help but feel a sense of contentment and warmth.

To become an unstoppable woman of faith, the essential components are similar to those required for starting a fire. You must possess something that is open, unguarded, and combustible. Your environment must be saturated with life-giving oxygen. And, of course, you must withstand a persistent heat that eventually sparks into ignition. My hope is that through revealing my small beginnings, under the guidance and protection of our Maker, you will discover the innate potential inside you to become a catalyst, who not only embodies an unwavering faith, but also sparks others to do the same.

Today, I am a Firestarter, fueled by the power of Christ and pursuing my dreams fearlessly. I took a leap of faith and left public education after a 20-year career to start my own Health Coaching business and later expanded to become a Christian life coach. Along the way, I also created a podcast and became an author.

However, I wasn't always so bold or believing. In fact, you could say for most of my life I was lost, undisciplined and unmotivated. If you feel that way now, be encouraged and lean in. Success leaves clues.

There are moments in life that stand out as markers which lay stakes in the foundation of who we are and create our shape. My inner drive to always strive for improvement and recognize the potential in others is fueled by key experiences in my past. Most of them are related to dreams that I believe God placed in my heart and were never realized. Some because others snuffed them out, others because I hadn't grasped Whose I was…yet.

I recall my first time stepping out of my comfort zone and into unfamiliar territory. It may seem trivial now, but it left a lasting impression. In third grade, there was a science fair with awards, but only the gifted students usually participated. Despite this, I felt a strong desire to test my love for science and create a project. Excitedly, I told my mom, but my mother quickly doused my dreams, saying it was for the "smart kids." Sharing our dreams is vulnerable, and if we choose the wrong person, it can be extinguished. My mom had just come home from a long, stressful day, so her timing wasn't perfect. It wasn't until high school that I pursued another dream.

During my time in middle school, I was an avid volleyball player and had hoped to continue playing in high school. However, I faced a major hurdle - my inability to execute an overhand serve, which was a requirement at the high school level. Despite this one shortcoming, I was a skilled volleyball player in other areas. My dedication to the sport was evident in my willingness to wake up at 6 am for practice, and even now, I can still recall the distinct scent of the gym mixed with the aroma of icy hot that we all used to soothe our aching muscles from our rigorous two-a-day practices. I remained on the team until my sophomore year, when a pivotal moment between my mother and I occurred. She was struggling to get me to the early morning practices, and I was still struggling to master the overhand serve. It was then that she suggested I quit, as volleyball was not my strong suit. Though I knew she was right, I couldn't help but feel upset at the thought of giving up. However, a part of me also felt compelled to see this challenge through, to prove to myself that I could overcome any obstacle. But eventually, I succumbed to my self-doubt and reluctantly bid farewell to volleyball. Looking back, I couldn't help but feel like I was "Halfway-Hilary," someone who never finishes what they start, especially when faced with difficulty.

In my sophomore year, my mother gave me the chance to start riding saddlebred horses. It soon became my passion and I spent most of my time at the barn, perfecting my skills. I was even invited to attend an Equitation camp with Olympic riders in another state. On the flight there, I excitedly bombarded my trainer with questions about competing at the highest level. I was thrilled to be in the same camp as a triple crown winner, easily recognized by her white gloves. The thought of earning my own pair of white gloves fueled me. I believed I had what it takes to achieve such a feat with my hard work and determination. But when I shared my ultimate dream of competing in the Olympics, my trainer's response crushed me. She glanced out the window and said, "Well, that will never happen." At that moment, my dream was shattered. I watched the smoke from my short-lived spark dissipate, feeling suffocated and defeated.

Attracted by the excitement of weekends and boys, I searched for fulfillment in romantic relationships like many teenage girls. Faith was not a part of my upbringing, but morals were instilled in me. Despite our strict upbringings, my friends and I often pushed boundaries and made mistakes. Looking back, I now realize that I defined myself through the lens of a boy. This unhealthy reliance on relationships led me into an abusive one.

In college, I lacked drive, motivation, direction, and self-worth. If not for my father's insistence, I may not have even attended. My roommate became my guide, helping me register for classes and pushing me to pursue education. It was a turning point in my life. I finally broke free from my high school relationship, only to enter an even worse one. This relationship led me to my darkest days and caused me to let go of someone I genuinely liked.

My journey towards faith began during my college years. I vividly recall taking a history course that filled me with animosity towards religion. I completely rejected my Catholic upbringing and made it my mission to uncover the truth. In my first summer at college, I enrolled in a course called "History in Art Context" in the beautiful city of Paris, France. Traveling to new places has a way of broadening one's perspective and introducing new ideas. Every day, we explored various museums, starting from the Paleolithic era and ending in contemporary times. It was during a visit to the Cluny Museum, surrounded by medieval statues, that I had a revelation. In passing, I made a remark questioning the existence of Jesus and my agnostic professor responded with, "Jesus was indeed a real man who walked the earth. There are records of him in historical writings from other cultures." I froze in my tracks next to a forgotten king's bust and thought, "If he truly existed and claimed to be the King of Kings, then I must delve deeper into understanding why." This encounter made me curious and open, flammable.

It took years of searching, and most likely prayer from countless friends and family, before I found the Truth. I went through dark seasons where the search paused. I took wrong turns that lengthened the journey. I continued to teeter-totter between near light and darkness, holding on to thoughts and ideas that I felt should create clarity and comfort but never did. I held on to people I thought would save me, but the tighter I held on to them the harder it was to breathe. I worked so hard to control, control, control, and all I had in the end was chaos. Years of no dreams, no visions, no self-worth, and no truth brought me to my knees. There comes a time when you just throw your hands up and say, "If you're real, show me the truth. No more hide-and-seek. I'm asking. Will you just tell me?!" And that's exactly what He did.

Post college, in my mid-twenties, one of my lifelong friends invited me to church for the umpteenth time. Sitting there in that room I screamed those words in my head to a creator I knew was there but didn't know. He answered. Not audibly, but it was Him. I heard Him say, "It is true. It is all true and I am Him." I understood it to be Jesus speaking to me. You ask how I know that for sure. I just do. And to this day I don't say, I believe that Jesus Christ is my Messiah. I say, I know He is. Oxygen.

In that moment of vulnerable, desperate surrender I met the rest of me. Where hope had been extinguished, faith reignited it. If I could gain access to the rest of me in one single moment, what more could I understand if I pursued my Creator? That's what I did! I was hungry to know Him and so I started making decisions that would help me know Him better. I joined Bible Study Fellowship, better known as BSF. It's a Bible study organization that runs very much like a college course and that's exactly how I tackled it. I was all in! I prayed for God's wisdom to help me understand His Word. I read, underlined, took notes, discussed questions with peers, and listened to sermons. I joined a church, got involved, and never missed an opportunity to be with the Body of Christ. What a glorious time of discovery! I thought I had finally figured it all out. I broke free from one of the most abusive relationships that I had allowed to steal so much of my life away and felt free. But I was still living off milk and hadn't learned how to put on my armor.

So with renewed hope and an underdeveloped identity, I entered what would eventually become a chain-breaking relationship. Did you know that just because a relationship isn't toxic doesn't mean it's healthy? I had never considered that idea. So, I dove head first into what I thought would be my forever. What I learned is that you can know God. You can believe that Jesus is your Savior. You can be in pursuit of Him, and you can still tuck a part of you away from Him because you want something else more than you want Him. Right away, I sensed that it was God's voice beckoning me to abandon my envisioned future. He made it evident that this was not my destined path, yet I was unable to envision a more fulfilling one. I just knew if I gave this up that I would be alone forever. I still had no self-worth. I didn't understand that my identity was in Christ alone. For two years I fought His call to obey. My understanding of God and my purpose deepened over two years through Bible Study, church engagement, and prayer. Despite initially failing to act on this knowledge, God's comforting hand and guidance ultimately led me to make a life-changing decision.

Interestingly, you can be in rebellion, but if you're still seeking Him daily, spending time with Him, and in His word, you become brave enough to surrender and obey. With great heartache, I let go. With no promise of something better, I let go. I surrendered to the idea of being alone forever. I told God I would keep my eyes on Him as long as He promised to keep His eyes on my life. I would serve Him and live for His glory and the building of His kingdom. I decided He was all I ever needed. My oxygen. He was enough. Crash. Chains broken.

Obeying can be overwhelming, bringing intense pressure and discomfort and leaving uncertainty. But as I freed myself from codependency, I embraced life with a new lightness, despite feeling foreign and uncomfortable. In the desert, I relied solely on God, challenging and forcing myself to withstand the heat. This heat was a result of my decision to follow God's path and live according to His will. There was no turning back, no escape from the solitude and I did feel pressure to return to my old ways. Yet, amidst the unsettling stillness, I found deep intimacy with God. His indescribable peace filled me, reminding me that in His presence, I am whole and lack nothing. I realized that I am seen and known by God, making me visible and significant. Though we may shy away from pressure and seek relief, it is through these challenges that we grow and evolve. Like a fire that needs pressure and heat to ignite, I was perfectly positioned in my most vulnerable state to be set ablaze by the Holy Spirit during that desert season. It was a time of ignition, transformation, and renewal.

By choosing to obey, the perfect conditions were set for a fire to ignite within me. He had molded me to be flammable, open, and receptive. His Word and Holy Spirit supplied the much-needed oxygen for my soul. His beckoning to step out of my comfort zone and trust Him created intense pressure and discomfort. And when all these elements came together, I was set ablaze. I finally grasped the true essence of not just knowing about God, but truly being in a profound relationship with Him. His trustworthiness, faithfulness, loyalty, and boundless love were revealed to me. I knew I could always count on Him to never abandon me, lead me astray, or change His ways. Having Him as my rock, my foundation, made me courageous and fearless. As the saying goes, there is a way that appears right to man, but in reality, it leads to ruin. How much suffering we bring upon ourselves when we choose this path instead of following the loving call of God towards a better way.

Inflamed by the Spirit, my dreams were ignited. During my time of independence, I took the opportunity to truly understand myself and my desires. I carefully crafted a list of qualities that I sought in a partner and experiences that I longed to pursue. This season was fruitful. It's remarkable how a soul is transformed when it is ablaze for the Lord. My relationships with colleagues, family, and friends took on a new dynamic. My conversations shifted, no longer craving shallow humor or crude language. Instead, I was driven to uplift and motivate others towards good deeds. I could clearly see when those close to me were straying from the right path, and all I wanted was to embolden them to trust and obey the gentle whisper in their hearts, urging them to have faith in God.

My career in education became my calling to serve not just my peers, but also my students. Though it was a strange turn of events, I can now see that this was the perfect time for God to bring my husband back into my life. He was the young man I had liked during our college years, but had walked away from. The moment I saw him again, my heart was reignited and we were engaged within months. Our life moved at a rapid pace once we were married. Within six months, we were expecting our first child and two years later, we welcomed our second. As teachers, our combined income brought on the familiar pressure that God often allows when calling us to greater heights.

Looking back, we both agree that our marriage began in a foxhole together. With financial struggles, it was hard to make ends meet, but this challenge brought us clarity. We quickly learned to rely on God and stand united in our trials. During this season, I can vividly recall falling to my knees beside our bed, my head pressed into the carpet, as I cried out to God. Though money cannot bring true happiness, the lack of it can certainly bring immense pressure. Balancing a full-time teaching job, raising two young boys, and rarely seeing my husband left me stressed and busy, but not fulfilled. It was difficult to bear fruit when I couldn't even see beyond my own struggles. But God planted a deep desire in my heart for more. I longed to leave the classroom and be at home with my children, creating lasting memories. I yearned for a greater purpose beyond the daily tasks that took away from the joy of teaching. I wanted, at the very least, to have more quality time with my kids than just bathing, feeding, and putting them to bed. Every time I cried out to God, I would feel a sense of peace wash over me, sustaining me until the next breaking point. But I never heard a clear answer, only the word "wait". And so, I remained in the furnace for four more years. During that time, we welcomed our third child. My husband eventually left the teaching and coaching profession, and I switched school districts to work in a less stressful environment. These changes brought some relief, but my desire to make a deeper impact and have more quality time with our children remained.

During this particular season, my pursuit of God was as urgent as if my very existence depended on it - and perhaps it truly did. My body was struggling with thyroid failure, causing me to spiral into extreme anxiety and paranoia, a state of mind that I wouldn't wish upon even my worst enemy. It felt as though I had lost my sense of self and there was no way to reclaim it. I vividly recall confiding in my doctor about the oppressive thoughts I was experiencing, wondering if they were normal. His answer was a resounding no, followed by a recommendation for medication. However, I stubbornly chose to rely on prayer to get me through this trying period. Day after day, I would go to work, cook dinner, bathe my children, and then collapse onto my side of the bed, finally allowing the tears that I had been holding back all day to flow freely onto the floor. After the unexpected arrival of our fourth child, I hit rock bottom. Alone at home with our newborn daughter, I fell to my knees and screamed out to God, questioning why He had burdened us with another child when we were struggling to make ends meet. Why hadn't He provided me with a job that could support our family and fulfill my longing for more in life? Why did I feel trapped in a cage of limitations, despite my constant searching for something greater? But there was no answer - only silence.

And so, I wiped away my tears, fed my baby, and continued on with my day. But then, everything changed the very next day.

One conversation set me on a path that would allow me to use my passion for health to not only improve my own life, but also to help others pursue the best versions of themselves. And perhaps, along the way, it could also bring in more income for my family. As I prayed and asked God if this was the answer I had been seeking, a sense of hope and peace washed over me, a gift from the Holy Spirit. Through this incredible opportunity, I have learned the true value of growth and the importance of embracing sanctification. I have been surrounded by like-minded women who have breathed life into my dreams and continually challenged me to strive for better. I have been encouraged to step out of my comfort zone, supported through the heat and pressure that come with such changes, and continuously ignited as a woman of faith. From being known as "Halfway-Hilary," I have transformed into an unstoppable force, driven by the realization that achieving all four elements of being your own firestarter requires intentional and ongoing pursuit.

You may sense a divine pull towards a dream, an aspiration, or a goal, but to truly spark it, four crucial components are necessary. I am confident that we all have the ability to ignite our dreams, yet it requires a recognition of these factors and a steadfastness in safeguarding them.

First, be flammable! Having an open and coachable mindset means being willing to let go of old ways of thinking and being open to new ideas and perspectives. It means being open to change and being willing to learn and grow. This mindset is essential when stepping out of the boat because it allows you to be receptive to new opportunities and possibilities.

Being flammable in this context means being able to catch and ignite the flames of change. It means being willing to take risks and embrace the unknown. Just like a fire needs an easily ignitable item to keep burning, a new journey needs an open and coachable mindset to keep moving forward.

However, it's important to note that having an open and coachable mindset doesn't mean being naive or blindly optimistic. It's about bringing your requests to God and listening. It's about acknowledging potential challenges and obstacles, but still having faith and hope that things will work out for the better. Scripture states, "And we know that for those who love God all things work together for good, for those who are called according to his purpose." Romans 8:28. This doesn't mean things aren't hard and don't go wrong. It means that He will work through it for His glory and good purpose and you will be better for it.

It's easy to fall into a negative and pessimistic state when you're stepping outside of your comfort zone. You may feel overwhelmed, uncertain, and even scared. In those moments, it's important to remember that your mindset and attitude can greatly impact the outcome of the transition. Instead of giving in to negative thoughts and limiting beliefs, choose to have a faith-filled mindset. Remember that you are made in the image of our Creator and have the strength and resilience to overcome any challenge. Don't let your past experiences or current circumstances dictate your future. Embrace the possibility and hope that change can bring. Just like the character Pollyanna, who always found the silver lining in every situation, your faith can create opportunities for good to come from any circumstance. By believing in the Scriptures and trusting in God's plan, you can navigate through the transition with a willing mindset and come out stronger on the other side. Be ignitable!

Oxygen is also needed to ignite a fire. Is your environment filled with oxygen or toxins that smother you? This element might require the most diligence to protect. You must carefully monitor your surroundings and remove any potential threats to your dreams. This means distancing yourself from negative influences and surrounding yourself with those who support and encourage you. It may not always be easy, but it is necessary if you want to achieve your goals. You can't expect to fulfill your dreams without purposefully posturing yourself around the right people. People who will fan your flame and breathe life into you when it's hard, and it will be hard. You need a strong support system, people who will lift you up and help you overcome challenges. These people may not always be obvious, but they are essential to your success. Surround yourself with positive, like-minded individuals who share your passion and drive. Their influence will help you stay focused and motivated, even during the toughest of times.

I only became an unstoppable woman of faith when I intentionally distanced myself from people who continually tried to stop me. This doesn't require over-the-top, dramatic, cutting off of relationships. Most of the time, it just requires reflection. Who builds me up? Who leaves me feeling drained and hopeless? Who spurs me on to good works? Who's advice causes me to shrink? Spend more time with the life-givers, fellow dreamers, and flame fanners. It will naturally limit your time with the snuffers, smotherers, and extinguishers. By surrounding yourself with the right people, you will create a positive and supportive environment that will help you achieve your dreams.

The journey to success is never easy. Nor is it a straight line; it's full of twists, turns, and unexpected detours. It's easy to get discouraged when our dreams seem impossible to achieve, but that's when we know we're on the right track so no one can boast. God's plans for us are always bigger and better than what we can imagine for ourselves. He wants what's good for us, and sometimes that means enduring the heat and pressure necessary to create a fire within us.

Just like coal needs to undergo extreme heat and pressure to transform into a diamond, we too need to go through challenging times to become the best version of ourselves. It may not be easy, but in the end, we will come out stronger and more equipped for the work He's called us to. We mustn't give up when things get tough because it's during those times that our character is molded and our faith is strengthened. So when the journey presents obstacles and the heat and pressure seem unbearable, remember that it's all part of the process. Trust in God's plans and embrace the challenges with a grateful heart. Embrace the heat! You were made to endure!

God has uniquely crafted each of us for this life, with all of its beauty and brokenness. He has called us to step out of the boat and equipped us to work within His boundless strength. We are never alone in the midst of challenges. As we persevere and are empowered by the Holy Spirit, others take notice. By embracing our identity in Christ and chasing after the dreams He has placed in our hearts, a fire is ignited within us. We become a shining light on a hill, inspiring others to see what is possible. Our passion burns bright and draws others in. As they draw near, they too are set ablaze. We become unstoppable women of unwavering faith, obediently following God's will. We are the catalysts of change, igniting a fire in others and setting the world ablaze with our unwavering faith and determination.

Jessica GourJess Gabriel

Divine Women Institute
Spiritual Life Coach & Motivational Speaker

http://www.linkedin.com/in/GourJessTV
http://www.facebook.com/GourJessTV
http://www.instagram.com/GourJessTV

Jessica GourJess Gabriel is an American author, motivational speaker, On Camera Personality and a Spiritual Life Coach dedicated to educating and empowering women to embrace their true divine identity and God given purpose.

Created Divine by Design: Awakening to My Divine Identity in Christ

By Jessica GourJess Gabriel

This chapter is dedicated to any person who has ever felt lost, unworthy, or inadequate. May you realize the immeasurable value of your worth, bestowed upon you by God, the divine Creator, who has made you in His image and in His likeness.

If someone had told me when I was younger that I'd be dead by age 35, I simply would not have believed them. Having had what I considered to be a wonderful childhood growing up in Hawaii, never in my wildest dreams did I think I'd be dead by 35.

"In the past you were spiritually dead because of your disobedience and sins. At that time you followed the worlds evil way..." Ephesians 2:1-2

Yet, there I was, alone on my bedroom floor, feeling helpless, hopeless, and defeated. I felt trapped with no way out. I had decided that death was my only option. Looking back, I realize that this period of my life mirrored my spiritual state at that time. I was spiritually dead, living a life apart from Christ and distant from God.

"Remember that at that time you were separate from Christ, excluded from citizenship in Israel and foreigners to the covenants of the promise, without hope and without God in the world." Ephesians 2:12

However, things were not always like this. When I look back, I remember how I used to communicate with God internally, seeking His direction and guidance, which kept me morally upright and on the correct path. What changed? Where did I go wrong? How did I stray so far off track? At this stage of my life, viewing things from an outside perspective, I appeared to be successfully managing two thriving businesses, assisting my future husband with his business ventures, balancing life's challenges, maintaining our lovely home, and nurturing a seemingly strong and loving relationship on the path to marriage. However, the truth was far from what it seemed.

> *"You were running the race well; who has interfered and prevented you from obeying the truth?" Galatians 5:7*

In reality, I found myself trapped in a toxic relationship while battling depression, overwhelming anxiety, and low self-esteem which looking back were all issues I had been dealing with long before meeting my ex. However, this was different, it was heavier, it was tougher, it was more intense. As a result, I turned to hard drugs as a misguided way to deal with the mental and emotional abuse that began to consume me.

I often wondered how my life and our relationship had reached such a disastrous point, especially during what should have been a joyful time in our lives. After all, we had finally gotten engaged after eight long years of being together, yet we were both still unhappy. He was often angry over money and no matter how much I contributed it was simply "NOT GOOD ENOUGH!" I often questioned if I was at fault, if his accusations had merit, if I was being "too sensitive," and if my responses were justified. The thing is, unfortunately, the mental, verbal, and emotional abuse I was experiencing was often subtle, disguised (masked), and hidden, making it extremely hard to discern though it was so incredibly painful. Over time, it slowly began to diminish my soul and crush my spirit long before I ever even realized what was happening. The mental anguish I felt from his harsh words began to take over my mind and make me physically sick.

As life went on, we stayed together, but his mood was unpredictable, often changing from light to darkness like shifting shadows. I eventually began to realize many recurring patterns of abuse emerging. For instance, he would be very joyful when he had money, he constantly went on trips, invested in new business ventures, as well as stocks and bonds, etc. Initially, I found this to be wonderful, I was happy for him until I realized it always took a turn for the worse. When he returned from trips out of town and or when these business ventures failed, the blame would shift to me, accompanied by criticism, insults, ridicule, shame, and blame. After some time, I began to expect and prepare for the mental beatdowns I knew were coming which caused me to live in full-blown survival mode. This began to have an extremely negative impact on my physical health which left me depressed and unable to get out of bed. He eventually began to express frustration and criticize me for staying in bed, but I was spiritually drained and therefore found myself physically exhausted.

"Death and Life are in the power of the tongue..."
Proverbs 18:21

The thing is he was so happy in public, but behind closed doors, he was emotionally unstable. Over time, I began to realize yet another pattern of abuse, whenever I was happy, it appeared to bother him immensely, leading to constant criticism, insults, ridicule, shame, and blame. I was often left confused by it and found myself stuck in this sick toxic repetitive cycle of trying to keep him happy (people pleasing) to avoid the abuse. It was so confusing and exhausting that I began to lose my mind. I found myself haunted by the relentless echo of his voice constantly insulting me and shouting "NOT GOOD ENOUGH!" both in reality and in my mind which kept me feeling hopeless and defeated. I began to internalize the lies and false statements he made about me being "NOT GOOD ENOUGH," and as I believed them, those lies gradually shaped the reality I found myself living in. I transformed into the very person that he perceived to be "NOT GOOD ENOUGH!"

I wanted so badly to pack my bags and leave, but fear held me back. He constantly made me doubt my own perceptions (gaslighting), leaving me feeling like nobody would understand my situation. How could anyone trust me when he seemed so perfect while I seemed like such a mess? However, beneath the layers of my own self-doubt and pain, I could hear a small voice within me insisting that this treatment was unacceptable. I recognized that, no matter how much I loved this man, I didn't deserve to endure such deep insidious mental and emotional pain.

I wish I could say that I left when I first began feeling suicidal, but the reality is I didn't. When the abusive cycle began, I would cry, threaten to leave him; he would apologize, make grand gestures (love bombing). I would turn to drugs, accept the apology, and eventually forgive him. It was just another toxic repetitive cycle and pattern of abuse that existed between us. We had formed our very own toxic trauma bond.

I wanted to leave so badly, but the reality was, we were both so deeply immersed in each others' entrepreneurial pursuits that it left little time for anything beyond work for me. Managing my businesses that included me juggling my role as an On-Camera Personality and Emcee, running a media production company, managing a demanding mobile salon, and assisting him with his business, which kept me incredibly busy and exhausted.

The continuous effort to satisfy him, the emotional and mental manipulation, and the control needed to stop. It was crucial for me to start being honest, especially with myself. I finally accepted the fact that I was in a toxic relationship, and instead of turning to drugs, I needed to turn to God. That sounded good, but for some reason, I just couldn't see a way out. All I could think was that my life was over.

"If my people, who are called by my name, will humble themselves and pray and seek my face and turn from their wicked ways, then I will hear from heaven, and I will forgive their sin and will heal their land." 2 Chronicles 7:14

It was at that moment that I found myself kneeling in tears on my bedroom floor that I decided that this would be the end. Death was my only option. I was going to do it, I was going to take my life... It was then that a voice deep inside me called out to God with what I truly believed would be my last breath, and just like that, everything changed. Something inside of me came alive, and what I had thought was my last breath became the beginning of a whole new life.

"Everyone who calls on the name of the Lord will be saved."
Romans 10:13

It wasn't until I came to the end of myself and cried out to God that I experienced an incredibly powerful spiritual awakening. Almost immediately I began to experience the transformative power of God's presence. Over the next few months, I began to have an insatiable hunger for spiritual food (God's word). I repented of my sins, drew near to God, and cultivated a deep meaningful relationship with Him. I felt an overwhelmingly powerful sense of being surrounded by God's love and His presence. Despite my circumstances, I was at rest, He had given me His perfect peace.

"For it is by grace you have been saved through faith. And this is not your own doing; it is a gift from God."
Ephesians 2:8

"God has called you out of darkness into his marvelous light." – 1 Peter 2:9

As I progressed in my healing journey, I came to the realization that the root cause of all my issues lay in my lack of self-worth due to past negative experiences and my lack of knowledge and faith in God. I struggled with valuing and trusting myself, and it dawned on me that I faced similar challenges that the Israelites (in the Bible) faced that led them to spend 40 years in the wilderness. Just like the Israelites, my disobedience (specifically my dependence on drugs) and my unbelief (my lack of knowledge and faith in God) during difficult times kept me stuck in my own wilderness. As my connection with God deepened, my comprehension of His nature expanded. This led me to discover more about Jesus, the Word of God made flesh (manifested), made alive and dwelling within me.

> *"And we all, with unveiled faces, beholding the glory of the Lord, are being transformed into the same image from one degree of glory to another. For this comes from the Lord who is the Spirit." 2 Corinthians 3:18*

> *"For those God foreknew he also predestined to be conformed to the image of his Son..." Romans 8:29*

By drawing closer to God and following Jesus, I embarked on a journey of divine self-discovery and the understanding of my purpose. Going deeper, I discovered a supremely powerful and all-knowing God, whose words are so powerful that He spoke this world into existence with them. I began to embrace the understanding that I am granted the same power and authority through the Holy Spirit to speak my world and reality into existence by declaring the truth that God says about all of His children.

This realization has led me on the transformative path of releasing negative self-perceptions rooted in past trauma and experiences by affirming the truth God declares about me. Scripture states that "the word of God is alive and active, sharper than any double-edged sword." By embracing and declaring the powerful truth of God's word over my life, it became alive inside of me and went to battle against the misconceptions and lies I previously believed about myself. Through affirming these truths, God's word the sword of truth began to cast down the imaginations, deceptions, and lies that I believed, enabling me to embrace my true divine identity, the reality that I, like Jesus, am a child of the most high God. I am royalty. I began to declare that I am blessed, prosperous, happy, whole, joyful, worthy, forgiven, redeemed, and restored. I AM a masterpiece, created in His image, whose value is far more precious than jewels and whose value is far above rubies and pearls. Yes, I AM the head and not the tail, I AM fearfully and wonderfully made. I AM more than a conqueror through Christ, who loves me. As I continue to believe and affirm the word of God by faith, I have received so many blessings including the revelation of my true identity found in Jesus Christ.

> *"Therefore, if anyone is in Christ, he is a new creature: old things are passed away; behold, all things* **have become new"**
> **2 Corinthians 5:17**

Moving forward with this new understanding has allowed me to forgive my ex and myself, understanding that our behaviors were shaped by our environment and past experiences. We were attempting to navigate life through self-preservation rather than self-sacrificing love, albeit foolishly and ignorantly. Wanting a better life, I turned to God, and through faith, I found salvation. By the grace of God alone, I overcame my struggles with low self-esteem and substance abuse, got my own place, and landed an incredible job. I am currently in the process of creating a platform that will help me further the kingdom of God by using my spiritual gifts and talents to educate, uplift, and empower others.

As I close this chapter in my life, I invite you to join me in saying this prayer.

Heavenly Father, We thank You for the wisdom found in Your Word. May your word serve as a mirror that reflects how your children perceive themselves. Looking ahead, I pray that your children will not shape their identities based on societal standards or others' opinions. Instead, may they see themselves as you do in alignment with what your word reveals and declares about them.

We ask for Your grace and wisdom to navigate our daily lives with purpose and dedication. As we move forward let our lives be a testament to Your goodness and a reflection of our commitment to living out Your principles.

In Jesus' name, we pray.

Amen.

Julie Lavia

Julie Lavia Coaching
Visibility & Digital Marketing Strategist

https://www.facebook.com/julie.lavia.1/
http://www.instagram.com/julielaviacoaching
http://www.juliechristinacreates.com/

Julie Lavia is a visibility strategist and digital marketer who helps women boost visibility in their online businesses. Julie is also a female empowerment advocate who helps women own their truth by being their authentic selves through the power of storytelling. Julie has her podcast, She Means Impact, on Apple and Spotify interviewing businesswomen on their business journey and how it is creating an impact in their lives. Julie is writing her first business-inspired solo book to help introverted women appear confidently online as first-time entrepreneurs. Julie is in the throes of creating her video podcast docuseries, Her Roadmap To Resiliency, on Fenix TV. Julie wants to empower more women to use digital and PR Marketing in their businesses for extra visibility through community building on Facebook, virtual networking, and a paying membership. Julie wanted to share her story of becoming an unstoppable woman by faith as a co-author.

Fragile To Fierce

By Julie Lavia

This brown-skin, browned-eyed black, curly-haired girl knew she was a little different since birth. In a sense, I had always liked to be alone and did not need any company around me. Aside from being an only child until 6, when my baby sister was born, I had to find my source of entertainment and happiness. I would line up my stuffed animals, sing, and teach them, but one behaviour stood out when I played with my toys. My mother noticed I was flapping, flailing my arms, and rocking back and forth. We were unsure what that entailed, but it was a behaviour I had done whenever I was playing, and I would just go off into my world. The arm flapping began at age two and has been a part of my life until now.

This was just one of the many behaviours that started as I grew into a young girl. I was timid to the point that if strangers came over to meet me, I would not speak, and my parents thought I was being rude and forced me to say hello to the person. I don't think I was rude, but I hid my voice and did not know how to express myself.

There were a few other incidents that challenged my reactions to social situations. I remember running away from the phone when it would ring in the house, and I'm guessing because I did not want to answer it since I never liked to talk to strangers or people in general. Also, whenever family members came to my house with their cameras, they would point them ready to take photos of me, and I would run away to avoid getting my picture taken. I was just a young kid who did not know any better but already hated to be the center of attention.

Eventually, when I got older, around 7 or 8 years old, I started warming up a little better to the camera. I allowed people to take pictures of me, but only for special occasions such as Christmas, first communion, or birthdays. Though I allowed people to take photos of me, I still needed to be more comfortable with being camera-ready and camera-friendly. I would avoid eye contact as much as I could. I would not smile much or just want to get it done. I was still really uncomfortable with being put out there on display, and I did not like to look at myself because I just thought of myself as an "ugly duckling" at the time.

Before the 3rd grade, I didn't remember how I behaved in school much. I went to my first elementary school, and I believe I got along with my peers. Though reserved, shy, and quiet, I felt accepted, and no one teased me. So, I was transferred to a new school after my second year.

Since the education system was not as strong and I was a baptized Roman Catholic, my mother felt it was only suitable to let me continue my studies in a Catechism environment. We had a church right across the school, and we would attend church functions and special mass ceremonies for our school. I adapted to my new school and fit in with the existing children who had already formed friendships with each other. However, the shy girl in me kept quiet, stayed alone, and did not talk to many people. I struggled with schoolwork, especially math, and did not like to raise my hand to ask questions or get help from my classmates. Being painfully shy and a loner did not serve its purpose when I was in my new class. I had to go to class every day to sit in a chair and remain focused on classwork, which was sometimes tricky.

Remember, I had mentioned that I would love to stim. Stimming is when a person performs a ritual behaviour to calm him or herself down. In my case, the arm flapping and rocking back and forth would help regulate me when I wanted to go off into my fantasy world. I can remember sitting still without trying to fidget in my chair, not letting on that I had these mild symptoms. It was bad enough that kids caught on to my shy demeanour and treated me like an alien.

This weird alien from out of space is alienated from many classmates. One particular boy who was not only the class clown but the class bully had control over these kids because he was forming some famous "club." One of the rules was to hate me for no apparent reason. Whenever they had to touch my papers, desk, or anything that belonged to me, they would cross their fingers and say "Ajax" as if I had some kind of germs they would catch. It was not easy to walk into school every day to face this ridicule and these kids' sense of immaturity.

I almost got beaten up by the same group of kids who were part of this club because they believed a rumour that some other kid in our grade had heard something terrible that was being said about their mother, which was not confirmed.

Since I did not talk much and was too shy to face people for confrontation, the best way to express myself was to speak to someone I was close with, my mom. She was the one that kept me grounded and told me it was ok. Whenever I told her I was nervous or did not want to go to school because I did not want to face the mean kids in my class, she would try to help me see the positive and that it could be a better day. However, she was my voice within; you know, she was the one person who stuck up for me by going to the school to face the kids and tell them to leave me alone.

This whole time, going through this crazy and dark journey in my life, I had managed to stay true to who I was and did not change to impress others. Of course, I did not realize it, but back then, I was not a follower but a leader and someone unique and different, even if my classmates were followers and wanted to be all the same.

After I had left the 3rd grade, the bullying continued because I was still a shy and socially awkward girl who barely spoke. I wanted to write short stories and was a good artist who loved to draw. Each year, as I moved up a grade, at least one annoying kid wanted to use my existence as a punching bag, and I mean that only figuratively. Whenever I felt a kid stop teasing me or what I thought was teasing, I would tell my mom, and she would come to my rescue again. I wonder now if I was just taking things that kids said seriously. I was so used to kids being so mean and phoney that I did not trust anything from their mouths, and I did not want them to speak to me.

The high school years approached, and I was a turtle in its shell by then. The reason for saying this is because I had severe trust issues. I did not want to draw attention to myself because I feared becoming a target for a new bully.

When I started my first high school, I remember intentionally giving my peers an attitude because I used it as a defence mechanism. My peers were nice to me, but I developed an attitude problem toward other kids who were not being mean to me. After a while, I realised I

needed to get out of my past, and from then on, I started acting nicer toward my classmates. Regardless of the shift in attitude, I was still very guarded towards people and stuck to myself.

I not only stuck to myself because of being guarded, but I was still socially awkward due to my undiagnosed Autism. In elementary school, avoiding getting teased was much more challenging because many children fed off other kids' energy. If one person in the group did not like you, it was a guarantee that their friends would not want you despite you getting along with them.

At least in high school, the students were just finding their walk in faith. These students were trying to survive another school year and were starting to develop their personalities. Therefore, meeting other students who were quiet and shy and kept to themselves, like me, became more manageable. I was such a pro at hiding my undiagnosed Autism that other students did not suspect that I had this intellectual disability. I wanted to fit in like other neurotypical children since I felt that no one would understand my disability. My inability to focus for long periods affected my schoolwork, and in turn, I felt overwhelmed with the piling up of work to do.

I attended three different high schools during my school years. The last two years were challenging because I had gone from the private to the public sector. The public school education was another culture shock because of the lack of education, funds, and how the kids behaved. There was occasional bullying from some mean girls and typical high school catty gossip. Other than that, I was still struggling to use my voice and dealing with social awkwardness from my Autism.

I started my first job in my early 20s. I was about to start university and needed support for my studies in human relations. Some new owners launched a healthy fast-food restaurant, and I applied. Finally, I had enough confidence to meet people for interviews in public spaces and wanted independence. The first start to my newfound freedom was earning money and gaining work experience. I was grateful they gave me a chance, even without work experience.

On my first day at my job, I met the owners and the on-site acting managers. They were not the friendliest of people. There were two women and a male boss. He did not speak much, but his wife was sure to be vocal and not shy about expressing her thoughts and opinions on how I was working. She was very stern in her voice, and it made me uncomfortable. By now, I should have known to speak up or just decided to leave the job. However, I wanted to stay to prove my worthiness that I could be a good employee, and I needed the job since getting one without experience took a lot of work. I was also somewhat pressured into going to university by my mother at the time since I would be the first in my immediate family to graduate with a university degree.

She was not the easiest boss to work with because she was controlling. My work situation was stressful a lot of the time. Still, I gained confidence in engaging with customers and other university students since the job was in the same building where I was studying. My work situation started to shift from bad to worse when I visited my doctor for a routine visit, and she noticed I had high blood pressure. I was working around my busy school schedule and dealing with

a moody and demanding boss, but I was still too timid to stand up to her and quit. Finally, it became so much that I started to experience mild chest pains at work and school. My health was beginning to decline from all the stress taking its toll on me.

I was finally diagnosed with Coronary Artery disease at the young age of 27 and had to take a cocktail of pills for the rest of my life to normalise my blood pressure and keep my heart healthy. As a result, I decided to find my voice to tell my boss I had to leave to take care of my health and that I would leave this toxic environment. That day, no matter which job I was working at, and if I felt that the working environment was toxic, I would have enough courage to leave the job before my health was once again affected.

I have always wanted to be self-employed, but more than ever after leaving my first job and its mismanagement and disrespectful employers. I learned a lot from my experiences and wanted to set a better example of how managers should treat and manage their employees. I wanted a voice, but I still had a way to go.

I enrolled in a university in Human Relations, and I have learned a lot about myself there. In this program, the main focus was to learn how to deal with groups of people in a business setting. I was to work with other students on group projects and presentations, and one of the keys was to teach us how to engage and confront our colleagues when there were conflicts within the group. It helped push me out of my comfort zone and become more open with people. However, I noticed that if I had to confront someone, I would feel guilty because I had this complex problem of being a people pleaser and feeling bad about possibly hurting their feelings. Although I had felt that way until I graduated from the program, I had done some growing, and my voice was slowly coming to light. I may not have used the degree to get a job in Public Relations, but I have no regrets about taking the program if it was just for self-awareness.

Another transformational process would be that I decided to pursue another career in Special Care Counselling to assist children and adults in adapting to this world with their unique needs. Since I had always thought I had a minor intellectual disability that I secretly hid from everyone except my family members. However, when I took a course in my first year, during the second semester, I discovered I might have Aspergers Syndrome.

This is a form of Autism that mainly impacts the social side, and it would be hard to notice because people who have it are solid with language and have average to high intelligence. We usually like to be alone as our social battery can get worn out quickly. We need time to regroup to avoid being overwhelmed by too many people in a room, and we are more comfortable interacting one-on-one or in a smaller group of 2 to 3 people. Autism can bring forth other behaviours such as arm flapping, rocking, and zoning out to comfort themselves.

Unfortunately, the program was not the right fit for me. I left in my second year once my internship supervisor noticed I was on the spectrum and did not feel that this was the right line of work for me to pursue. However, she mentioned something in our meeting that I had always remembered. She says, "You are trying to fit into our world; you should go back and get more hours at your restaurant job and see someone for your anxiety."

For those unaware of Autism Symptoms, you can go through anxiety. For example, you can ask the wrong questions without thinking it through your head first, and it can come across as being too anxious to have your questions answered at an inappropriate time.

I went to a therapist under my instructor's recommendation, which I felt did help a bit but did not need to take six months. However, she was not the right person to handle someone with a disability, and she felt that nothing was wrong with me since I knew how to mask my disability, which I had done for many years. So, in the end, I went for six months until I felt I had learned how to cope with my so-called anxiety. I say this because I thought I did not have high fear as some people have, but this teacher decided to put me in a box with all the other children with disabilities and thought I should be on medication, etc.

It took me from my early 30s until presently to try my hardest to hold myself accountable and embrace who I am. I used to be upset with myself and ask why I had to endure these limitations. I lived with a disability I had been hiding for years and never spoke about until now. On top of that, I had to be on a cocktail of medications because I may have almost had a heart attack, and being on meds had its side effects, such as hair loss. It was depressing to deal with this, but I realised two things.

It could have been a lot worse, and I'm still alive and surviving these obstacles.

Maybe God has his reasons for creating me like this. I have always believed that we all have different life purposes. He is trying to show me that this is my superpower and what makes me unique in a positive way.

Therefore, these two choices have made me decide that I could choose to take two completely different paths, which are:

1. I can sit around wallowing in self-pity, questioning why these adversities are happening to me, and maintain a negative attitude.
2. I can use my experiences to help educate others who are introverts, empaths, and struggling to have their voices heard.

Of course, it was a no-brainer as I am here sharing my story and hoping to inspire you never to stop believing and not give up on yourself despite life's challenges.

I have overcome these challenges by simply learning to put myself out there as I write. In recent years, I realized that I still wanted to make a difference, and I was not happy with going to a 9-5 every day and having to be friendly to my co-workers and phony to people I could not stand.

I am a true introvert who loves to be at home. Due to my mild autism and discomfort around people I do not know well, I am socially awkward around large groups of people. In addition, I have realized that my social battery gets drained after 1 or 2, and then I am ready to retreat to my tight space. In this case, you may wonder if someone like me, who is not an extrovert, still wants to be seen and heard from everyone.

The difference is that I am ready to grow as the best version of myself. The pipe dream of owning a restaurant is different from what I want to do now.

As much as it is all I have known, and I am great at providing exceptional customer service, my heart was no longer in it.

If you are someone reading this and want to go from fragile to fierce, you can start that journey to heal that inner child. Here are some tips to get you on that roadmap to resiliency. The roadmap to resilience will help you get on the right path to forgiveness, reframing your mindset, and accepting your adversity until eternity because it is a part of your story. Most of all, how to amplify your voice to create the right choices in life. Once you have learned to change your mindset, you can learn how to master the art of storytelling to elevate your business brand.

1. Let Forgiveness Become Limitless.

You should learn to forgive people but also forgive yourself.

Yes! The way it is, just how it should be. A good example would be that I had to learn not to be angry with myself for not retaliating against those bullies, no matter how upset they made me. Although I did not know any better then, it was a learning process for me, and I became stronger. I had to forgive to heal that inner child still affected by this. If I did not do this, I would not be able to move forward with my life and experience great things coming my way.

2. Accept Your Adversity Until Eternity:

If you are going through challenges, trauma, and even facing

Disability the best thing to do is to own it and make it a part of you. I would never think that embracing my adversities and uniqueness could be used to provide support, empowerment, and gratitude. I want to give that strength to others who don't talk about their personal stories or are too ashamed to show the world because of fear of being judged.

As I mentioned previously, I thought I had to hide my Autism to conform to everyone else's standards of what is expected and perfect. However, I have realized that we are all born with challenges and imperfections, and we must decide whether it will work for us or against us.

3. Start Reframing Yourself From Shaming Yourself.

The message is about forgiveness and not putting shame on anything that happened to you and why you were born to be different. I hated that I had to deal with living with autism and what life could have been like if I had not dealt with social awkwardness and prevented myself from stimming outbursts. In addition, I blamed myself for not getting out of my toxic work situation earlier to avoid the stress l I put on my body.

However, I have learned to reframe my mindset; Autism is a part of who I am, and living with premature heart disease, I will no longer be ashamed to let my voice be seen and heard and advocate for it. I know I am not alone; others may need me to be their voice.

4. Amplify That Voice for That Life-Changing Choice

It is not always easy to allow your quiet, inner thoughts and feelings to get noticed. It has taken me until I am 41 years old to finally express how I did not have the confidence to do so many years ago.

I wanted to be a business owner, and the best way to connect and grow my audience and followers is to get comfortable with being uncomfortable. Unfortunately, I was too self-aware about how people would perceive my appearance and how my voice sounded. I had always hated public speaking in class as those pairs of eyes looking back at me with possible judgement or glazed over from boredom made me feel like I was wasting my time, and no one wanted to hear from the least popular and most timid one. However, once I stopped caring what others thought about me, found my confidence, and grew a thicker skin, there was no stopping me. I want to amplify my voice over more podcasts, digital magazines, and books, and I want to tackle my public speaking skills on digital and physical platforms.

Learning to walk more in my Faith

When you realise you are not happy living the life you are taught to follow, you must learn to walk in faith and trust the process. In my 40s, I have just started to understand that all the suffering I have encountered was not all for nothing. Somebody put before me to learn to stand up for myself and others. It gave me more compassion and empathy for others who have walked the same path and gave them that voice I had to learn to use.

I realised that all of this pain and purpose would lead me to something great. I was not meant to sit back in the corner, do what somebody told me, and not voice my opinion. I was meant to help people by teaching them how to build the ideal business, even if you are introverted. Introverts like myself can struggle the most because we don't like being in the spotlight. However, faith has carried me to step out of my comfort zone and speak my truth.

To find your voice, start with storytelling to your friends, co-workers, and family, and you can take it a step further when you are ready to step out of your comfort zone. You can start by sharing your story on a blog post or writing in your journal to get those feelings out. If you feel comfortable with social media and are ready to share with an audience, you can slowly post content without showing your face or photos, but you just want to test the waters. So start with that and see where it takes you. That is what I did.

Today, I am a visibility strategist helping women like me learn to show up for their businesses through organic marketing and authentic storytelling.

I have recently started sharing my story through podcasts and writing books to spread my message and inspire other readers and listeners to get out there. Here are some tips I have learned about storytelling to help you find your voice within and make a difference.

Elevate your storytelling with these steps to create a powerful personal brand and build brand awareness.

Defining your audience: You want to make sure that you have the right audience who wants to hear your story and can benefit from it.

Defining your purpose: What difference do you want to make with your audience? My purpose is mind-shifting if I am on a podcast or summit sharing a life or business story. If I am talking about my life story, I want to emphasize that you can do anything you want to despite your shortcomings. If I am talking about business, I will share valuable tips in my industry because people want information from an expert.

Be Authentic: To become more likeable and authentic, you will want to show transparency by showing the human side. People gravitate to you when you are honest with them and can show the human side in your storytelling because they can relate to you and your struggles.

Providing value: You will want to provide value while telling your story. If you share a reel, a story, or a YouTube video, you want to talk about your personal story and then provide the value. Providing value gives you more credibility and teaches others how to avoid mistakes or take actionable steps that they have been putting off.

Encourage two-way communication: When telling your story online and on social media, you want to encourage your audience to interact with your content. You can use various platforms to share your content for more exposure and engagement.

Be a guest speaker at an online summit.

Podcast guesting
Magazine article publishing
Solo book author

If you are someone who, like me, has gone through pain, found their passion, and wants to showcase their purpose, I sure hope my story and these gold nuggets sparked a fire in you to start moving the needle to play that vinyl record for everyone to listen and enjoy!

Kim Groshek

Founder and CEO of Lifeful Habits

https://www.linkedin.com/in/kgroshek/
https://www.facebook.com/groups/pauselive
https://www.instagram.com/pausepowerchallenge/
https://kimgroshek.com
https://opt-in.kimgroshek.com

Kim Groshek, an International Best Selling Author, has spent over three decades shaping industry standards, driving $20 billion empires with her systematic solutions and a focus on intentional living. Today, Kim dedicates her expertise to empowering leaders who want to make a difference but feel overwhelmed by demands and time constraints.

Her message is clear: Pause to truly understand and love who you are. Embrace solo experiences—whether flying, dining, or simply enjoying your own company—and discover the power of self-connection. Once grounded in your own strength, Kim guides you in mastering the art of creative collaboration, bringing people together to create extraordinary outcomes.

Wake up to Your Inner Compass

By Kim Groshek

Have you ever felt a nagging sense that there's more to life? A yearning for purpose, meaning, and a deeper understanding of who you truly are? This feeling is a call to **awaken;** it certainly is a process of self-discovery. This will be your guide, and I offer practical tools and insights I learned to help you dive deep into your inner wisdom and create a life filled with purpose and fulfillment. These experiences are not about reaching some distant destination but rather a continuous exploration that unfolds throughout our lives. Through challenges and triumphs, we learn valuable lessons about ourselves, our strengths, and our potential.

I share some powerful practices to help you ignite the inner guide. We'll also talk about overcoming obstacles, trusting your intuition, and living authentically. This awakening cultivates a state of conscious awareness, gaining greater clarity, purpose, and connection.

The superior man is modest in his speech,
but exceeds in his actions. (Confucius)

Our meticulously planned retirement - a lake cabin and sun-drenched escapes - crumbled when reality intervened. My husband's abrupt departure from his beloved police science career left a gaping hole, and my career ended, leaving a crushing disappointment. Initial attempts to fill the emptiness with busyness and extravagance felt hollow.

A revelation showed up: True luxury wasn't material possessions but connection and experience. Meditation and walks by the lake became my refuge. We discovered new passions through volunteering and hobbies. The dream cabin faded, replaced by the joy of watching sunrises paint the sky, not just the water, and a newfound resilience. Retirement wasn't the ending, but a chance to rewrite our story, finding deeper connections, a richer life, and the simple joys that had always been there for the taking. And in that **awakening**, in that space, we found a deeper connection, a richer experience than we ever imagined.

Here's my story, my transition journey; it took a lifetime and I start here.

Peace reigns forever, with a king of endless justice! Gratitude for guidance and angels. Listen closely. Create amidst challenges. We lead brighter days ahead! (Kim Groshek)

Finding Courage to Act

Rain lashed against the bookstore window, mirroring the tempest brewing inside me. There, on the counter, gleamed the acceptance letter from John Grisham's writing masterclass—a dream I'd held close since childhood. Raised in a household where faith and hard work were the foundation, I'd always believed in taking calculated risks and trusting in a higher purpose.

Leaving behind the stability of my well-paying corporate job was a daunting prospect. For nearly three decades, I'd thrived in the fast-paced world of technology, tackling complex problems and influencing industry standards. My skills had helped build empires worth billions, a testament to the systematic problem-solving honed throughout my life.

Taking a hiatus to pursue writing—books, documentaries, animation, art exhibitions—felt reckless, bordering on irresponsible. Raised in a faith-based household, I understood calculated risks, but this felt like a plunge off a cliff.

A relentless voice echoed my doubts: "What if you fail? What if this is just a foolish dream?"

That evening, I found myself seeking solace in the familiar embrace, sitting at a solo table in the cafeteria. Pen in hand, I poured my anxieties onto paper, the letter a silent plea for guidance. As I prayed, a familiar passage surfaced: "For I know the plans I have for you, plans to prosper you and not to harm you, plans to give you hope and a future," (Jeremiah 29:11).

These words weren't a guarantee of success, but a promise of purpose. Was this the "hope and future" whispered by a higher power?

Leaving the table, a newfound calm settled over me. Fear remained, but it no longer held the reins. A quiet voice whispered, "You will not fail."

The next morning, with trembling hands, I emailed my resignation. The following weeks were a whirlwind of anticipation. The masterclass was demanding, a crucible that tested my skills and resolve. Yet, with each hurdle crossed, my faith grew stronger. Late nights fueled by coffee and belief yielded results.

Whispers of solaced prayer remained a constant companion. I expressed gratitude for my supportive husband and the beautiful life we shared.

Then came the email—acceptance for a short story in a literary magazine. Tears streamed down my face as I reread the message, a validation of the path I'd chosen. It wasn't a bestseller deal, but a significant step, a testament to the power of trusting my intuition and faith.

Years later, with a published novel and a flourishing writing career, I look back at that rainy afternoon with immense gratitude. The leap of faith wasn't easy, but it led me to a life filled with purpose and passion. It's a constant reminder that while the future may be uncertain, with faith as my anchor, I can navigate the storms and embrace the adventures that lie ahead.

"Every setback on the entrepreneurial path is a lesson in resilience, teaching us to find strength within and push forward despite the challenges." (Kim Groshek)

The Entrepreneurial Spark: A Crucible for Self-Discovery

Leaving the security of a steady job after three decades meant facing financial anxieties and the fear of failure. This initial awakening underscored the importance of **courage** and **perseverance**. Every setback, from underwhelming responses to financial hurdles, became a crucial lesson. It wasn't about external validation but about building **resilience** and discovering an inner well of strength. Overcoming these challenges fostered a sense of **self-belief** and determination, essential for staying awake on the path toward my goals.

Collaboration with my nephew on *Nate the Dragon* was a turning point. It exemplified the magic of **community** and the impact we can have on each other. This project, along with others, solidified the importance of **collective effort** and the interconnectedness of our lives. These experiences reinforced the idea that awakening is not a solitary pursuit but one enriched by connection and shared purpose.

Lessons Learned: The entrepreneurial journey, with its triumphs and failures, served as stepping stones to self-discovery. Through facing challenges, I discovered a hidden strength and a deeper trust in my **intuition**. This journey mirrored the message of awakening—the power lies within us, waiting to be unearthed.

The journey of a thousand miles begins with a single step.
(Kim Groshek)

Awakening Within: Entrepreneurship's Unexpected Journey

My entrepreneurial ventures became an unexpected path of self-discovery. Each project, success or stumble, unveiled a deeper connection to myself and the world.

Traveling opened my eyes to diverse perspectives, mirroring the Buddhist proverb, "Travel is the only thing you buy that makes you richer." The warmth I received as Africa's Women's Ambassador showcased the power of storytelling, echoing the Hindu concept of "Vak", the divine creative force. Collaborating with my nephew on *Nate the Dragon* cemented the importance of community, a core principle emphasized in the Gospel of Matthew: "For where two or three gather in my name, there am I with them."

Facing initial challenges—funding and marketing—became lessons in resilience. Each hurdle wasn't a dead end but a test of **courage**, revealing a hidden strength within. Like Dorothy in *The Wizard of Oz*, I had the **power** all along. This experience resonated with the Bhagavad Gita's message of "yoga karmasu kauśalam," meaning "skill in action"—overcoming challenges through focused effort.

Nate the Dragon reignited my love for storytelling and the impact it can have. It reminded me of empathy, family, and the power to touch lives, reflecting the Islamic concept of "rahma," universal compassion.

This journey wasn't about external validation. It was about embracing my inner strength, intuition, and the power within. It mirrored the timeless message across many spiritual texts: the key to fulfillment lies within ourselves.

"In the stillness of the mind, we find our true self." Kim Groshek

Finding the Inner Compass: Practices for Self-Discovery

The human spirit yearns for more than just existence. We crave a life filled with purpose, wanting a sense of belonging and a deep understanding of who we truly are. There is no end, or it's not trying to achieve a destination but a continuous exploration that unfolds throughout our lives. But where do we begin? Here are some practices for your inner compass and guide:

- **Mindfulness Practices:** In the constant busyness of life, it's easy to lose touch with our inner selves. Mindfulness practices like meditation and deep breathing can help quiet the mental chatter and connect with the present moment. Start with five minutes a day, focusing on your breath and bodily sensations. This practice cultivates self-awareness, allowing you to observe your thoughts and emotions without judgment.

- **Journaling for Clarity:** Our thoughts and feelings can often feel jumbled and unclear. Journaling provides a safe space to explore these inner landscapes. Write freely every day, allowing your thoughts to flow without editing. Re-reading your entries over time can reveal patterns, hidden desires, and areas for growth.

- **Gratitude as a Guiding Light:** Cultivating gratitude shifts our focus from what's lacking to the abundance already present. Take time each day to reflect on the things you're grateful for, big or small. This practice fosters a sense of contentment and opens your heart to receive more blessings.

- **The Power of Reflection:** Regular self-reflection is key to self-discovery. Ask yourself questions. What truly matters to me? What are my strengths and weaknesses? What brings me joy? Devote dedicated time each week to this introspection. Journaling prompts or guided meditations can be helpful tools for deeper reflection.

- **Stepping Outside Your Comfort Zone:** Growth often lies beyond our comfort zone. Challenge yourself to try something new—a class, a hobby, or a solo adventure. Embrace the discomfort; it's a sign you're expanding your horizons and discovering hidden potential.

- **Nature as a Mirror:** Immersing yourself in nature can be incredibly grounding and insightful. Spend time in quiet contemplation, observe the natural world, and listen to the whispers of your inner voice. Nature can offer a sense of peace and clarity, allowing you to reconnect with your true essence.

Incorporating these practices into your daily routine and remembering that this exploration is a lifelong process. Be patient with yourself, celebrate your progress, and trust that your inner compass will guide you toward a life filled with purpose and authenticity.

They sought peace, they sought tranquility... a perfect life...
(Popol Vuh)

Personal Growth and Self-Discovery

Then, even after three decades of self-leading, I hired an elite coach who used challenging methods. I learned the valuable art of enrollment conversations; however, she used bullying and psychological undermining techniques and used them to leverage to her advantage. Looking back, the experience proved pivotal in my personal growth. The coach's guidance, although demanding at times when I had to learn to set emotional **boundaries** with her, helped me develop crucial sales, marketing, and new enrollment communication skills. I also stood up in power, and **used my words** to tell her, "Who are you to be an expert when you don't have any experience, especially when it comes to working out as an athlete." I still didn't consider myself an expert, even as an athlete, despite completing over 112 half marathons, including one in each of the 50 states, and an Ironman. Yet, she, an overweight and unhealthy person, was claiming to be one. Of course months later, after much of my standing my ground, she shifted and partnered with an athlete and started a co-campaign to validate her expertise in some way. Besides taking back my power, the one thing I did get from this coach is I discovered a hidden strength in the importance of business aligned with money. I remember the coach she assigned me to, which again, I was misled into thinking she was going to be my direct coach when I signed on, I used to state how out of integrity this coach was. And she'd joke with me stating, "I'm going to start calling you the Integrity girl." I laughed with her and liked that a lot because being in **integrity** is very important to me. Integrity is doing what you say and agree to do and, actually, doing and being what you say. Something important to remember here. Integrity is always on **focus**.

Many people are attracted by this coach's no-nonsense, tell-it-like-it-is, and direct demeanor. I'm that way too. But, her behavior, words, and abrasive interaction can be demeaning and too harsh, especially when the receiving person does not know and is just learning. She uses this technique, the "fears," to her advantage. And those hypnotized in her wake with starry-eyed filters may disagree. It was a form of "psychological bullying," and this coach took advantage to "steal ideas," push them down, and overshadow growth tactics. But, I eventually learned, "The way you do one thing is the way you do everything." And because of this, I was certain she was practicing.

She was pushy and abrasive, trampled over people, and even stole their ideas—something she openly admitted on many occasions. In my house, we emphasize the importance of how you act and behave. She was a bully who bragged about the expensive things she'd buy with our money. There was more to it—she even claimed she was "raising soldiers." Yikes! That was the final straw for me. I decided I had enough and left.

This experience was a wake-up call for me, a **spiritual awakening**. I realized I had been letting too many people walk over me, just like this coach did. What hurt the most was that there was no effort to retain me, yet she bullied others into re-enrolling. It was sad to watch.

He who finds happiness and misery within himself is truly wise.
For happiness and misery come from contact with objects, which
are impermanent. (Bhagavad Gita)

From Passion Project to Financial Powerhouse: A Story of Refocusing

You know that feeling deep down, that nudge towards something bigger? It's like a wake-up call from the universe, a call to **eternal wakefulness**. A chance to be truly present, mind and body, and discover what we're really capable of. It's a powerful thing, that's for sure. But how do we cultivate this awakened state? **Eternal wakefulness** isn't about constant vigilance; it's about shedding illusions and seeing the world with clarity. It's a journey of self-discovery, a peeling back of layers to reveal the authentic self that lies beneath. This section will guide you on this transformative path, offering practices to cultivate awareness and awaken the wisdom within.

The Seeds of Awakening: Overcoming Challenges

Early retirement dreams took a detour. Chasing creative pursuits, I neglected my finances, drawn to every "shiny object"—courses, events—that promised artistic fulfillment. This detour became a financial wake-up call. It showed me that success, even in personal endeavors, requires focus alongside passion, just like a business.

At 58, after a successful career, I retired early. My initial artistic ventures felt empowering, but financially, I spiraled. Thankfully, a financial advisor helped me refocus on my strengths: connection and time management. Now, I'm exploring self-connection through spirituality, all while prioritizing financial awareness. These, together, guide my future.

Debt, once a lurking monster, stole my peace. It was a constant loop of worry, doubt, and regret. But instead of dwelling on it, I took action. Meditation and self-reflection cleared my mind. I actively sought solutions, no longer letting fear dictate my choices.

The results were transformative. By shifting my mindset and taking concrete steps, I eliminated my debt in record time. The weight was lifted, replaced by financial security and even wealth. This experience solidified the power of focus and positive action. By cultivating inner peace and love, I attracted abundance and broke free from the cycle of debt.

Here's what changed:

- **Cleared the Clutter:** Negativity and distractions are gone. My path is clear.
- **Sharper Focus:** My vision is a powerful one—a debt-free future. It's within reach!
- **Proven Techniques:** Meditation helps me achieve the mental clarity needed for success.

- **Action-Oriented:** No more sitting on the sidelines. I'm taking concrete steps towards my goals.
- **Positive Reinforcement:** Secured a financial accountability expert. This journey may present challenges, but together, we can accomplish anything.

Debt repayment can be tough, and we're all in this together! I've gone through it myself, and now I specialize in helping folks conquer their debt, move them forward when stuck, and help remove the chaos through focused accountability. Think of me as your partner in success. So, if you need support, reach out anytime. Let's celebrate every milestone on your path to financial freedom! Much like dedicating myself to completing my first novel or crossing the finish line in an Ironman, this experience highlighted the importance of a well-rounded approach that considers both financial security and self-awareness.

You can't get to Narnia by wishing for it. You have to know the way. (The Lion, the Witch, and the Wardrobe)

The Power of Reflection: Our Inner Compass

Self-discovery thrives on introspection and action to achieve your goals. Regular reflection allows us to step back and observe the patterns in our lives. Questions like "What truly matters to me?" or "What are my strengths and weaknesses?" or "What do I know about myself?" Spark self-awareness and guide us toward our authentic selves. Journaling or guided meditations can be powerful tools for deeper reflection illuminating the path to a more awakened life.

Wrong will be right, when Aslan comes into sight. (From The Lion, the Witch, and the Wardrobe)

Embracing Vulnerability and Growth

True awakening requires embracing vulnerability. Vulnerability allows us to be open to new experiences, connect with others on a deeper level, and step outside our comfort zones. When we push past our boundaries, we discover hidden potential and expand our understanding of who we can be. This growth is crucial for staying eternally awake on the path to self-discovery.

Toto, I have a feeling we're not in Kansas anymore. (Dorothy)

Eternal wakefulness is not a destination but a continuous journey of exploration. By incorporating these practices into your life, you'll cultivate a state of conscious awareness, navigate life's challenges with clarity, and ultimately, discover the authentic you. This awakening journey promises a life filled with purpose, meaning, and a vibrant connection to the world around you.

"As a dynamic change maker, staying true to yourself is the compass that directs your journey. Embrace your unique path, and you'll inspire genuine connections and transformation in the world." — Kim Groshek

Living Authentically: Unveiling Your True Self

Imagine a world where everyone wore masks, hiding their true selves behind facades of expectation. Maybe the masks thing isn't unimaginable since COVID, but you get the idea. It wouldn't be a very fulfilling place, would it? You peel back the layers, uncover the essence of who you think you are, and now comes the time to live authentically, in your integrity—aligning your actions, values, and beliefs to create a life that feels true to you—doing what you say, and saying what you mean.

Living authentically isn't about being perfect; it's about embracing your imperfections, quirks, and all. It's about honoring your values, even when they differ from others, and speaking your mind and through your actions, too. It's about expressing yourself openly and honestly, even when it feels uncomfortable. It's about living a life that resonates with your core being, a life where your actions reflect your inner compass.

But why is authenticity so important? Here's why:

- **Increased Happiness and Fulfillment:** When you live a life true to yourself, you experience a deeper sense of purpose and satisfaction. You're not constantly trying to fit into a mold but carving your path, which leads to lasting happiness.
- **Stronger Relationships:** Authenticity fosters genuine connections with others. People are drawn to genuine and transparent people. It allows for deeper, more meaningful relationships built on trust and mutual respect.
- **Enhanced Self-Esteem:** Embracing your true self, flaws and all, leads to a more positive self-image. You stop comparing yourself to others and start appreciating your unique strengths and contributions.
- **Reduced Stress:** Living a life of inauthenticity creates internal conflict. By aligning your actions with your values, you reduce inner turmoil and experience greater peace of mind.

Living authentically isn't always easy. It may require stepping outside your comfort zone, challenging societal expectations, and even facing disapproval. But the rewards far outweigh the risks. Here are some tips to embrace authenticity:

- **Know Your Values:** Reflect on what truly matters to you. What principles guide your decisions? What kind of life do you want to lead?

- **Embrace Your Uniqueness:** Don't be afraid to express your individuality. Celebrate your quirks, talents, and passions—they make you who you are!
- **Set Boundaries:** Don't feel pressured to conform to expectations that don't align with your values. Learn to decline requests that go against your core beliefs politely.
- **Communicate Openly:** Express your thoughts and feelings honestly, even when it feels difficult. Authenticity thrives on open and transparent communication.
- **Be Kind to Yourself:** Living authentically is a journey, not a destination. There will be bumps along the road. Be patient and kind to yourself throughout the process.

Remember, authenticity is a muscle that gets stronger with practice. As you embrace your true self and live with integrity, you'll attract like-minded individuals, cultivate fulfilling relationships, and experience a deeper sense of happiness and fulfillment. Your journey of self-discovery has led you here, to the threshold of living authentically. Step boldly forward, and embrace the life that awaits you—a life true to your unique and beautiful self.

Kindness is a language everyone understands. (Kim Groshek)

Finding Strength in Faith and Community

To explore the intricacies of communication, I engaged in an eight-way process focusing on what could, couldn't, should, and shouldn't be said between my mother and me. This exercise opened my eyes to the many layers of our relationship.

You might say this has nothing to do with the Bible, the Torah, or any other written word of the spiritual realm, but I correct your thinking, point blank, it does because:

Spiritual Teachings on Persistence: Many spiritual texts emphasize the value of **perseverance** and faith in the face of adversity. The Bible, for instance, teaches in James 1:2-4 that trials produce perseverance and maturity. Similarly, the Torah speaks of the perseverance of figures like Moses and Joseph, overcoming hardship to foster spiritual growth. My journey, filled with challenges and persistence, mirrors these teachings and underscores the spiritual growth that comes from enduring and learning from hardships.

Community and Unity: The Torah and the Bible both highlight the importance of community and supporting one another, echoing the value of community in Ecclesiastes 4:9-10; the Bible states that "two are better than one...if either of them falls, one can help the other up." Unity and collective effort contribute to success and spiritual connection. My experiences of collaboration and community in my projects resonate with these spiritual principles. They demonstrate the power of unity and collective effort in achieving success and fostering spiritual connections.

Effective Communication and Connection: Spiritual texts often emphasize the power of words and effective communication. Proverbs 15:4 mentions that "the soothing tongue is a tree of life," highlighting the impact of positive and effective communication. My learning of enrollment conversations and effective communication aligns with these teachings, showing how connecting authentically with others and the universe can lead to profound personal and professional growth. There's more here, but that's for another chapter.

My entrepreneurial journey, filled with obstacles and lessons, culminated in a powerful conversation with my mother that unearthed both relationship dynamics and deep spiritual truths.

Only love is real. Nothing else exists. (A Course in Miracles (Helen Schucman, 1975))

Connecting to Myself and the Universe

I decided to approach a challenging conversation with my mom by using the principles of NLP (Neuro-Linguistic Programming), some call it Clearing Methods. Talking to Mom brought up a lot of challenges in how we communicate, but it also opened doors for us to grow closer.

One of the biggest hurdles was finally addressing the unspoken truths that had been hanging between us for so long. I remember feeling really vulnerable when I brought up how distant she seemed and how it made me feel undervalued. But that conversation opened the door to a whole new level of honesty and truth, which was a huge step forward. It was sometimes challenging. Talking about how she treated me differently than my siblings, my oldest sibling specifically, brought up a lot of old feelings of resentment and inadequacy. But facing those tough issues head-on helped me start to deal with the hurt and work towards making things right.

There were even some surprising moments of clarity. One time, she actually admitted to regret not giving us more freedom when we were younger. The "us" was resonating with the fact that even she could not come to the truth that it was me she was talking about. But, it was good enough. And hearing that really helped me understand why I picked her in the first place.

The more I talked out loud, the more I noticed a shift in my body. As I spoke, I started to be more open to my consciousness, I felt light. I treated others with more respect. For example, Mom even admitted that she felt intimidated by me, which helped me break through. I started to see things I couldn't before, things when I was two, three even four years old. I knew my choice, understood my intention, and chiseling away, piece by piece, like working through a solid mason wall, has enabled me to start recognizing my superpower, while also deepening my connected relationship with Christ and the trusted archangels.

When you are content to be simply yourself and don't compare or compete, everyone will respect you. (Tao Te Chin)

The Unfolding Lotus

My yoga practice has been a big part of finding myself. It's like the Buddhist idea of always learning and looking inward. Understanding chakras, our energy from within, and the blocks made lots of sense. Yoga helped me get **grounded** and **focused,** and **breathe**. I experienced an inside-out flow each morning I practiced. I was strong when things got tough. Money problems, rejections, people misunderstandings, and business ups and downs—they all tested me. But just like untangling a knot in a hard yoga pose, each setback became a chance to grow. I learned to keep going, never give up, and bounce back even stronger. It wasn't just about work; it was about feeling more **connected** to myself and the world around me. Even the bad stuff taught me something, and that helped me find meaning in everything.

Another practice that helped me connect with myself and the universe was being **mindful** and **present**. Just as taking deep breaths before a yoga pose calms you, **meditating** and focusing on my breath became my anchor in the chaotic world of business. It helps me quiet my mind, connect with myself, and discover **inner peace** and **clarity**. By being fully present in each moment, I gained a deeper understanding and intuition, which enabled me to make wise decisions and take inspired action. Mindfulness became my anchor, grounding and connecting me to myself and the universe.

Finally, **practicing gratitude** and **letting go** plays a big role in deepening my connection. Just like a yogi goes with the flow of a challenging pose, I learned to be grateful even when things were tough. I changed my way of thinking to appreciate the good things already in my life instead of focusing on what I didn't have. This gratitude opened my heart to receive all that the universe offered and helped me trust the flow of life. By letting go of control and accepting what happens, I learned to trust that everything unfolds in the right time for the best reason. Through gratitude and letting go, I felt a deeper connection with the universe and a sense of trust in life's journey.

In the past, I was drawn to coaches and experts I looked up to who seemed too good to be true. From the somatic coach who blurred boundaries to the aggressive ones who took advantage of my eagerness, each experience, however negative, proved to be a valuable lesson. These encounters gifted me with awareness, strength, and refined judgment. I can now identify red flags, like manipulative friendship tactics or pushy salesmanship. I've developed the inner strength to walk away from people who don't align with my goals, and I have a clearer vision of what I seek in a human relationship.

Finding yourself is like a lotus flower blooming—it's a never-ending process. It's about facing challenges head-on, finding peace even in chaos, and going with the flow of life with an open heart. As we continue on this lifelong journey, let's hold these yoga principles close so we can all feel more connected to ourselves, the universe, and everything around us.

These practices have not only transformed me but have also enriched my life on a deeper level, guiding me in navigating the complexities of existence with grace, wisdom, and inner peace.

Unmask your truth. Live awakened. - Kim Groshek

A Call to Live Awakened

These stories emphasize the importance of living **authentically** with **integrity** and **connecting** with ourselves, the universe, and the divine, which ultimately makes each of us **dynamic**. When we slow down, we give ourselves time to listen and then become dynamic. When we embrace our values and express ourselves openly, we shed societal masks and insecurities, akin to removing the Tin Woodman's rusty exterior in Oz. This authenticity allows us to connect with others on a deeper level and build genuine relationships, fulfilling the Christian principle of loving your neighbor as yourself. There's a profound impact of practices like mindfulness, gratitude, and surrender, aligning with the Torah's call for living a life of purpose and service. By quieting the external noise and tuning into our inner selves through practices like NLP clearing techniques or Reiki meditation, we cultivate peace, trust, and a sense of belonging. This mirrors the Buddhist concept of universal interconnectedness, where we can see the beauty and purpose in all of life's experiences, even the challenging ones like Aslan's sacrifice in Narnia.

Looking back, this awakening feels like a second wind in my late 50's. Who knew there was so much more to discover after all these years? By slowing down and taking the time for mindfulness and reflection, I finally unearthed the person I was always meant to be. Each day feels like a fresh start, a chance to live authentically and pursue what truly matters. It's a constant work in progress, but the sense of purpose and fulfillment is unlike anything I've ever known. This may have begun late for me, but it's never too late to awaken, a chance to rewrite our story, find deeper connections, and a richer life filled with the joy of simpler moments and a newfound resilience.

Kimberly Tyler

https://www.linkedin.com/in/kimberly-tyler-a8849539/
https://www.facebook.com/kimberly.tyler.161
https://www.instagram.com/kimmijotyler
http://www.brokenvesselholylight.com/

Kimberly Tyler M.Ed is a seasoned educator and leader with over 30 years in education and children's ministry leadership. A retired Special Education Director and dedicated teacher, she possesses a wealth of knowledge and experience in supporting students with diverse needs, advocating for inclusive practices, and fostering positive learning environments. Kimberly is a compassionate author with a profound gift for seeing others succeed despite any challenges that they may face. Residing in Northern California with her husband and extended family, she draws inspiration from the beautiful surroundings and close-knit community. Kimberly's writing reflects her genuine desire to uplift and empower readers, as she shares stories that resonate with faith, hope, and resilience. Her unique blend of storytelling and encouragement has positively impacted the hearts of readers worldwide. An accomplished creative, her favorite mediums are fabric arts such as quilting and embroidery. She can be found at www.brokenvesselholylight.com

Embraced: Fully Known and Fully Loved

By Kimberly Tyler

Hello and welcome, sisters! I want to take a few moments to talk about something truly beautiful and profound—how God embraces, loves, and blesses women. This is not just a distant theological concept but a deeply personal and relatable truth that can empower us all. Understanding this can increase our joy and give us abundant strength and marvelous power to navigate our personal and business challenges with increasing grace and positive purpose. I want to explore this together like friends having a heart-to-heart conversation. As we delve into this, let's also think about how we can practically live out God's incredible love in our relationships and communities, whether through acts of kindness, forgiveness, or simply being a listening ear.

From the very beginning, God's special love for women has been evident. Consider Genesis 1:27, which says, "So God created man in His own image, in the image of God He created him; male and female He created them." This tells us that women, just like men, are made in God's image. I find that incredible; to me, it means that every woman is made in the blueprint of God and carries a piece of God's nature and spiritual DNA. This inclusivity of God's love for all women, regardless of their situation or past, is a testament to His boundless grace and acceptance.

Take Eve, for example. Created as Adam's partner, she wasn't an afterthought but a crucial and integral part of God's perfect plan. Adam needed her in order for God's perfect plan for humankind to be fulfilled, and she was always there in His plans for humankind's future. This shows us that God's love is intentional and inclusive, embracing all women with perfect faithfulness and a magnificent plan for each of us. And then there's Hagar, Sarah's servant. Her story is especially touching because God saw her in her darkest moment when she felt utterly abandoned and alone. In Genesis 16:13, she calls Him "El Roi," which means "The God who sees me." How comforting is that to us? To know that even in our loneliest moments, God sees and loves us. His eyes are always on us, loving us and waiting for us to call on Him for what we need in our individual situations because nothing in our lives is beyond His notice and care; he desires to increase our joy so we can rejoice before him.

But God doesn't just distantly love women; He embraces them fully as His beloved, beautiful bride and the object of His love. The Song of Solomon is a lovely example of this. This poetic book reflects God's amazing love for all people but especially addresses his intense love and passion for women. In Song of Solomon 2:6, it says, "His left hand is under my head, and his right hand embraces me!" This isn't just about physical closeness but a deep emotional and spiritual connection. God says, "I'm here; I've got you. You are mine; I'm holding you close, and you are precious to me." He says this to each of us individually, reminding us of His personal and deep love for us, making each of us feel cherished and significant in His eyes.

Jesus' interactions with women reinforce this and are some of the most heartwarming parts of the New Testament. His love and respect for women is evident throughout the Old Testament, but when He was walking the earth as Jesus, God made it even more transparent and established with His interactions with women. Remember the woman at the well? She was an outcast, someone most people would avoid; she was shunned not only as a Samaritan but also as a woman living in sin, but Jesus saw her, really saw her, not just her past but her future; he valued her and wanted to offer her a beautiful future that was not based on her past mistakes or current life choices. When He spoke to her, He offered her "living water" (John 4). He provided Himself and a personal relationship with Her that transcended her current situation and was not dependent on her past.

Think of it: The Creator of the universe. The one who calls the stars by name and holds them in place by His hand offered her a new beginning, a new life based on her relationship with Him. The Lord looked past her mistakes; He saw her future, full potential, and what she could be. He embraced her with compassion, respect, and deep love and loved her as she was, as He offered her a new and different future. In that encounter, Jesus demonstrated that He fully knew and loved her, showing her and us the transformative power of His mighty love. This transformative power of God's love gives us hope and inspires us to live our lives with faith and courage.

Another important story is that of Mary Magdalene; after Jesus freed her from seven demons, she became one of His most devoted followers. After His resurrection, Jesus chose to appear first to her, not to any of His other followers (John 20:14-16), showing how deeply Jesus valued and embraced her and the future He had planned for her. The love Jesus showed Mary was protective. Jesus not only freed her from a terrible existence but then offered her a place close to Himself, an intimate relationship where she knew she was safe from the old life that had tormented her. Never again would Mary suffer the way she had; instead, each day was fresh, walking with Jesus and trusting His protection.

Throughout the Bible, we see that God's protective nature is immense, powerful, and profound. In the Old Testament, we see laws specifically designed to protect women. Widows and orphans, who were particularly vulnerable, were given special consideration (Exodus 22:22-24). God ensured they weren't left out or exploited and blessed those who protected them.

Think about Ruth's story. She was a widow in a foreign land, but God provided for her through Boaz, who acted as her kinsman-redeemer (Ruth 2:8-9, 4:9-10). It's a beautiful narrative of God's provision and protection. Boaz's kindness and care towards Ruth reflect The Lord's father heart for protecting those who are vulnerable. Not only was Ruth's story one of love, redemption, and protection, but Ruth's love and respect for her mother-in-law has been a story passed down through generations.

Jesus, too, demonstrated God's protective love. One of the most striking examples is the woman caught in adultery (John 8:1-11). The religious leaders wanted to stone her, but Jesus stepped in. He challenged the accusers and protected her from harm, affirming her worth and dignity despite her failure to make a good choice. He was saying, "You're worth protecting, and your life matters." Even in moments of despair brought on by our own mistakes, He stands, ready to redeem us and point us to a new future, blessed by His love.

God's blessings on women are abundant and varied. In the Bible, we see numerous instances where The Lord blessed women with their heart's desires. This was often children and occurred after long periods of waiting and hoping for motherhood. Sarah, Hannah, and Elizabeth are just a few examples. Sarah's story (Genesis 21:1-7) is particularly moving because it shows that God's blessings often come when we least expect them, reminding us of His perfect timing.

But God's blessings aren't limited to children. He also blessed women with roles and responsibilities that had significant impacts. Take Deborah, for example. She was a judge, a leader of Israel, and a prophetess, leading Israel with wisdom and courage as a woman (Judges 4-5). And then there's Esther, who saved her people from destruction with her reliance on God and the bravery and strategic thinking that He provided her in answer to her prayers and fasting (Esther 4:14-16).

Mary, the mother of Jesus, received one of the greatest blessings of all – to bear the world's Savior. Her humble acceptance of this role ("Behold, I am the servant of the Lord; let it be to me according to your word" – Luke 1:38) reflects the profound honor and responsibility God entrusted to her and knew she would fulfill.

God's Continued Work Through Women

God's love, embrace, protection, and blessings for women didn't stop with the stories in the Bible. Throughout history and even today, we see countless examples of how God continues to work through women. He's writing new chapters in His story daily, and women are vital to that glorious narrative.

Think about the early church. Women played crucial roles in spreading the Gospel and supporting the church. Lydia, for instance, was a successful businesswoman who opened her home to Paul and other believers, helping to establish the church in Philippi (Acts 16:14-15). Then there's Priscilla, who, along with her husband Aquila, was a crucial figure in the early Christian community, teaching and mentoring others (Acts 18:24-26).

In more recent history, we have inspiring examples like Corrie Ten Boom, who risked her life to protect Jews during the Holocaust, and Mother Teresa, who showed the poorest of the poor His love through her service. These women show us that God's love and power are not bound by time or circumstances. The Lord continues to use women to accomplish His supreme purposes and demonstrate His love to the world.

Personal Reflections

Now, let's bring this closer to home. Think about the women in your life – your mother, sisters, friends, mentors. How have you seen God's love, embrace, protection, and blessings in their lives? For me, I think about my grandmother. She was a woman of deep faith, constantly praying and trusting God no matter what. Even in the most challenging times, she had an unshakable belief that God was with her, loving and caring for her. Her faith inspired me and showed me what living under God's loving embrace and trusting His will looks like.

Or consider the women in our communities who quietly and faithfully serve others. They may not always be in the spotlight, but their impact is profound. God's love shines through them in how they care for their families, support their friends, and serve their communities. They remind us that God's love is active and alive, working through ordinary people in extraordinary ways.

Take my friend Rachel, for example. Despite the challenges she faces, she's always quick to offer a helping hand or a listening ear. Rachel's strength and kindness clearly show God's blessing and presence in her life. Seeing her in action reminds me that God's love and blessings often manifest through the everyday acts of love and service we extend to others.

God's love, protection, and blessings don't mean we won't face challenges. Many women in the Bible and throughout history have faced significant hardships. What stands out is how their faith sustained them through those tough times, allowing them to emerge stronger and more deeply rooted in God's love and impacting the world around them in lasting ways.

Even today, we can draw inspiration from women who navigate life's difficulties with grace and faith. Whether battling illness, overcoming personal loss, or facing societal challenges, these women demonstrate that God's embrace is a mighty source of strength and unwavering hope. Their stories encourage us to trust God's love and believe He is with us, even in the darkest times.

I have been fortunate to have had many women in my life who have demonstrated what it is to walk through difficult times and still see and experience God's love and deep embrace for them. These women have shown that God's unstoppable love and precious grace surrounded them and enveloped them with comfort, strength, and a sense of deep trust as they leaned into His embrace in their season of trial.

One example is my friend Sarah, who lost her husband unexpectedly. Despite her grief, she found solace and strength in her faith. She often shares how she felt God's comforting presence during her darkest days and how the support of her church community helped her navigate her loss. Sarah's confidence in the Lord's love for her and unwavering faith in His goodness remind me that God's protection and blessings are ever-present, even in the most challenging times. We all have that same assurance that we can face the future and whatever it may bring with peace because we know we are not ever alone and that we are adored and cherished by our Creator, who is nearer than a brother.

It's important to celebrate and support one another as we face our daily challenges and remind each other of the Lord's splendor. Recognizing the ways God works in and through women's lives can deepen our faith and inspire us to live more fully in His love. This celebration can take many forms, from sharing stories of faith and resilience to simply being there for one another in times of need.

One way we can do this is through community and fellowship. Gathering together with friends, family, and church members to share our experiences and encourage one another can be a powerful reminder of God's presence and love. Whether it's a Bible study group, a prayer circle, or a casual coffee chat, these moments of connection help us to see and celebrate God's work in our lives.

Another way to celebrate is through acts of service and kindness. When we serve others, we reflect God's love and extend His blessings. Volunteering at a local shelter, supporting a friend in need, or simply offering a word of encouragement can make a profound difference. These acts of love not only bless those around us but also strengthen our faith and deepen our connection with God.

A beautiful way to celebrate one another is by honoring the women who have been a source of inspiration and strength in our lives. Write a letter of appreciation, share a heartfelt conversation, or simply spend quality time with them. These gestures, though simple, can profoundly impact and reinforce the message of God's love and appreciation for them.

Reflect on the countless ways women contribute to our lives and communities, both in big and small ways. Sometimes, we might overlook the daily acts of kindness and support women provide. Taking a moment to recognize and appreciate these acts can deepen our understanding of God's love at work in our lives.

We need to celebrate God's love. Sharing stories of faith is a powerful way to celebrate God's love with joy and gladness. When we hear about how others have experienced God's embrace, protection, and blessings, it strengthens our faith and encourages us to look for God's hand in our own lives. These stories can be shared in various settings, from church gatherings to personal conversations.

Consider creating a space in your community or church where people can share their testimonies. Hearing how God has moved in the lives of others can be incredibly inspiring. It reminds us that we are part of a larger story in which God's love continually unfolds.

Another critical area is passing on all the stories of God's love and faith to the next generation. By sharing with younger women and girls the marvelous ways God has worked in our lives and shown us His perfect faithfulness, we can help them build a foundation of trust and faith in God's love. Mentorship and discipleship are excellent ways to encourage and support the next generation.

Think about the young women in your life – daughters, nieces, students, or neighbors. How can you invest in their lives and help them grow in their faith? Sometimes, it's as simple as being a listening ear, offering guidance, or sharing your own experiences of God's faithfulness.

Living out God's love in practical ways can transform our relationships and communities. Here are some ideas to get started:

- **Listen and Support**: Be present for the women in your life. Listen to their stories, support their dreams, and be there in times of need. Your presence and support can be a powerful reflection of God's love.
- **Pray Together**: Prayer is a powerful way to connect with God and each other. Organize prayer groups or prayer partners. Praying together can deepen your faith and strengthen your bonds.
- **Celebrate Achievements**: Take the time to celebrate the achievements and milestones of the women around you. Acknowledge their hard work and successes. This not only encourages them but also shows that you value and appreciate their contributions.
- **Offer Help**: Sometimes, practical help is the best way to show love. Whether it's babysitting, running errands, or offering a helping hand, these acts of service can make a big difference in someone's life.
- **Encourage and Affirm**: Words have power. Use them to uplift and encourage the women in your life. A simple note, a kind word, or a heartfelt compliment can brighten someone's day and remind them of their worth.

So, as we wrap up this heart-to-heart, let's remember that God's love for women is deep, personal, and unchanging. He sees every woman as His beloved, embraces her with tenderness, protects her with fierce passion, and desires to bless her abundantly. These truths aren't just historical facts but living realities that continue to unfold in our lives and the lives of women around us.

May we all take comfort in knowing that we are seen, loved, and incredibly cherished by God. May we reflect His love in how we treat the women in our lives, honoring them, protecting them, and celebrating the incredible gifts they bring to the world. Whether we're looking at the stories of women in the Bible or the women we interact with daily, we see a God who is passionately in love with His daughters. And that, my friends, is something truly worth celebrating.

As we go about our lives, let's keep these truths close to our hearts. Let's be reminded that in every moment, God's wonderous love is with us, guiding, protecting, and blessing us. And let's make it a point to share that love with others, creating a world where everyone feels embraced and cherished by the God who loves us more than we can imagine.

In these conversations and reflections, we find not only God's love but also the incredible strength, resilience, and beauty of women who, through their faith and actions, continue to inspire and uplift those around them. God's love story with women is a testament to His enduring commitment to all His children. This love transcends time, culture, and circumstance, always inviting us to see and celebrate His unstoppable, marvelous work in the world.

May our lives be a living testament to the Lord's amazing love. May we embrace others as He embraces us, protect those who are vulnerable, and share His blessings abundantly. Let's continue celebrating and honoring the remarkable women who enrich our lives and reflect God's enduring and beautiful love daily.

As we close, let's make a commitment to carry these reflections with us. Let's strive to be beacons of God's love in our communities, shining His light through our actions and words. Together, we can create a world where every woman feels seen, valued, and loved, just as God does and intends us to be to each other.

Lynda Malka

Lynda Malka Intuitive Mindset Coach
Coach, Speaker, Author

https://www.linkedin.com/in/lyndamalka/
https://www.facebook.com/lyndamalka/
https://www.instagram.com/lynda_moore_malka/
https://www.lyndamalka.com/
https://linktr.ee/lmalkamindset

Lynda is a Certified Intuitive Mindset and Life Coach with a rich background in education and entrepreneurship. As a former teacher and co-founder of an award-winning charter school, she deeply understands people and their unique patterns. Her varied experience extends into network marketing, where she achieved a ranking position as she honed her skills in mindset and self-development. A sought-after speaker and workshop presenter, Lynda empowers women through divine insights and experiential wisdom to transform their minds, rediscover purpose, renew passion, and overcome obstacles. She also runs J29virtual, a niche virtual assisting business that supports entrepreneurial women by providing assistance tailored to help achieve their business goals. Lynda's latest project, "Mindful Moments: A Mindset Reset Adult Coloring Book," which combines relaxation with personal growth is available on Amazon. Her passion for guiding others and her diverse experience make her a powerful advocate for women striving to reach their fullest potential.

Whispers of the Soul

By Lynda Malka

"And we know that in all things God works for the good of those who love him, who have been called according to his purpose." Romans 8:28

Little Girl Lost

Sitting here with my hands hovering, sometimes literally shaking, over the home keys, I hesitate to share my story of how I overcame challenges, defied expectations, and embraced my God-given inner strength to become the resilient, determined and confident woman I am today. My story is not something that I have shared outside of a small group of trusted family and friends, and only a few of them know the details I am sharing now.

As I embark on this journey, it is suddenly not lost on me that my fingers are resting on the home keys on my keyboard. A safe and familiar place to land as I type my message to you. Sometimes loudly and furiously as I deal with the emotions that come up. Sometimes, softly and introspectively as I struggle to find my voice and share something that for a lifetime I have tried so hard to dismiss, minimize, and forget. Yet, I have come to realize that it is often in the act of owning, fully owning, these things that have been put in our paths that we can fully grow and discover the true purpose of this life that we have been blessed with. So, here I sit with my hands on the home keys ready to move forward. You should know that in creating the title for this section and sharing my story, I have literally reached my fingers to the far corners of my keyboard/my past and been able to safely return home. Try it yourself so you know that it's entirely doable before you read on.

My name is… My name is… Wait, my name is not important in sharing my story. I could be you. I could be your closest friend. I could be your distant relative. I could be the person in front of you or behind you in the checkout line at your local store. I could even be someone you haven't met yet. Few of us go through this journey we call life without experiencing challenges or trauma in one form or another. We don't always know why. We don't necessarily need to. It's what we learn from these moments that is important. Steps forward are only possible because of what we actively leave behind. And so begins the sharing of my journey…

The night t we moved into our rental house in Hawaii, a Navy acquaintance of my Dad's, invited us for dinner. While dinner was being prepared, their two children, my two sisters, and I were taking turns riding in a wagon down the sidewalk on a hill near their house. We were giggling and laughing as we pushed and pulled the wagon back up the hill. Glancing at the palm trees swaying in the breeze and inhaling the sweet smell of flowers, I thought, "I'm so glad we moved here!"

On my last bumpy trip down the hill, a car slowed down and a man who was about the same age as my Dad asked all five of us where the "Moores" lived. "My house is up there," I said as I pointed up the hill. "We live up there." He asked if I could show him. I looked around and saw that everyone else had begun to head back up the hill with the wagon. I had been warned about talking to strangers. In that moment of trying to be helpful, I forgot everything I had been told. I got into the car. I had met a lot of strangers because the Navy had relocated our family to different cities and states since I was born. My parents liked to entertain so this stranger didn't feel any different at first.

"That's our house," I said pointing as we approached it. He didn't stop. He didn't stop the car. "Hey, it's back there. You passed it." The panic started in my chest. It tightened. It was hard for me to breathe. The alarm bells started to go off deepening my panic as he turned right at the end of our street. This was wrong. It was the wrong way. The message on repeat in my head was, "I'm going to be in so much trouble." "Do you have panties on?" He asked. I tried to hide, to disappear as I flattened myself against the car door to get as far away from him as possible. The smell of leather and his cologne dove deeper into my nostrils as I struggled to breathe. I gripped the armrest so tight that my fingers ached, and I didn't let go even when he eventually stopped the car overlooking a cliff.

As he turned toward me, his sweaty hand snaked out and grabbed my left calf. He yanked me toward him and pulled my panties down and shoved his fingers inside me. "Ow!". I screamed. I began to sob uncontrollably. Mercifully, my brain won't allow me to remember the rest. Just a memory of his contorted, angry face as he shoved me out of the car onto a deserted street near a cliff, "Get out! You cry too much!" He drove away leaving me in a heap on the ground. I struggled to my feet and cupped my burning crotch with my hand. I turned in a circle to look at what was around me. There was a cliff overlooking some city lights in front of me and street lights in the distance in the other direction. Tears blurred my vision as I stumbled toward them, crying and sobbing and whimpering, "Mommy. Mama. Mom-eeee."

An older woman out with her dog heard me and called out to me walking toward me. "What's wrong honey?" When she reached me, she bent down to look me in the face and asked, "Are you lost?" I WAS lost, I didn't know where I was. I nodded yes. She reached down to hold my hand. Her gentle touch helped to calm me. She led me down a nearby street and toward a house that seemed to be exploding with laughter, voices, and music. She knocked on the door and asked if anyone knew who I was. Fortunately, someone there recognized me and called my Dad. The woman and everyone else assumed that I had taken a walk and gotten lost.

I didn't correct them. I was more worried about being in trouble and being treated differently because of what happened than I was about listening to the whisperings of my soul. My inner little girl voice who needed the comfort of her Mom. A little girl who needed to know that everything was going to be okay despite what had just happened. A little girl who needed me to speak up and tell what that man had done to me as an acknowledgment that she mattered, that she was worthy of the care, concern, and attention.

But I didn't do that. Instead, I pretended that nothing had happened and stuffed all that trauma and fear deep, deep down inside me. I didn't say a word to my parents as they rushed into the house to hug me and ask me what happened. I repeated the story that had been assigned to me. I was walking and got lost.

Sometimes I think that it's so odd that my sisters don't remember me getting into the stranger's car, but they don't. Why would they? They were just kids too.

It must have been easier as a 6-year-old to pretend it didn't happen. But my brain didn't forget. It would program encrypted beliefs into my subconscious and nervous system to "keep me safe". Anything new and unfamiliar held hidden dangers. The pattern of crying and being unable to sleep the night before school started each year was one of the effects of this internal alarm system. Not surprisingly, over the course of my life, I would react and/or make choices out of that fear-based operating system that ultimately didn't serve me well.

"The Lord is close to the brokenhearted and saves those who are crushed in spirit." Psalm 34:18

Hide and No Seek

Because of my inability to acknowledge and release those deeply buried wounds, emotions, and trauma from my childhood, my body and brain learned a pattern of withdrawing as a protective mechanism. With my inner child's whisperings muted, my brain heard subconscious messages on loop, reinforcing in a variety of ways, over and over again, my need to fade into my surroundings. I hid to stay safe. I hid because of a camouflaged belief that I had no value. To reinforce those beliefs, my mind continually gathered and showed me evidence from my life experiences to support them.

My sisters and I are one year apart in age. Because of our closeness in age, I was often compared to my sisters. My older sister was dubbed "the pretty one". My younger sister was dubbed "the funny one". I was dubbed "the quiet one". A chubby, awkward ugly duckling, I found it easy to believe I didn't matter and should fade into the background to let others shine. My sophomore year in high school, when I was chosen to be on the drill team, should have been my open door to shine, to embrace that I mattered. Something inside me whispered, "Shine!" but my mind wouldn't allow it even when I was co-captain in my senior year.

As I went on to college, though I had been raised Catholic and made to go to church every Sunday, I soon realized church attendance was optional and my participation trickled off. God was nudging me to grow and learn myself, but I hadn't yet formed a relationship with Him, so I missed the signals. Instead, I questioned every facet of God I was ever taught. Though I didn't realize it at the time, these questions flowed up through my buried inner child. Did God truly exist? If so, was God truly good? Then why did He allow what happened to me? Was He truly a loving father? If He was, why did He seem to love me less? Did He truly provide for his children? Then why didn't he provide protection for me? And on and on and on. What I failed to recognize was the fact that BECAUSE of His protection, I didn't die when I exercised my free will and made a bad choice that day.

We Attract What We Are

"As water reflects the face, so one's life reflects the heart."
Proverbs 27:19

Two months after I graduated from college, on a blazing hot August day, with a bilingual education degree in my pocket and my little blue Toyota Tercel packed to the gills, I took the only job offered to me and moved to Bakersfield, California where I eventually met my first husband.

He was wrong for me in every way and somehow instinctively reinforced every "I don't matter and I'm not worthy" belief I had about myself. I was broken, he was broken, we just didn't realize it at the time. The combination of his unhealed childhood wounds and mine were like Dynamite and matches and he seemed to crave chaos and explosions while I craved security and calm. When we argued and I stood up for myself, I paid dearly as I experienced the verbal, mental, and sometimes physical repercussions of his temper. The messages in my mind played louder, "You don't matter. Just fade away. Disappear."

To those with knowledge of what was really happening inside my marriage (and there weren't many), I probably appeared to be an incredibly weak woman as I stayed and worked to keep the vows that I had made the day I said, "I do." I stayed because I knew the difficulties that co-parenting would present with a man who opposed my wishes at nearly every turn. I stayed because I knew that I didn't want to see my daughters part-time. And here's the thing most people don't think about, it takes incredible inner strength to stay in a war zone where each new argument creates new trauma and wounds from the fall-out.

It wasn't like I was doing nothing. I sought God and leaned on Him more intensely as I prayed for remedies. At first, I prayed for God to change me so that I could be the wife he wanted. Then, I prayed for

God to change him. Ultimately, I prayed to God for release from the marriage if the cycle wasn't going to change.

One year during my summer break, I was asked to help co-found a program for a charter school in my district. It seemed a better alternative than summer school teaching. As summer turned to fall, I found myself working full-time doing two jobs. One week, I was job-sharing as a second-grade teacher. The next week, I was meeting with homeschooling families. Something had to give, my original intention was to be able to spend time with my daughters and that was happening less and less.

I didn't want to give it up, this charter school program job I had helped to co-create was seemingly the only place where my value was recognized and acknowledged. It was the place where God built a net of supportive friends underneath me to catch me when the bottom dropped out of my life.

As we grew our enrollment, I made the choice to resign from my classroom position and become the Program Coordinator of Natomas Charter School's P.A.C.T. Program. Weeks after making the decision, I learned that the board had not yet approved our charter which meant they could possibly shut us down and I would be unemployed. When that didn't happen, I felt God's provision. It was a sign that I was where I was supposed to be.

Two years later, my husband chose to remove himself from my life. 13 ½ years of marriage and two daughters later, I saw a glimmer of proof that a God I struggled to trust and believe in loved me. He set me free.

The 4-year divorce was extremely painful, the price tag placed on my freedom was steep. Still, I was free! The process left me raw and unsure of what to expect as I walked a path I never expected to walk alone. The day I was ordered to pay him child support and alimony, I walked out of the courthouse in tears, "Lord, what just happened? Where were you?" I heard an audible voice near my ear say, "Trust me, I have a plan." I whirled around looking for who had said that and saw no one. Not anyone in sight anywhere. Part of me doubted what I had heard while part of me hoped and prayed for rescue.

In the first few months after our parenting plan began, to avoid the emotional impact of only seeing my daughters every other week, I kept busy so I wouldn't have to face the deafening silence. The constant reminder that they weren't there made my heart ache. In the beginning, I bolted into action the moment I woke up and didn't stop moving until I fell into bed at night. I built a retaining wall in my backyard, hauling stones from construction projects nearby. I painted each of our bedrooms. The doing helped me to avoid dealing with the being part of my life.

"For I know the plans I have for you," declares the Lord,
"plans to prosper you and not to harm you, plans to give you
hope and a future." Jeremiah 29:11

There's a Hole in My Life Raft

In this place in time, where everything around me seemed to be falling apart, the whispers of my soul grew louder. As I began to hear their stirrings, I understood that I had been given the gift of a safe space to start to recognize who I was and who I wasn't. A place where I could stop hiding or pretending to be someone I no longer wanted to be and listen to what those whispers were telling me. I could stop being who others were knowingly or unknowingly manipulating me to be though, I went along with their requests willingly…to keep that little girl I had muted long ago safely hidden and in good graces. This was the start of my rising…my rebuilding…my reclamation process.

Every other week, when my daughters were with their Dad, I began to take time to ask myself what I wanted, what I liked, what I was passionate about in this phase of life. I got to peel off what no longer fit me, and put on those things I had been restrained from pursuing as I subjugated myself to the wants and needs of others.

This wasn't an instantaneous process. Much like Lot's wife who kept looking back at the past, it took me a while to let go of the familiar in order to embrace a better future. It was a slow process at first because my mind questioned anything new, it kept screaming that danger lurked in the new and unfamiliar. This was a lesson not forgotten from my experience in Hawaii. I first had to re-open the emotions and feelings I had all but completely shut down during my marriage in order to survive the constant button pushing. If you've ever had one of your limbs fall asleep, you will understand that this awakening process was painful at first. That uncomfortable pins and needles feeling as my heart reawakened, processed, owned what was mine to own, and forgave. There were LOTS of things I had to forgive. LOTS. When I was taught the forgiveness process by my parents, I was taught how to forgive others but never to include myself in that process. I had to learn that too. I made many poor choices along the way that wounded myself and my daughters unnecessarily. However, grace was a welcomed gift that helped me to understand that I was doing the best I could with limited tools to navigate the trauma fallout.

As the months passed, through the process of rediscovering myself, I clung to my life raft…my job that clearly came from God. Together with innovative, expert teachers, talented staff members, and dedicated, supportive families, we created an AMAZING environment for homeschooled kids to learn and grow. We offered classes in everything from classes for the younger K-2 grades, to writing, to computer science, to dance, to musical instruments, to home education. If the parents asked for it, we tried to find a way to support it, if it made sense for curriculum and state guidelines that is. P.A.C.T. was a crowning jewel for us all. The process of creating it as we moved from a strip mall, to a business park, to a campus, and eventually to a custom constructed 14,000 square foot building made us family.

I even met my current husband through P.A.C.T. when his job brought him to my campus to install the mirrors in our dance studio. A job that was extremely unusual for the company he worked for, I might add. He is truly the embodiment of Song of Solomon 3:4, "I have found the one my soul loves." God had prepared me by healing me enough to attract him. I never knew life could be this good!

As I struggled with the lack of integrity of some of my coworkers within the charter school administration, I continued as Program Coordinator not only because I needed the income but also because of the positive impact of our program.

Then, in June of 2010, with no explanation, my job unexpectedly ended. My P.A.C.T. family I loved was ripped from me. Once again, my soul went into hiding with this new evidence that I didn't matter. A good friend of mine, who knew the struggles I had been having regarding staying or leaving, tried to lessen my pain as she told me, "It's a gift. It's a gift wrapped in sandpaper but it's a gift nonetheless." I wanted to believe that, but my brain bombarded me with rationale and scenarios of why I didn't matter. "Your staff didn't fight for you." It screeched. They needed their jobs every bit as much as I needed mine, I reasoned. "The families didn't fight for you," it taunted. They had been told I wasn't returning, why would they question it? Though I did my best to cut off every false belief as it sprouted up, I was losing the battle because I wasn't dealing with the roots of those beliefs. At the time, I was unaware of them, and still, the whispers bubbling up from inside me persisted, "Acknowledge me." "See me." "Love me."

"When you pass through the waters, I will be with you; and when you pass through the rivers, they will not sweep over you. When you walk through the fire, you will not be burned; the flames will not set you ablaze." Isaiah 43:2

Out of the Valley of Shadows

Just before my program coordinator job ended, I had begun dabbling in network marketing. Network marketing, for me, was truly a self-development course wrapped up in a business. I was fortunate enough to land on a team that cared about us as individuals as they coached and grew our business and people skills. This doesn't always happen. I had so many great mentors in one place! They would call me often just to connect with me and help me process anything I was wrestling with. One day as I was still trying to make sense of my job loss, my mentor Judith said to me, "Don't you see Lynda? You weren't meant to be there anymore but you wouldn't leave so it was removed from you." Whoa! The tumblers turned and something clicked. So much shifted in that moment I could nearly feel the earth moving beneath my feet. And for once, I was excited for what was coming next in my life.

Enter Visions in Education where I was hired to work with High School Independent Study English Language Learners. Try to say that one fast! I was the teacher for 26 students grades 9-12. I had never taught High School. Nor was I familiar with the curriculum. And it had been a while since I had been in high school. I didn't sleep the whole night before I was to start my job. The next morning I told my husband, "They are so going to fire me when they figure out that I don't know what I'm doing." His response, "God has a reason for giving you this job." And he was SO right.

I met with my students in groups of 4-6 once a week for 2-3 hours to help them complete their online courses. There was no way to cover all 6 of their classes in that amount of time, so I had to find the carrot, that thing that they wanted to do, have, or be once they finished high school. And then it was about helping them believe in themselves and their abilities while giving them ideas on how to conquer their distractions. I was more of a coach to my students than I was a teacher, though I didn't realize it at first.

It wasn't until I was asked, through my newly created Virtual Assistant business, to edit and format a friend's instructional guides in exchange for participating in her coaching course that the light bulb went off. "Oh, wow! I'm coaching my students over the finish line! I love that!" And I truly did love it. God had created me for this!

A year or so later I was introduced to mindset coaching. As I worked on my mindset coach certification, our instructor paired us up to practice what we had been taught. At the end of our session, my partner did what she was supposed to do. She gave me homework at the end of our practice session to further the mindset work we had covered. My assignment? Complete a Ho'oponopono meditation for healing and forgiveness. It seemed simple enough, but the memory it triggered…oh lordy, was anything but.

I pulled my knees close to my chest and wrapped my arms tightly around them, rocking back and forth trying to lessen the impact of the intense grief that flooded in as I struggled to breathe through the seemingly unending sobs. In just a few minutes, my path was forever altered until my mind learned to overcome the stories and illusions created to protect it. I was meant to get to this place where I could identify and deal with my triggers/shadows and fully embrace myself in the process. That's why my traumatic childhood memory appeared when it did. Healing opportunities arise when we are ready to deal with them. In that moment, we have the choice to deal with it and heal it (Deal and Heal), or we have the choice to stuff it back down until it resurfaces another time, and it will. I chose to heal. To embrace all of me. To listen to that lost, lonely, invisible little girl inside me. I often wonder what would have happened if I hadn't taken this path God opened up for me? Who would I be?

"Therefore encourage one another and build each other up, just as in fact you are doing." 1 Thessalonians 5:11

Spread the Good

Having seemingly been a late-bloomer all my life, I have sometimes lamented the amount of time it has taken to fully embrace all of who I am and how God has uniquely created me to be. Then my soul lovingly whispers, "It takes as long as it takes, my love. You didn't give up. Well done."

I now see that God used every choice, EVERY choice, I made to grow me, prepare me, and teach me something about myself. To show me that I could trust Him to use it all for my good. The faster I learned the lesson, the less painful the growth process. The more I resisted, the harder the lesson was. Every phase I've gone through, whether growth or healing, has brought people to me who were a few steps behind me on a similar path trying to find their way. More than a coach, mentor, or guide, the tools forged by these experiences allow me to help other women process, reframe, and understand their value and the purpose behind their life's experiences. Armed with this knowledge, they become empowered to understand how to align with their God-given path. Then as they, like me, know without a doubt who they are, what they were born to do, and that they are valued and loved just as they are, they become unstoppable.

Nedra Reid

CEO of Signet Professional Services

http://www.linkedin.com/in/nedra-reid
https://www.facebook.com/nedra.reid
http://www.instagram.com/msintentionalpeace

Nedra Reid is a woman whose life is deeply guided by her unwavering faith. Her strong belief system has been the cornerstone of her journey, influencing both her personal and professional endeavors. As a dedicated Speech and Language Therapist, Nedra has a profound passion for working with children and families, striving to make a significant positive impact in their lives. Her commitment to her own family and friendships is equally fervent, reflecting her belief in the importance of close-knit relationships and mutual support. Beyond her professional role, Nedra continually seeks ways to contribute meaningfully to her community, embodying a spirit of service and compassion. She is also the author of "Grief Mode," a book that showcases her empathy and insight, offering guidance and support to those navigating the difficult terrain of loss. Her work and writing serve as a representation of her faith, resilience and dedication.

Resilient Faith

By Nedra Reid

"I knew you before I formed you in the womb.
Before you were born, I set you apart and appointed you as my
prophet to the nations." Jeremiah 1:5 NLT.

I stood at the edge, just where the sand meets the ocean, the early morning sun casting a warm glow over the calmness of the waves. I closed my eyes and breathed deeply, inhaling the scent of salt water mingled with whatever pollen was in season. This was my sanctuary, a place where I felt closest to God. As I lounged with my toes dangling in the water, my fingers moving deftly through the sand, I whispered a prayer. The heaviness of life appeared to be overtaking me. Here I was at another juncture of life's vicissitudes.

Born to young and unprepared parents, their lives had their own challenges. They found themselves unable to navigate their relationship, family, and finances. Using familial support to nurture their child seemed like the best decision in their current situation. My developmental years have handed me nurture, abandonment, isolation, love, and feelings of unworthiness. Despite the upheavals and growing pains, faith was the bedrock of either home.

The countryside offered a haven of tranquility, with its rich vegetation, sandy beaches, cold and refreshing rivers, beautiful scenic hillside views, and a host of family members within proximity. Living with my grand aunt and grand uncle gave me a large family. The change was drastic with new names to learn and more demands to meet, the change was overwhelming and it took time for me to acclimate. Eventually, I made strong bonds with family and had special cousins and friends in the community and church. The school year was exciting as I loved my teachers and they loved me. The routine of the day, special projects, learning activities, and opportunities to bond through play provided stability. However, that stability and routine were always accompanied by a pause in time known as summer. The sounds of laughter, frolicking, and goodbyes, as we closed the chapter on our current grade indicated the long-awaited summer was just around the corner. It's the season that children anticipated the most; however, nothing could be further from the truth for me. The dreaded summer vacation was to be spent away from my norm and in a place of isolation, adult despair, and unfamiliar neighbors and or workplaces. Anxiety, dread, and fear were just a few emotions that flooded me, resulting in physical illness each summer. Not even the picturesque mountain peaks, glistering blue ocean, and powdery sand were not enough to distract me. The scenic four-hour journey was frequently met with tears, sleep, and the contents of my stomach in a bag. Subsequently, my anxiety increased as embarrassment was added to the plethora of swirling emotions.

The waves of my life seemed to have calmed during my preteen years, but little did I know it was merely a calm before the storm. As I attempted to navigate the ebbs and flows of life, my grand aunt was diagnosed with cancer. I wasn't quite sure what that meant, but I knew I didn't like it. I could hear the adults around me having conversations as they attempted to research, prepare, and plan. It seemed dismal to me. Was I to lose my stability in this life? It was time for me to take some responsibility for myself. My caretaker who was insistent on a summer spent with my biological mother was now ill. I vowed I would be spending another summer in emotional turmoil and was traveling, so I emphatically declared I was not going away for another summer, and if I was made to do so, I would be making alternate arrangements. My adult cousins had enough to deal with and so they agreed with me. It seemed clear to my mind that the plans were set and I'd experience some normalcy from here out. They focused on helping my grand aunt recover, when she did I'd be able to present a winning case for not traveling over the summer. But, oh, how incorrect was I? The script had been altered, and not even my adamant demands could prevent the future as it was orchestrated. The years ahead were met with obstacles, seemingly a familiar, endless rhythm as steady as the seasons. It seemed age was no respecter of persons when it came to life's unpredictabilities. I was well acquainted with the joys and disappointments life offered and knew this chapter by heart.

During this season of my life, my faith community became essential to my survival. Unknown to most, the calm that was observed was all I could have done. I sat in the wings, observing and engaging with others, behaving as a typical teen within the boundaries of my household expectations to get through days that left me drained and bewildered. My teen years appeared to be demanding more of me than my mental development could handle. Not knowing how to react to a parent figure being ill, the axis that I knew as stability facing the most significant event of her life; I was left scared and unsure of God's plan. There was no room for dubious faith in my culture. It seemed that my faith needed to be solidified to hold the strength of the adults. As expected, I fell in line with the norm. I busied myself with church activities and school. School became a daunting task; known and unknown emotions needed to be processed, but there was no one to do so with. My routine involvement served as a decoy, seemingly sufficient. Maybe it wasn't, but the situation at hand took precedence. Life as it was currently, demanded their attention, and I couldn't be caught sitting in nonchalance. There was no time to sit in the pittance of life's turmoil and contemplate the unfortunate events and their impact.

My grand aunt's story was not one of healing; she lost the battle. As I watched a strong woman of faith declare the words of the Lord, even in her pain, I was perplexed. How could she be thankful to God when her death was sure? Unknown to me then, while her current reality sucked, the hope that God provided extended her will and solidified her faith and that of those around her. As her life came to a close and her last breath escaped her lungs, those surrounding her were overcome with emotions expressed through audible wails and tears. Feeling lost, I stood there with tears streaming down, unsure of what would happen next. But God!! God has an interesting way of meeting my needs. While staging normalcy, God placed a few people on my path, helping me to understand personal development and friendships. They offered a respite from my chaotic thoughts while creating new experiences.

Closing a chapter of loss and sadness to open a new one became a welcomed distraction. The loss of my grand aunt mandated a permanent relocation to live with my parents and siblings. The anticipation of a new journey filled me with excitement. I was in for a surprise. My transition was not as easy as I thought. I never factored in the magnitude of this move and the loss that was associated with this transition. I recall quietly crying and dealing with the loss of my "parental figure," loss of access to friendships of many years and familiar routines was devastating. As usual, I used my faith community to fill the gaps. This process took some time, but again, God provided some solid friendships, which helped me navigate these uncharted waters. I trusted him to carry me, but unbeknownst to me were the spectacular blessings he had in store. At 15 years of age, when life should be focused on figuring out mid-teen age scuffles, pre-dating sagas, and other teenage dramas, my parents had the brilliant idea to gift me with godparents. I didn't receive one, but two sets. I had a godparent who was a parental figure, and the others, spiritual guides. I don't think they knew the magnitude of their decision. I have been indelibly blessed by these two couples. Immediately, they took an interest and excelled at being godparents. I had a mentor, teacher, financial advisor, spiritual guide, employer, and even a newfound family. God had shown himself to be a provider. He knew that at this age, with my experiences, there were topics and insights I'd require for healing. He showed me so much intentionality through these years that he turned a perfect stranger into a family member.

Swift was the years between high school and college. So much had consumed me in prior years, and now I was at a pivotal juncture. Career decisions were to be made and I was ill-prepared. A nurse or a teacher? That should work! Nah, I was indifferent to both fields. I possessed attributes in both fields, but none was a conviction. I sat in bed one night with thoughts of being a failure. How could I have gotten to this age with an unsettled career path? I did the one thing I had learned to do; pray. After praying, I was reminded of the catalog I'd picked up at the local college fair. As I read the description and requirements, my heart became settled. He had directed me to the perfect blend of the two paths I struggled to select. Communicative disorders explored my curiosity for medicine and embraced my passion for education.

In a few short years, I experienced several changes, a new country, and all that is associated with such a move. Here a short time later staring down was yet another inevitable change and transition; college called. Blindly I embraced the responsibilities and unfamiliar terrain with the understanding that my only course was holding fast to my faith. Prayer became my source of direction, strength, and peace. I became more appreciative of my friends, especially those who walked the prayer journey with me. It was on faith that I asked God to provide the job needed to pay for housing and cover my automobile. He delivered. I grew in understanding of the phrase "His grace is sufficient." I frequently found myself thanking him for his small mercies. Those small mercies were quickly translated into enormous blessings when God led me to a church home and into the welcoming arms of a family with three female adults and their parents. The timely encounter with this family proved that God is all-wise. Not only did I have a family away from home, but I also had sisters. A lifelong relationship allows us to share memories, from milestones to consoling each other and soothing the thought of that, which hurts us deeply.

Life as a college student was successful, and another chapter was closed. The natural progression of securing employment and then marriage was a part of my story. A union of bliss quickly crashed as the reality of being unequally yoked was realized. There were days when the shame of having a failed marriage overwhelmed me into a state of depression. Knowing I had failed myself in this area of life was heavy. The thought of isolating myself from my faith community was tempting. The whispers, looks, comments, hearsays, and advice: I didn't need any of it. While they weren't directed to me they were communicated to loved ones. But God showed up. He allowed me to experience his protection through those He had assigned to me. My well-being, soul, and mental health were their priorities. I saw the grace of God through their acts, words, and gifts of kindness.

Plans had to be made and executed as the marriage dissolved. I decided not to return to my parents' home as it would only serve as an endless reminder of my failure. Still a fairly young professional, a single life was not in my plan. I hadn't been saving for my own housing. I hadn't been keeping funds aside for that "rainy day," and now it was storming. Unprepared, I had limited resources and God to rely on. "For I know the thoughts that I think towards you, saith the Lord, thoughts of peace and not of evil, to give you an expected end," (Jeremiah 29:11 KJV) His thoughts towards me were evident in this season of my life. He orchestrated a plan that not even I could ever envision. The best part was his timing. Not only did I have a place to stay, but within three months I was signing loan documents for my first home. But God! It wasn't my financial or intellectual acumen, nor was it generational wealth. Only the goodness of God could have done what I was experiencing in this moment.

Grateful for the opportunity of restart, I continued my fee for service employment. The roller coaster of financial stressors would attack often. While trying to maintain a job and a roof, I told God in the midst of my uncertainties, "You took me here, I am going to trust you to get me through." Then the economic crash of 2008, was this a joke? Nope, we were all feeling it. This was real! How was I going to get through this one, Lord? Yep, this time I was going to lose it all. The minuscule finances were insufficient to meet my needs. The crushing pressure of life continued to weigh on my heart, and I sat with God. We've been here before. The situation is different, but the Deliverer is the same. You have this one. I continued to serve in all the capacities he required of me.

My mortgage holder reached out and offered an assessment proposing a verification of my file and the possibility of a modification. As a novice to all these proceedings, I acquiesced. I had nothing to lose but stood to gain. A notice of approval for modification was received, and thus the process was started. In this process, I learned to trust God. I understood what patience was. The many requests for documents that were provided multiple times prior, followed by their silence, were anxiety-inducing. I soon realized my anxiety was building and my fear of another loss was staring me down. A representative called on a day when waiting on them for a response was overwhelming; he requested yet another document. On completing the call, I remained in my car, tears streaming down my face, I had it. I told the Lord, if this house is getting between you and me, then take it. I was done. Done fighting and submitting papers. Several minutes later, I dried my eyes, collected myself, and returned to my office. There was a peace that I couldn't explain after such a bold declaration. I had no other plan, but God did; after all, he is omnipotent and omniscient.

The daily rigor of life continued, and I fell in step. While visiting my cousin, I received a call, which I answered with hesitation. It was the bank. I awaited the request for document number one million plus, but the request never came. The voice on the other end said they reviewed my file and had agreed to grant me the modification. There was a plane passing overhead and I just knew I hadn't heard him correctly. He proceeded to explain how the modification worked from that date on. With eyes filled with tears and a heart filled with gratitude, I simply expressed my thanks and disconnected the call. I sat in the driveway, staring at the sky, being thankful to God for his blessings.

I was assured of God's plan for me. What was my plan for myself? I decided that my job no longer sufficed. I needed to position myself for more. I updated my curriculum vitae on one of the job sites. Sitting in my office, I received a call. It was from a recruiter, and he had a job for me. A place I had never heard of; it was in my state, and the relocation would be within an hour of my parents. Again, he was presenting my needs on a platter before me, with a salary and benefits.

Calm were the winds in my life. The shift was welcomed. I decided to maintain the assignment he had given me while getting adjusted to my new city. Life had its own rhythm, and I was enjoying the smooth sail. Then one day, the winds increased, and life was once again out of kilter.

The phone rang: "Hello, I'm on my way to the hospital with your brother. He went to work but never made it in due to a severe headache and vomiting." "Ok, let me know what's going on." A few hours later, the phone rang. "Hi, Mom." "The news is not good. Your brother has brain cancer." I responded, "That sucks!" My brother was diagnosed with glioblastoma. After doing the research, I realized those words mom had said on the phone weren't just words. Glioblastoma is one of the worst forms of brain cancer. The prognosis was not good!

Mom, being a nurse, got into action, and a plan of care was shared with the family. We were hopeful; there had been cases of success. A few months prior to this event, we all gathered to celebrate our mother's retirement with some of her associates. At that event, he had spoken some very positive and uplifting words to me. He offered affirmations of God's hand in my life. Here I was asking God to deliver my baby brother. We have so much more life to live. We hadn't taken a siblings' trip, and our relationship was evolving. We needed more time to establish who we were as adult siblings.

The surgery date was set, and we believed in God for healing. There was no way all the talent he had gifted him would cease so soon. He would pull through, and I'd have multiple opportunities to see him in the capacity of a worship leader. During his late teens, I'd identified that he would be a powerful worship leader, I requested the prayers of a friend for him to walk in alignment with God's path. This diagnosis was a stumbling block. He had a determined spirit. He was optimistic, standing in faith that God would heal.

The morning of the surgery, I decided to meet God on the beach. In the quiet hours of the morning, as the dawning, pleading in prayer for all the medical professionals and a successful outcome. I needed to understand the trials of a Christian, as they seemed continuous and in some cases brutal. God led me to Job. A journey through Job as I journeyed with my brother was surreal. I had so many questions about Job and Kris' experiences. With each question came assurance and more questions. The beach became my place of solace, where God would provide answers and remind me that my questions were important to him.

Kris' surgery left us hopeful. His treatment at the cancer center went well. He appeared to be healing. His resurgence indicated a promising progression. He requested to go to Jamaica to spend Thanksgiving and Christmas on the island. We obliged. Multiple visits would prove to be pointless only offering minimal improvement. After landing in Jamaica in November, his health began to shift downward. This change was odd because he was medically cleared before departing the state of Florida. Multiple visits to the doctor would prove to be pointless, only offering minimal improvement. In mid-December, he deteriorated quickly. Returning him to the US, so we could seek specialized treatment for him confirmed our worst fears. His organs were now failing.

Decisions were to be made. But before we do so one more valiant effort to seek God's miraculous intervention. I needed to have this conversation with God. The day I landed in Jamaica and saw him, I was in visible shock at how impacted he was by this illness. He hugged me as I held it together, he said, "Sis, I know God is going to heal me. I just don't know when." He believed, and so, I hoped linking my belief and prayers with his would shift this trajectory into a breakthrough. The answer was clear, no. Mom took him home and a few days later he breathed his last breath.

The cataclysmic crash of this wave rocked me but I couldn't release my faith. He was already gone and I needed the promises to lean on. I needed the comfort of God to heal me. The many days I spent reading the scriptures, meditating, questioning, and journaling revealed that God is more than a judge waiting to convict me but a friend. A friend who wants to be in a relationship with me in spite of me. One who will hold and comfort me in those spaces of hurt regardless of how harshly I've communicated my feelings. He continues to protect, provide, and align His plans for my life. I've found an authentic relationship with Him, so I stand relentlessly holding on to my faith and believing His promises and plans for me will always exceed anything I can dream or imagine for myself.

Norma Jeffers

https://www.facebook.com/profile.php?id=100074537377998
https://www.instagram.com/jeffers3347
https://www.viewbug.com/member/normajeffers

Norma is a compassionate mother, devoted sister, loyal friend, dedicated nurse, and passionate photographer. Her journey of overcoming immense challenges, including a profound personal crisis in 2019, has been fueled by her unwavering faith and the relentless support of her family. After returning to the church she had distanced herself from for 20 years due to her ex-husband's beliefs, Norma found strength in her renewed faith and commitment to inspiring others. With her sister Mary by her side each day and the encouragement of her daughters, who continuously motivate her perseverance, Norma embodies resilience and hope. Her professional life in nursing reflects her dedication to helping others, while her love for photography allows her to capture and cherish life's beautiful moments. Norma's mission is to inspire women to embrace their strength and faith, following the inspirational example set by 'Women of Unstoppable Faith.'

Women of Unstoppable Faith

By Norma Jeffers

Introduction

Breaking Chains

My faith in God has never wavered but I did not practice my Catholic religion for over 20 years. Now I live my life with purpose and try to do all things with gratitude and in service to God. I hope and pray that by sharing my story I can inspire and motivate others that with God on our side, all things are possible. His never-ending love keeps me going now. But I have not always felt this way. My struggles with depression and anxiety for over 20 years sometimes were overwhelming. I have been on and off antidepressants for the past 20 years. It is through my faith that I have been able to overcome childhood traumas and challenges during my recovery process physically, emotionally, and financially. In September 2019, my life took a dramatic turn that led me to the deepest and darkest valley I have ever encountered. After a suicide attempt that left me in a coma and resulted in the loss of custody of my beloved daughters, I found myself at a crossroads. It was my unwavering faith that pulled me from the abyss, inspiring a journey of recovery, resilience, and purpose. This is my story of how faith, family, and friendship became my pillars of strength and guided me to rebuild my life.

My Background

I come from what I saw as a broken family. My parents divorced when I was 3 years old, which deeply affected my perspective on family and relationships, growing up one of seven children raised by a single mother in the 70s. My mom did not take us to the Catholic church after her divorce. We went to various churches intermittently. Her faith in God was strong but she felt rejected by the Catholic church after her divorce. My mother was a beacon of strength amidst the turmoil of domestic violence and alcoholism. She too suffered from depression. We moved frequently as my mom tried her best to provide for us, taking odd jobs like a bricklayer, custodian, and door-to-door saleswoman. My mother did her very best to raise us on her own. Her dream was to open a restaurant, a goal I was able to help we were able to help her accomplish. However, lacking the business background she struggled to keep it open. Nevertheless, she instilled in us the valuable traditions and the importance of hard work.

One of the most memorable examples of her determination was during a particularly hard Thanksgiving when our power and water were shut off. Despite these challenges she managed to prepare a Thanksgiving dinner over an open fire outside, showing us that even in the hardest times, family and tradition were worth preserving. She loved the holidays and always tried to make them special despite struggling financially. I have carried forward these traditions and values. Trying to instill them in my girls. Her determination inspired me to break the cycle of providing a better life for my daughters. When I was 12, I turned to God to deal with my childhood trauma. I would walk to church every Sunday. I went to religious education and made my First Communion and then my Confirmation. I got married to my first husband Paul three days after I graduated high school. I was the first of seven children to graduate high school. I applied to nursing school immediately after graduating high school. I completed nursing school while married to Paul. I had my oldest daughter Gabrielle while in nursing school. Unfortunately, my marriage to Paul ended after three short years. We were both incredibly young and drifted apart, then I met Chris, my second husband, while working in a small rural emergency room in Del Rio, Texas. For over 20 years, I distanced myself from the church due to Chris's beliefs. He grew up in a deeply religious household and did not want to do the same to our girls. We agreed to expose the children to religion when they were older. This period of separation was filled with numerous challenges during that time, I was a dedicated stay-at-home mom, focusing on the upbringing of my daughters. It was not until after my suicide attempt that I found my way back to faith. The day after I woke from my coma, I clung to my faith in God as the anchor to pull me through. This pivotal moment marked the beginning of my journey towards healing and redemption.

During my recovery, the unwavering support of my family and friends became my lifeline. My sisters played a crucial role during my darkest hours.

My Relationship with My Faith

I have always believed in God, I was baptized in the Catholic church but after my parents' divorce, I was not taken to church. I returned to the church on my own. After my childhood trauma became known, I reached out to God to help me heal. I started going to church, I would walk to church every Sunday and pursue my religious education. I made my First Communion when I was 12 and then continued and received my Confirmation. My first husband Paul and I tried to get married through the Catholic Church, but the priest refused to marry us at that time because Paul was 17. We went to church intermittently. We had our oldest daughter baptized in the Catholic church. I clung to my faith but despite our efforts to make our marriage work, we divorced after 3 short years. I did not feel welcome in the Catholic Church after my divorce but my faith in God never wavered. In 1992 I moved out of my hometown in pursuit of better opportunities for my daughter Gabrielle and me. I found myself a single mom just like my mom. God was ever-present in my life. On my way to San Antonio, I got in a wreck the week I was supposed to start work. I was blessed with an amazing cab driver who after the first two trips back and forth to work stopped charging me. For three weeks while my car was in the car repair shop, he took me to and from work every day and refused to let me pay him.

I had an excellent job working in the San Antonio pediatric emergency room when tragedy struck our family and shook my faith to the core. My sister Virgina, who was 3 years older than me, was killed by her husband when she was 24 years old. She left behind four beautiful children. My faith in God was shaken as I questioned how or why he allowed terrible things to happen.

I drifted from the church as I entered a relationship with Chris. I married Chris in a small chapel in Tennessee in a small wedding. Chris embraced and took Gabby in and raised her as his own, which brought us even closer as a family. We were blessed with three amazing daughters. Ashley was born while Chris was in graduate school. I had to return to work when she was 5 weeks old. I put my faith in God that he would help me find a good daycare for her. I was blessed to find an amazing daycare for her. She thrived and I was at peace at work knowing she was well cared for. Chris was raised in a deeply religious household which turned him away from religion and he did not want us to indoctrinate the girls with it. I respected his wishes and raised our girls without religious teachings.

My girls are seven years apart; I saw my sisters struggle with babies close in age and we decided to space ours out. I did not want to have to put our girls in daycare at such an early age. I was a stay-at-home mom for four years after Isabelle was born and five years after Katie was born, doing my best to be a great mom.

He was a scientist and looked at things differently and my faith was shaken after the death of my sister. I stopped going to church and praying regularly. My depression and anxiety worsened, and I was prescribed an antidepressant.

While I was in the hospital, a priest came and prayed for me with my sister Delia every day. Their unwavering faith and prayers created a sense of calm and hope during the darkest hours of my life. When I finally woke up and was able to, I started going to the chapel. The spiritual awakening felt like a miracle of God, reinforcing my belief that I am here for a higher purpose to help others through my painful experience.

Upon my release from the hospital, I continued attending church regularly. My renewed faith became the cornerstone of my recovery, and I passionately believe that trusting god can empower us to overcome even the most challenging circumstances. Through my story, I hope to inspire others to realize that God has a plan for each of us, even when we may not understand it at the moment, Faith can guide us through anything.

My Involvement with the Legion of Mary

Joining the Legion of Mary deepened my understanding of the Catholic faith and offered a sense of community and purpose. In October 2023, I became a member of the Legion of Mary, marking a significant milestone in my faith and guiding me in daily practices and community involvement. Every day I pray the Tecera and the Rosary finding solace in these sacred rituals. My faith is further nourished by attending weekly Legion of Mary meetings and participating actively in church services every Sunday. These regular spiritual engagements are integral to my ongoing recovery and resilience. The monthly Patrician group meetings where we discuss and deepen our understanding of our faith. I also have the privilege of taking the Pilgrim Virgin Mary statue to parishioners' homes. An activity that brings me immense joy and a sense of purpose to my life. Sacred Heart enthronements are a practice that strengthens community bonds and brings faith into people's living spaces, and visits to the sick. Through these activities, I encourage others to seek God and their faith hoping to inspire them just as I have been inspired.

The growth of my faith and my active involvement in these spiritual practices have significantly contributed to my journey of healing and empowerment. They have equipped me with the strength to overcome challenges and have allowed me to be a beacon of hope guiding others towards their own spiritual awakening.

Unfortunately, after 26 years of marriage, Chris and I drifted apart leading to our divorce in 2018. We co-parented well but the summer of 2019 brought new challenges, Belle our 13-year-old started struggling with mental health issues.

The end of my marriage, the loss of my job, and my daughter's mental health struggles felt like too much to bear. My mental health was at its lowest point. In the depths of my despair, I attempted to end my life feeling hopeless.

On September 3, 2019, Chris came into my home after I had missed an appointment and he called me multiple times to no avail. He found me unresponsive and called 911.

While being transported to the ICU, I went into cardiac arrest and after several minutes I was revived but was in a coma. I was in a coma for over two weeks. I remember having a vivid image of my deceased mom and dad sending me back, telling me. "You still have shit to do."

Through my faith in God and the support of my sister Delia, I had to re-learn how to speak, how to eat, how to walk, and how to write. My recovery is nothing short of a miracle and I give all thanks and praise to God. I was released to a rehab facility where I continued my recovery but had a setback and was returned to the hospital. On October 13, I was finally released to go home but my recovery was far from over.

I had many doctor appointments and I found an incredible mental health support group through NAMI. I started walking daily while praying and meditating.

My path to healing has been far from easy but through his grace, I am now able to work and spread His word.

I have leaned into my faith and given all my struggles to Him.

After I woke up from my coma, my sister Delia had been at my side day and night, I realized I had been given a second chance in life thanks to God.

As soon as I was able, I started going to the chapel in the hospital and my faith in God grew stronger every day.

Overcoming Challenges

My journey to independence has been fraught with challenges, financial setbacks, enormous medical bills, and mounting credit card debt added strain to an already difficult path. My journey to independence was marked by small victories and significant milestones.

My struggle to find the right working environment with my new limitations was challenging. I was supposed to start a new job at a local emergency department in September 2019. When I got out of the hospital, I called and was able to start in January,

In hindsight, it was still too soon for me to return to the emergency room. I did not realize the cognitive implications of the brain infarct I sustained during my cardiac arrest. I was not able to function in such a high-stress environment. I tried several other jobs, but none were the right fit. When we went into COVID lockdown, I was able to get a job as a long-term care liaison during the pandemic. This allowed me to work from home while I focused on my recovery,

In addition to financial and emotional challenges, I encountered legal challenges. Despite my best efforts and support, I lost custody of my girls and had limited visitation rights. This was one of the hardest blows to my spirit. Nevertheless, my faith and unwavering support from other friends and family kept me going. My focus shifted to becoming resilient and finding new ways to connect with my daughters and their continuing healing journey. This was heartbreaking. I felt like I had lost my identity as a mom. The custody battle was challenging. I had to undergo intense scrutiny, cognitive evaluations, mental health screenings, and medical clearances.

I leaned into my faith, prayed daily, and went to weekly support groups and weekly therapy sessions. Daily phone calls with my sisters.

In addition, a high school friend Sonya came to help me with my recovery. While her intentions may have been pure, our relationship became strained in the beginning. She developed a holistic plan for my recovery, focusing on all aspects of my recovery and fighting for custody of my daughters. However, as time went on, our relationship grew strained. She became very controlling and often yelled at me, triggering past traumas and creating a toxic environment that I could no longer endure. In a moment of difficult realization, I asked her to leave. Our relationship ended in bitter disagreement, adding emotional turmoil to an already challenging period.

In response to my attempt, Chris made significant changes in his career to help our daughters cope. He left his job at a law firm and started his own business, allowing him to be more present for them during such a critical time. Chris has ensured that the girls receive extensive therapy, providing them with the support they need to navigate their emotions. My daughters have leaned on each other, their therapists, and friends for strength and understanding.

I have made many attempts to reconnect with my girls including meeting with their therapists. Despite my efforts, our relationship is still strained and we don't visit as often as I would like. The path to rebuilding these bonds is slow and challenging, but I remain hopeful and pray for them daily.

Throughout my journey, my primary goal has been to inspire my daughters and others through my experiences. My family has been a pillar of strength, and their support has been invaluable.

My Daughters: Gabby, Ash, Isabelle, and Katie

My daughters, Gabby, Ash, Isabelle, and Katie are the center of my world and the driving force behind my determination. Despite the estrangement that has kept us apart since my darkest days, they are always in my heart and on my mind. Each day, I work tirelessly not only to rebuild my own life but also to help them heal from the pain I have caused. Their love and the hope for our reconciliation inspire me to keep moving forward, no matter the obstacles.

Gabby, my oldest has shown incredible dedication in supporting my ex-husband, Chris, in caring for our girls. Her resilience and unwavering love have been a constant source of comfort to her sisters. She is kind, loving, and encouraging. My hope for reconciliation with Gabby is strong. I pray for her and thank her for all she does for her sisters. She has stepped into the role of a surrogate mother in my place.

Ash has had her own struggles with mental health and anxiety but her passion for writing and theater has continuously amazed me. Her focus on the arts drives her to new heights, and her talent shines brightly She has always had what I used to call "an old soul." Her intelligence and ability to process complex subjects at an early age always amazed me. I reach out to her often and pray that one day our relationship will be stronger than ever.

Isabelle, despite her struggles, owns a strength that inspires me every day. I am committed to helping her navigate her journey and find her own path. Her grit and perseverance are admirable. She has also struggled with depression and anxiety and I pray that with God's help, she will overcome each trial that comes before her. Isabelle, my wild child, I pray that one day we will have a strong relationship.

Katie my youngest with her articulate nature and exceptional public speaking skills has made a mark as a debater. Her ability to convey her thoughts eloquently and confidently is truly impressive. As the youngest, she has been affected differently than her sisters. She is processing and learning to cope with my actions as we try to reconnect

I have struggled with each one of my girls as they transition from child to adolescent, despite reading many parenting books, therapy, and parenting classes. My mother struggled as a single mother of seven. I don't feel I had the best example of parenthood and was determined to do better and be a great mom. Unfortunately, my suicide attempt left them with great trauma that will take a long time to heal. My attempt was during the week of three of their birthdays, which I feel added to their sense of abandonment. I pray for them every day and pray for God to intercede and help with reconciliation. I can't undo what I have done but I can become the best version of myself and show up for them as much as they allow me.

I am committed to proving to them that, through faith and perseverance, we can all rise above our past and create a brighter future. My journey is as much about them as it is about me, and I long for the day when we can be together again, stronger and more resilient than ever.

Unwavering Support from the Family

Delia's Role in My Recovery

During my coma, my sister Delia never left my side. As I navigated the challenging road to recovery — relearning how to eat, drink, write, and walk — Delia's unwavering support was my constant. Despite my stubbornness to be independent, which often resulted in frustration and concern from Delia, she remained devoted to my healing. Her selflessness and love were evident every day, and one memorable moment was when she got mad at me for trying to get up alone after waking from my coma, fearing for my safety. Her presence was a testament to the incredible power of sibling love, especially as we celebrated our grandmother's 93rd birthday together during this tumultuous time.

Collective Family Prayers

In my darkest times, the prayers and support from my entire family — siblings, nieces, nephews, and my brother and friends near and far — enveloped me like a warm blanket. Their collective faith gave me hope and the strength to carry on. Each prayer was a reminder that I was never alone in my struggles. The outpouring of love, support, and encouragement I received while I was in the hospital gave me the strength to keep fighting.

In November 2019, Sonya drove me to Texas to see my grandmother for her 93rd birthday. We stopped in Georgia to pick up my sister Juanita and her husband Edward. She drove from Maryland to Texas. It was a gift from God to be able to see my grandmother and my cousin Blanca who gave me a rosary, a Catholic Bible, and a statue of Mother Mary. She was a devout Catholic and encouraged me to lean into my faith. The next year she died of COVID. My sister Mary, my brother, my aunts, and my nieces and nephews were all there to welcome me and celebrate my grandma's birthday and my second chance of life.

Mary's Unconditional Love

My oldest sister Mary was a beacon of unwavering love and support. Almost daily, she would call, write letters of encouragement, or send greeting cards. Her unconditional love lifted me during my darkest days, reminding me that I was valued and cherished.

Lifelong Friends: Jen and Abria

Jen's Faith and Encouragement

My dear friend Jen has always been an anchor of faith. Her strong belief in God and her words of encouragement were vital as I navigated my journey back to wholeness. Jen's faith and visits provided me with the spiritual sustenance I needed to remain steadfast.

Abria's Strength and Protection

Abria, strong and fiercely protective, stood by me like a fortress. Her strength and determination to see me through my recovery were invaluable. On days when I felt weak, Abria's tenacity gave me the courage to face another day. Her unconditional love, support, friendship, and advice are invaluable.

Achieving Independence Through Nursing

I knew I wanted to be a nurse since I was a little girl. I watched the movie *Nurse Where Are You*. It left such a profound impact on me. I wanted to be the person there to help those in need of medical attention. I graduated from Nursing School in 1992 with an Associate's Degree. I worked in a small rural hospital in the Emergency Room. I learned from the paramedics, especially Dex. I learned so much in my first years out of nursing school that I knew I made the right choice. I was a pediatric emergency room nurse in San Antonio and Corpus Christi. While living in Corpus Christi, I learned from some of the best pediatric specialists. Then, I moved to Houston and worked at The Methodist Hospital Emergency Room. While working at Methodist Hospital, I worked with some of the best specialists. I was a charge nurse, mentor, and Sexual Assault Nurse Examiner. My experience was invaluable as I worked with an incredible team. Chris was accepted to law school so we then moved to the DC metro area and I worked at several emergency rooms. Currently, I am working three jobs as my financial situation is still not where I would like it to be. I am a school nurse and a home health nurse. My years as a nurse have allowed me to care for others when they are in their most vulnerable state. It gives me a sense of purpose and fulfills me.

It aligns with my core values of empathy, compassion, and loving my neighbor as God loves me. I did stay at home for several years to care for my children in their early years. But I always knew I would return. Providing care for others brings me joy and satisfaction that I am doing God's will.

I want to take my experience as a nurse and my painful experience to help others. As a nurse, I can only help one person at a time. Giving each person the best care I can give. My mission now is to help as many people as possible through sharing my story.

Conclusion

My journey from the brink of despair to a place of renewed faith has been profoundly transformative. Inspired by the love and support of my family, friends, and faith community, I have rebuilt my life and dedicated myself to helping others find their way through similar struggles. My story is a testament to the unshakable power of faith and the incredible strength of the human spirit. To all the women out there facing their own battles, my message is clear: Never lose faith, for it is the beacon of hope that will guide you to a brighter tomorrow.

As I continue my path of service and healing. I draw strength from the love and support that envelop me. Every step I take and every person I help is a testament to the blessings I have received. I am eternally grateful for the opportunity each new day brings allowing me to serve others and uphold my faith.

Pamela Kurt

Best Version of You
Coach

https://www.linkedin.com/in/pamela-kurt-41a26ba/
https://www.facebook.com/pam.kurt
https://www.instagram.com/best_version_you/?hl=en
https://pamkurt.com/
https://bestversionyou.com/

Pamela D. Kurt is an attorney and professional womens' life coach. She received her associate degree, bachelor's degree, Master's in Public Administration and Juris Doctorate in December of 2003. She lives in Ohio with her husband and two black labs. She also enjoys time with her adult son and grandson.

As a professional, Pam has added several additional certifications and advanced training. As an attorney, her area of practice is in family law and juvenile law.

Pam is a very active business owner in her community, and as a result, has held multiple leadership roles, including as a board member and advisor for several nonprofits and agencies. She also recently was named the Leader of the Year for Lake County, 2022.

Through her community involvement and personal passion to empower women, she created a new company: Best Version of You, LLC. This company is to empower and elevate women to their next level and be the best version of themselves. It is about collaboration and not competition. You can reach her at pam@bestversionyou.com or https://pamkurt.com.

Faith came early in life by Pamela Kurt

By Pamela Kurt

"Be Still and Know I am God" Psalm 46:10

My name is Pam Kurt. I am sure from the brief introduction of this chapter you learned a little bit about me. I want to share more about me. My faith journey started quite young. I grew up in a rural community in Ohio. There were some small farms around but no sidewalks and few streetlights. My grandparents are from Canada and moved to the US when my father was in middle school. They owned a 125-acre farm about 20 miles away that we visited frequently.

I was born on an Army military base in Killeen, Texas (my father was in the Army and honorably discharged shortly after my birth due to some medical complications from his surgery while enlisted). He did serve in the US Army (although he came from Canada) during the late 60s and early 70s. Immigration laws were very different back then, especially, during the draft.

My father never finished high school but was very talented and could fix anything. He primarily worked on cars and motors to anything. I grew up (at least as memory serves) very much a "daddy's girl." I would be outside with him a lot! I learned a lot from him—the basics from swimming, fishing, batting a ball, throwing a frisbee, ice skating, and playing billiards to how to catch worms, how to use a knife, how to use basic tools and more. I look back sometimes and things that I learned as a child I learned to do left-handed.

My other set of grandparents lived within a few miles from our house. My mother's parents were great and a huge part of my life growing up too. They were there through the majority of my childhood and adult life. I am ever so grateful for them. Family has always been very important to me and was my foundation.

The reason some history and background about my family and especially my dad is significant is because my father passed away in a car accident when I was 8 years old. It wasn't an instant car accident. He was hospitalized for over a month before passing away. We didn't get to see him once he had the accident. My mom did bring us to the hospital parking lot once and said my dad was going to be looking out the window to see us in the parking lot. But I never got to see him again after his accident. As a child, we (me and my brother) only heard updates fit for children. It was weird and felt like I never got to say goodbye.

The morning of his accident, he left to go to the corner store for tomato soup. Me and my brother were left home playing in plastic tunnel (they used to look like an accordion) while he ran to the store. My mom wasn't home she was at the hospital visiting my grandmother who was in the hospital because she had just had surgery. This "corner store" was a mile away. He went to get soup because that's what I wanted for lunch. Somehow, when my dad would make the Campbell's soup, it was the best ever. He just added a splash of milk and heated it up but it was the best because he made it.

Later, as I got older and found out or even figured things out, his accident happened before he even got to the store. He was driving a Ford Mustang, the tie rod broke and the car went off the road and smashed into a telephone pole. He was cut out of the driver's side of the car with the "jaws of life." From the pictures, if you only saw one side of the car; the passenger side wasn't harmed.

My grandfather (we called him Papaw) called and asked where my dad was and I told him he was at the store. See, as I mentioned, I lived in a very small community. The fire department and rescues were already called and they called my grandfather because it looked like my father was in the accident. My grandfather didn't know if it was my dad or not until that call.

As a child, I still didn't really know what was going on. My mom came home and told me and my brother and my dad stayed in ICU for quite some time. Our house was chaotic with people coming and going. My mom was coming back and updating us kids.

Then one day, I will never forget the image burned into my head. My Aunt was over watching me and my brother and my cousins were there. At this time, we were all young so there was some even in high chairs. My grandfather (who was a tall man over 6 feet and back then seemed even taller to me) came into the house and put his head down. No one said anything to me. I looked up and all of the women of my family, my grandmother, mom, and Aunt were all in his arms crying. I just knew. It was such a sight. All of the women in my family were being held and comforted by my grandfather. I ran to my room and literally didn't remember speaking for days.

My faith background was that I was baptized Lutheran and grew up Methodist (the church closest to where we lived). I grew up with my paternal grandmother (we called her Granny) taking me to church. I was baptized Lutheran and went to Sunday school regularly. I later was confirmed Methodist and baptized my son Methodist as well. But when I ran to my room at 8 years old, I just started praying and asking why. None of it made sense and felt so alone.

I have learned about religious holidays and stories so much that my father passed away in April on a Friday. I remember as a child, I thought he would rise on Sunday. It was around Easter time. But I also learned fast that religion and faith aren't always the same.

There were many religious things we did for my dad and traditional funeral-type things. But there was such a void and emptiness. Sometimes, I still feel it and earn for him today. I didn't learn what the faith part even meant until I was older.

This was the first time I questioned God and tried to reconcile faith, religion, and simply why.

I would review my life when my dad was in and when he wasn't around. It became a life timeline and marker for the rest of my life. Anything he taught me I learned before 8 years old was one of my markers. I was left-handed at that time. Later in life, I was taught to become right-handed; so I could print (writing) with both hands. I do something as a lefty and most other things with my right hand. So I have both sides of my brain working at all times. At least that's how I explain my creativity and logical thinking at the same time. When I was growing up, we didn't have many of the "diagnoses" they have today.

I followed my Father in several things from creative and curious to also struggling with seeing things backwards. I am sure I would have fit several other diagnoses but they didn't diagnose back them. But pretty sure I had some level of dyslexia. My father also had this. Of course, all I learned later in life as an adult and trying to put things together.

My mother later remarried my stepfather, Jim. They are still together today. He was 8 years younger than my mother but (as my grandmother would say…) bless his heart, my mom gives him a run for it. Later, they had a son, my wonderful stepbrother. So today, I have two brothers who I love to death!

Throughout my childhood and teenage years, I was a classic overachiever. I had to get good grades and be #1. I played piano, sang in choir, and tried to be a "good kid." I look back and I was always busy. My busyness to fill the void came quite young. There were times I would go into my room and wonder if anyone cared. I would feel lonely and out of place and would pray to God to show me the way even back then. I started journaling even at a young age and those pages would turn into prayers to God.

I knew and believed that God had never left me. But the pain of feeling sad or empty had stayed with me for a long time.

Another marker in my life was when I turned 18 years old. I had always been the traditional good kid. And I realized at 18 years old, I could leave my mom's house and not come back. So after a few arguments, that's what I did. I stayed at my best friend's parent's house until I graduated (I turned 18 years old in March and still needed to finish high school). Those were dark times, but I had scholarship opportunities, college tours, etc. I had no idea what I was doing. I even missed the opportunity for any funding because my father was in the military.

So at 18 years old, I started working two jobs and attending college, again fulfilling the need to be busy. I didn't know really what to do but I knew (at least, I thought) I was supposed to go to college. I didn't have any financial help and it was hard. Any guidance on filling out FASFAs, etc. wasn't there. I fumbled through and "made payments" towards any tuition at a local community college. I was trying to start college all on my own. A path of unchartered territory.

I got a job offer in Washington DC. I thought if I got here to make some money, I could move to California with my friends. I thought I could go to school there cheaper if I moved to California. I never made it to California; I met my ex-husband in DC. I was alone in DC. I wasn't afraid because I was so naïve. God kept me safe in scenarios I didn't even realize were dangerous. I got pregnant and moved back to Ohio and had my son. We later moved to Miami, Florida, after the baby was born.

At this point, I again started feeling those lonely feelings. I started attending church in Miami and even had my son baptized in Florida. When he was baptized, my family never came nor to my wedding in DC. So somehow, with my Father missing, I simply dismissed it. It didn't matter since no one else came either. My marriage wasn't that great and. actually, was quite abusive. I prayed and knew God would get me through. There were many days I wanted God to reveal this grand plan. I was very alone inside. But I would pray for strength. It worked.

One day after a bad fight, I packed up the crib and came home to Ohio with not much. I had to stay at my mom's and grandmother's long enough to work and save up for a car, apartment, etc. Short version, my husband did move back and we tried (to no avail). Things got worse and I woke up and knew God would take care of me and my son.

I have had many bad times, but I knew and have never doubted today that God provides for me. Struggling on and off at one point as a divorced single mom without education, I was let go from my job. I was offered another position thousands of miles away. I elected to be terminated. I heard I could go to school while unemployed. I remember another God moment.

I was at the local community college (the one I left earlier years ago). A lady was talking to me and said, where do you want to be in 5 years? I was giving her reasons why I can't go back and finish school. God put so many right people in place during these years from scholarships. supportive friendships, and more. Needless to say, I went back to college in the fall, and five years later, I graduated with my associate's, bachelor's, master's, and Juris doctorate. I took 20 or more credits a semester and unusually few classes in the summer but did it.

God taught me many lessons through those struggling times. One time, I had a stick-shift Chevy Cavalier for sale. I had gotten another car and wanted to sell the Cavalier. I went and got the title notarized etc. because a lady said she was coming and bringing her daughter to test the car as her first car. I was asking $1,500. Well, the daughter didn't want to drive a stick shift and, of course, in my head, I had already spent that money on bills. I was so upset because I even had the title notarized, now what? I was so angry. About a day or so later, another person called for the car. They came. I wasn't excited and still so disappointed. The man came, looked at the car, and stated something about what God provides. He was looking for a car to drive back and forth to work. I dismissed it and his words. But then he offered me $2,200 for the car, I knew that God again took care of me and I just needed to trust.

Fast forward some more to when I was licensed as an attorney. I was still substitute teaching until I could find a job. I started my practice and was scared to death but was trying to do that and teach to keep an income. I walked into my little law office and remember saying out loud. God, what am I doing, am I supposed to be a lawyer or a teacher? I said it out of frustration and fear of not knowing anymore. I asked and I received…

Literally, the next day I was coming in from teaching my phone was ringing. It never stopped. There were two people lined up to come into the law office. What is going on? It exploded. I recruited my son and his teenage friends to help with phones and letters and I worked later each night. As I grew, God brought the right people and opportunities. There were so many of those kinds of stories. I just needed faith to do as I was to do.

I ended up with over 15 attorneys and 8 support people with four offices. I grew and grew. It was a success. All because I had the faith to do it. I took many business chances and just did it.

I had one attorney (an older man, I bought his practice as he retired) say I had more "balls" than most men. I took it as a compliment. But later, while processing, realized I didn't even see it as a fear. I knew God was going to get me through.

Time continues to go forward, and my life has many little times (can be daily, in fact) that God shows me the next steps and comforts me when I am open to hearing him. I am on my next journey and I know I will be taken care of and successful. It's scary to change careers and "start over" but I know God has given me a new direction. I am welcoming this journey. Never give up faith. Life is hard and can be overwhelming. But give that away, God is ready and always there. I know when you're in the throes of it, it's hard to even see the light at the end of the tunnel or ever acknowledge there's a way out. But when we can't see how to get through those storms, let go and have faith that God will get you through.

"My God will supply every need of yours according to his riches in glory in Christ Jesus" (Phil. 4:19).

Renee Ozier

Founder of The Next Step- with Neuro-Coach/
Consultant Renee Ozier

https://www.linkedin.com/in/renee-o-43535ba5/
https://tinyurl.com/reneeozierfacebook
https://tinyurl.com/reneeozierinstagram
https://www.thenextstepcoach.com

Renee Ozier is a lifelong educator, former school principal, trainer, neuro-coach, speaker, writer, and retreat leader! She combines unstoppable faith with growth opportunities, and GOD to facilitate lasting transformations for women in their 2nd half of life- to make it their BEST HALF OF LIFE! Today, Renee is a full-time neuro- coach... coaching women who are experiencing significant life transitions that produce uncertainty, upheaval, fear, or scarcity. Her clients come away with skills to successfully rewire their brains, mend broken beliefs, transform their results, change their limiting mindsets, and prepare them for greater success and joy! Renee helps women reframe, refocus, re-purpose, and renew their God-given talents, abilities, and genius to help them create their NEXT STEP in life!Renee is most blessed to hold the title of "Mom" to her 6 children and "Nana" to her 7 grandchildren who are the "loves of her life!"

JUST KEEP STEPPING UP!
Transformation through Resilience
By Renee Ozier

I raised six children as a single mother, and there was not a day that went by without my daily "chat with God" about what I was struggling with—why my life had taken these twists and turns—and how I was to carry on as a single parent with 6 young children to shepherd and nurture into adulthood! Quite honestly, my usual chats with God began something like this, "Really, God—was this setback (loss, hurt, disappointment) really necessary for my survival and growth? Really? Haven't you tested me enough yet? Are all the things I am going through as a single mother really "your will?" I often remembered St. Mother Teresa of Calcutta's powerful quote, "I know God will not give me anything I can't handle. I just wish that he didn't trust me so much!" Golly gosh, I felt this way every day of my life while raising my children as a single mother!

Furthermore, invariably, when one of my children was hurting, physically or emotionally, whether or not they skinned their knee, lost their favorite toy, their best friend moved away, had a car accident, had a breakup with a girlfriend or boyfriend, or endured the loss of their grandparents whom they loved, one child or the other would often ask me, "Mom, why did this happen? Why is there pain like this in the world? Why would God, who is supposed to love us, allow us to feel so much pain and sadness? Why can't we just grow up without all the pain and disappointment? Wouldn't we be stronger if we could just stop this suffering?"

These were really hard questions to face and confront and even harder to answer lovingly, with grace and intelligence! I was the mom, and I was supposed to know all these answers! However, the truth was—

oftentimes, I myself wrestled with this dilemma and these existential questions about life! How could I explain to my children—those I loved more than life itself—that pain was a part of the journey? However, I also knew another pivotal and crucial truth for all of us to remember… that suffering didn't have to be the final answer!

Pain, loss, and disappointment—all necessary parts of life—but not ones that are meant to triumph over faith and grace. Nor are they to be ignored or covered up with distractions! Rather, I learned over time that suffering was meant to teach, refine, and solidify our inner character—like gold tested in the fire! It was meant to ultimately transform us into our God-given potential through the property of resilience!

Unfortunately, in real life, growth most often follows some kind of setback or pain. As the famous saying goes, "No pain—no gain." While we may not have total control over the "pain" portions of our life, especially when that pain is caused by others' actions or words—we most definitely have control over the *how* and *what* we "gain" from the pain we experience! Enduring suffering, coming through it, and ultimately growing and triumphing over setbacks creates "setups" for resilience and tenacity, unlike any other lesson in life! We learn to have "unshakable and unstoppable faith" and we build tenacious character as a result! The majority of our learning and growth in life does not originate from our happy and carefree moments, but rather from the tough times we encounter, all that we endure, and everything that we walk through! Years ago, I had heard a story about the great Itzhak Perlman—the inimitable Israeli-American concert violinist! At one concert that he gave, as he was warming up, he accidentally broke a string on his violin—something that could be very costly in terms of performance quality! Rather than leave the stage and cancel the concert, he signaled to the conductor to begin the overture. Somehow, through determination and patience, he managed to bring beautiful sounds out of the remaining strings, and he completed a performance worthy of a long-standing ovation! When asked afterwards about the concert and his performance, Perlman said, "You know, sometimes it is the artist's task to find out how much music you can still make with what you have left!" Flexibility and adaptation are crucial elements of success, as evidenced by great stories such as the one above about Itzhak Perlment!

I once asked an older and wiser friend for some meaningful and insightful advice on how to make the best decisions possible, and how to judge situations wisely and prudently. I was going through one of the toughest times in my life at the time. I had just endured the death of my father, my husband of 20 years had left our marriage, I was alone raising 6 children, and my mother was dying of pancreatic cancer! I had just applied for a job as a teacher in a Catholic school, was homeschooling my children at the time, and had been traveling around the country with them as my oldest daughter was a vocal recording artist and attempting to launch her singing career! All of this was happening in my life at the same time—and to be frank, I was over the top with OVERWHELM! I had no idea what I was going to do or how I was going to do it!

This particular friend and fellow educator had raised her children and was now a counselor at the school where I applied for a teaching position. She had weathered her trials in life with apparent grace and wisdom and I wanted to know her secret! She answered my request and question quickly and thoughtfully, "Good judgment and sound decision-making ability usually come from one thing, and one thing only... a difficult experience, lived through and overcome!"

She reminded me of a story that I had heard when I was a child—the story of the donkey in the well. This was a parable that I had heard early on in my Christian walk with God, as a young girl in Catholic grade school. A story which, up until now, held very little meaning for me other than pure entertainment. But at this point in my life, I had just endured a terrible divorce and became a single mother to 6 children, lost both my parents within one year, and lost all of my financial resources. This parable of the donkey grew to have a profound effect on me as I heard it repeated once again by my wise and sweet friend.

She reminded me that every now and then life is going to shovel "dirt" on me, all kinds of messy dirt. Dirt like the loss of a best friend, divorce, the loss of a parent, or worse—the loss of a child! Life will shovel all kinds of dirt upon us in the form of loss, accidents, and illnesses... These times will feel dark and deep like being in the pit of a deep well, unable to see the sky or feel the sunshine! Yet, the key to getting out of these dark "pits" is to sit in silence, soak up the lesson being taught, stand up, shake off the disbelief, and take a step up! We can get out of the deepest pits by not stopping, and by never giving up but rather continuing to LOOK UP towards Jesus and learning to lean on HIS strength, gather our own, trust in HIS plan, shake off the dirt, and take that NEXT STEP UP!

She retold me the story of the farmer who had a donkey.

There was an old farmer whose donkey fell into an empty well. The farmer was elderly, and the donkey was past his prime as well. The farmer knew he didn't have enough strength to pull the donkey out of the deep hole. So, he reasoned to himself, "This donkey is old. I am too. I can't get him out of this mess. It is better for the donkey and me if I just bury him here in this hole. He's had a good life and served me well, but I can't do anything with him now. It is better to bury him and put him out of his misery." So, the farmer grabbed a shovel and started throwing in the dirt.

The dirt felt like raindrops on the donkey's face, only it was messy and it hurt a little. He wondered what was going on. He was already bumped and bruised from the fall. His body ached and he felt tired. Everything around him looked dark. He couldn't make sense of what was happening to him. He felt scared and alone. "What more could go wrong?" the donkey thought to himself. That's when the second pile of dirt hit him. It seemed to come out of nowhere—and this time it really hurt. "Why is this happening to me?" the donkey groaned. He was angry and confused.

The farmer could hear the donkey's cries from below. The donkey cried louder and louder with each pile of dirt that was thrown upon him. And then the cries stopped! The farmer felt relieved. He didn't want the donkey to suffer and was glad he was no longer in pain. "This is for the best," the farmer reasoned. He continued to fill up the hole.

The donkey stopped groaning for a moment. "All this complaining isn't getting me anywhere," the donkey reasoned. "I'm still in this mess and it is only getting worse. I need to do something different so that I can get out." So, the donkey thought, "I can't do anything about the dirt being thrown at me, but I can change how I use the shovelfuls of dirt! I don't have to let others put me down, bury me, or steal my hope of survival. I do have a choice." The donkey decided to shake off the dirt and not let it affect him.

Something amazing happened. When he shook off the dirt, it no longer covered him up and affected him in the same way. The dirt fell down around him. Then something brilliant happened… The donkey decided to use the dirt to STEP UP and GET UP on top of it.

As I sat with and pondered the meaning of that parable once again, I began to craft an outline for the steps that needed to be taken to endure, walk through, and triumph over any pain, setback, suffering, or disappointment. As women of unstoppable faith, we must begin to see periods of trial as periods of preparation for transformation! In that moment of trial, the donkey made 6 critical choices and strategies to change the odds of his survival and ultimately become transformed!

STOP. BE STILL. SIT IN THE SILENCE. STRENGTHEN. SHAKE IT OFF. STEP UP AND OUT.

1. He chose to STOP letting his circumstances dictate his outcome and took back the control of his life.

2. He chose to BE STILL and take the time he needed to craft a plan, an attitude, and a way to get around his present circumstances. He chose to be still in order to prepare to be active!

3. He chose to SIT IN THE SILENCE. Sitting in the school of silence frequently allows us the space to sit with our circumstances, sit with God, pray, craft a plan, and rise above what we are currently living with using God's strength as the foundation. The donkey had to deal with the pain from the dirt being thrown at him. He had to recognize, through silence, that the pain, negativity, and discouragement all kept him "buried" under the mounds of dirt and kept him prisoner in the well.

4. He chose to STRENGTHEN his resolve. He chose to not be buried alive under the weight of the dirt but rather use the weight of the dirt to build a strong mound upon which to raise himself to freedom!

5. He chose to SHAKE OFF the dirt being heaped upon him, and he allowed it to fall around his feet! He used the dirt—the very thing meant to destroy him—to overcome the pain and the challenge! He used the weapon thrust upon him to regroup and recover, to become the victor and NOT the victim! Isn't that how God uses our broken pieces and our broken circumstances? He uses all of our "brokenness" to strengthen us for the road ahead, for it is in our brokenness that God is unleashed! As Ernest Hemingway so beautifully wrote: "We are all broken—that is how the light gets in!"

6. And finally, the donkey chose to STEP UP AND OUT of the well! He acknowledged what was happening to him, gathered his wits about him, showed faith and determination,

strengthened his resolve, used the dirt to rebuild his options, and ultimately, pushed past the obstacles confronting him and STEPED UP AND OUT to freedom and triumph!

STOP. BE STILL. SIT IN THE SILENCE. STRENGTHEN. SHAKE IT OFF. STEP UP AND OUT. He did these 6 steps over and over again. With every step, he got stronger and more determined. The more dirt he shook off, the higher and higher the mound and the closer and closer he got to the mouth of the well! The struggle built his confidence. "I can do this," the donkey thought. "I can do this as long as I don't give up."

The farmer couldn't believe his eyes. Instead of being buried, the donkey was very much alive! With every pile of dirt, he was getting closer and closer to the surface. The farmer mistook the donkey's silence as a sign he had given up. However, he had forgotten that as a rule, donkeys are stubborn creatures and rarely give up without a fight! The farmer had clearly underestimated the donkey!

The donkey refused to let a negative circumstance determine his survival and the quality of his life. He did not allow his circumstances to influence his outcome or steal his character. He stepped out of that hole—that deep, dark well—one step at a time! The very thing that was meant to bury him, actually, served to rescue him and helped him gain his freedom once again! By not giving up, the donkey overcame a hopeless situation. The donkey emerged stronger and more confident, as we will if we use the painful or difficult circumstances of our lives to shape our hopeful attitudes, create resilience, allow ourselves a renewed and reinvigorated outlook, and finally, craft a revamped perspective on pain, inconvenience, stumbles, and challenges!

When life throws challenges at us, we have a CHOICE. We can feel sorry for ourselves and cry and complain like the donkey in the well originally did… "Why me? God, get me out of this mess!" Or, we could stop, become still, sit in silence, gather our strength, shake it off, and step out and step up to meet the challenge and overcome the obstacle! We can either give in to the enormous amount of "dirt" we have on top of us, or we can shake it off and ask these 3 critical questions:

1. What is God teaching me through this situation?
2. What can I do now in my life, given the new circumstances that have arisen?
3. And most importantly, how can I rely on God's strength and providence to carry me through, to lift me when I stumble and fall, and to renew me when I am broken and struggling to see the light?

Life can certainly throw a great deal of "dirt" our way—no doubt about that! Negative people can throw dirt with their critical comments. Negative circumstances can make us feel like we are being buried alive. It is easy to get discouraged when life doesn't go as we've planned. Sometimes the struggles we face can cause us to lose hope. But as we persevere, we are "exercising" our flexibility and adaptation muscles, just as we would exercise all of our other muscles in a workout. Real flexibility and adaptation come from trials and "emotional workouts" whereby we are given the opportunity to practice using our new set of muscles: to bend, to change, and to cultivate emotional, intellectual, and spiritual resilience. When we are resilient we may be pushed and pulled in uncomfortable directions, but we do not break and we do not fall into despair. We may get "windblown" and knocked around quite a bit, but we are like the cypress trees on the Pacific coast or the bamboo trees in Asia—bendable, but not easily broken. The cypress and the bamboo bend with the changes in the wind but continue to grow "in spite" of the wind and in fact, strengthen in the process! Heavy winds serve to only strengthen the root system and create a more resilient, hardy, and immovable structure!

- Do you feel like there is "dirt" being thrown upon you?

- Are you feeling lost, broken, windblown, and confused? Are you asking, "Why is this happening to me?" or "Where is God in all of this?"
- Do you feel like "Life is not fair?" or "I try so hard to be a good person, wife, mother, friend, co-worker, etc. Why is God doing this to me?"
- Have you lost hope that things will ever change?

As tempting as it can be to feel as if God isn't listening, that He is not present, or that He may not care... Don't allow the enemy the satisfaction of going there! As strong women and faith-filled followers of Jesus, we can't allow difficult or painful circumstances or people to steal our outlook and give us a negative mindset. As I reminded my children many times as they were growing up... We do not have to STAY discouraged, down, or despairing. We can make the choice to change our outlook, despite what is happening around us. We can choose to never give up, to always "get up" and to always keep "stepping up and out" of the "dirt" life can sometimes throw our way!

How do we rise above these tough circumstances that life will inevitably throw our way? We can rise above by making the same 6 critical choices that the donkey did!

1. STOP.
2. BE STILL.
3. SIT IN THE SILENCE.
4. STRENGTHEN.
5. SHAKE IT OFF.
6. STEP UP AND OUT.

Someone once said, "The definition of insanity is to continue doing the same thing over and over again and expecting different results." If we stay stuck in a negative situation and don't do anything differently to change it, we will never be free. Simply hoping things will get better is not enough. We need to have "unstoppable faith" to make the radical choice to change whatever we can change, whether it be our attitude, our outlook, our spiritual life, or our circumstances!

One of my favorite children's books of all time is the "Velveteen Rabbit." In this moving story about a worn and ragged stuffed bunny who desperately wanted to be real, the moral of the story is powerful indeed. In this story, the rabbit can only become "real" when the boy has worn him out with love and "loved his fuzz off," literally! It shows us that those who thrive in the midst of suffering, thrive because they have allowed challenges and losses to make them more "real" because they have been flexible and adaptable enough to bend with the winds of change and grow in spite of the setbacks and circumstances—just like the velveteen rabbit did!

One of my favorite quotes is so deceptively simple yet uniquely profound at the same time... Let this sit with you for a moment: "IF NOTHING CHANGES, THEN NOTHING CHANGES!" If the donkey hadn't changed his outlook and his plan, nothing would have changed, and he would have been buried alive under the weight of the dirt!

Don't let negative circumstances hand you a negative outlook or outcome in life. As Steven Covey once stated, "I am not a product of my circumstances. I am a product of my decisions!" So, make the decision to SHAKE it off and STEP UP AND OUT! Don't stay stuck in your pain. With God's help, with *"UNSTOPPABLE FAITH,"* you can overcome any obstacle that you are facing. As my wise friend reminded me when I was a young, single mother and as St. Teresa of Calcutta most certainly understood—often the difficult circumstances of our lives that we think should "kill us," serve instead to only make us stronger, more faith-filled, more reliant of God, more resilient, and ultimately totally transformed! Nothing is hopeless! Nothing we go through is ever useless! Turn everything over to God! Maintain unstoppable and unshakeable faith! And always GET UP, STEP UP, AND STEP OUT into what God has planned for your life! It may not be what you had envisioned but it will always be better than what you had planned! God's plan for us is perfect if only we choose to use the "dirt" heaped upon us, not as a cause for despair, but rather to bring us renewed resilience and transformation!

So many scripture verses address this exact concept, and they are worth reading, pondering, praying over, and remembering:

- "Weeping may endure for a night, but joy comes in the morning." (Psalm 30:5, AMP)
- "Why, my soul, are you downcast? Why so disturbed within me? Put your hope in God, for I will yet praise him, my Savior and my God." (Psalm 42:5, NIV)
- "I have learned how to be content (satisfied to the point where I am not disturbed or disquieted) in whatever state I am." (Philippians 4:11, AMP)

Life is going to shovel dirt on you, all kinds of dirt. The trick to getting out of the well is to shake it off and take a step up. Each of our troubles is a stepping stone. We can get out of the deepest wells just by never stopping, and never giving up! Just keep stepping up… Take that NEXT RIGHT STEP UP AND OUT into your bigger and brighter future! God has this—God has YOU!

Despair, sadness, and suffering have always been a part of the human condition. However, these trials we undergo never have to have the upper hand or the final word. The final word is God's indeed! Triumph, Joy, and Transformation are God's answers to suffering, well-endured through unstoppable faith!

Roberta Quimson

Quimson Coaching
Bible Teacher, Empowerment and Self-Discovery Coach

https://www.linkedin.com/in/roberta-quimson-m-psy/
https://www.facebook.com/qtquimson/
https://www.instagram.com/robertaquimson/
http://www.robertaquimson.com/

Roberta has been coaching and empowering women for over two decades. As a Bible Teacher and Bible Study Leader she has helped women from all walks of life discover their true identity in Christ. As a speaker she invites her audience on an extraordinary voyage of uncovering their own God given greatness through engaging storytelling and practical, real-world applications. After spending time with me, women will leave with a deeper sense of confidence in who they are and what they can do. This ultimately leads to a greater ability to step out in faith and step into their greatness.

Embracing Change:
A Story of Resilience and Faith

By Roberta Quimson

I was never one to like change. It's a word that can evoke a multitude of emotions, from excitement to fear, anticipation to dread. For me, change was a constant companion throughout my life, shaping my experiences, challenging my resilience, and ultimately, leading me on a journey of self-discovery and faith. My first major life change happened when I was 6 months old. I was quickly weaned and sent to my grandparents, as my mother needed to return to full-time work because my father had left us. Of course, I have no memory of that, but I have no doubt it affected me.

Each parent remarried by the time I was two and I was shuffled between two houses, two sets of friends, and lots of grandparents and cousins. Before the age of 5, I was in a whirlwind of chaos and uncertainty, so I had to learn early on to adapt to ever-shifting circumstances.

As I had various people in and out of my life, there were different rules, different cultures, different languages, and lots of change. Through it all, one constant remained: the solace of nature and the warmth of the sun on my face offering a sanctuary from life's storms. Whenever I was stressed, confused, or felt out of place, I would go outside to feel the warmth of the sun. Being barefoot in the grass with the sun on my skin would feel like God wrapping his loving arms around me like a blanket. Even in the winter during the snow, as long as I could see a blue sky and feel the warmth on my face, I knew it would be ok.

So many times I would hear comments like "You are so lucky to have two houses" or "Wow, two moms and two dads, twice as much of everything." Despite the outward appearance of abundance – I grappled with internal turmoil and a sense of disconnection. I felt like two different people, navigating disparate worlds depending on the day of the week. My stepmother created an environment for me to be free of worry and chaos. I was allowed to be a child, not burdened by responsibility. I quickly learned who to be and how to behave depending on whether it was a weekday or weekend. That all fell apart when I became a teenager and my father and stepmother divorced, I no longer had a safe haven to let my hair down and feel seen. Once again I was faced with my nemesis: change.

The people in my life who offered a safe place to land were gone. The family members I depended on for support relocated to Florida. I had to begin to navigate my world on my own. There was not a lot of guidance and support and this was when my extreme panic attacks and anxiety started. Every chance I got, I would sit in the grass outside allowing the sun to warm my face.

As the years went on and the anxiety and challenges grew, I found myself no longer able to continue living in the chaos and longed to be in a place where I felt my truest self and safe.

I reached out to my stepmother and family that had relocated to Florida. I desperately longed to be with people who made me feel safe, seen, and heard. I was welcomed with open arms and told to pack everything up and come on down to the place where it is always warm and sunny. My heart was exploding inside my chest. I was beginning to feel hope well up inside of me at the thought of being in a place where I not only would be loved, but also be able to absorb the sun in all its glory. Florida became Heaven on Earth to me. I felt wonderful.

For the next seven years, through college and beyond I began to rediscover who I was again. I lived with my siblings and extended family and began once again to laugh and enjoy life. I sought counseling and the correct medicine to help with the anxiety and depression. I learned things about myself that had been long hidden: my love of writing, creating, and cooking. I felt like I was slowly beginning to emerge as the person who I was originally supposed to be.

After I married my husband in October of 1996, we began our life together trying to decide which Florida town we wanted to settle down and raise a family in. As long as I was within 30 minutes of my family and lived near a beach, I would be fine. I was finally my truest self. Married, happy, safe, and with my whole life ahead of me. Unbeknownst to me, things were about to drastically change.

Five months into our marriage, my husband came home and announced, "We are taking a week to visit California." I was curious as to why. We don't have any reason to go to California. My husband's company was opening a new office in Northern California, outside of San Francisco, and wanted him to run it. They were sending us on a fully paid, week-long vacation to check out the area and make sure we liked it. I fell apart at the news that we might be uprooted and move across the country. I sat outside on our porch, allowing the warm Florida sun to cover me as I held my face in my hands and sobbed for hours. Change was upon me once again. My deep-seated pain of abandonment and chaos came rushing to my mind as I thought about what this move would look like and how I was entering, once again, into an unknown world of chaos, alone.

Later that month I was listening to the sound of seagulls flying overhead mixed with the barks of the sea lions below. We were visiting San Francisco. My heart was broken. Northern California seemed like a really great place, but my life, business, and family were all in Southern Florida. I was standing at the Pier, looking at sea lions, wrapping my head around the fact that this would become my new home in a few short months. No warm beaches, no palm trees, and most of all, no family or friends. Just my new husband, our three cats, and me. The excitement and dreams of my imagined future in Florida began to fade. It was being replaced by the uncertainty of a new future in California. My old friends, anxiety and panic, were starting to show up again. Memories of feeling abandoned and alone from all those years ago started to haunt me again. I was petrified that all the healing work I did was going to disappear. I could not go through this giant change and lose everything again. There was not enough sun in the world that could make this better.

I chose to support my husband and his career, so I left behind all the things that defined me: My Mary Kay business, my friends, and most importantly, my family.

This cross-country move was a true test of resilience. I felt alone, deceived, and depressed. Every day my husband would go off to work and be around people he knew, meanwhile I sat at home unpacking an apartment and not even knowing where the closest Target was. One time, I decided to take a drive to learn about our new area. I have a poor sense of direction, GPS did not exist, and cell phones were still new to the scene and were used only to make phone calls. After about 30 minutes I realized I was going the wrong way because nothing looked familiar. I was completely turned around, lost and confused. This was a real-life experience playing out the feelings of my heart. I had lost my bearings. I had no sense of which direction I should take. Nothing was familiar. Nothing. At one point, I called my husband in tears and afraid. "I can't get home, I don't know where I am!" My words rang true of my physical location, but the deep truth of being lost and just wanting to go home was symbolic to my heart. I just wanted to go back to Florida, to all that was familiar. After following my husband's directions, I arrived at the apartment about 45 minutes later. I was tired, scared, angry, and upset. This was all his fault. All of it. He moved us here, I didn't want to move to California, his stupid job made us move. I never wanted to leave Florida. I hated him, hated California, hated life, hated everything at that moment. I crashed onto our bed and cried. I yelled out to a God I wasn't sure was listening and asked, "Why? Why is this happening? I want to go home."

But God knew, of course. He knew how to get my attention and bring me into a relationship with Him. He had to isolate me and make me uncomfortable. Neither my husband nor I would have considered ourselves Christians at this time. I was raised both Lutheran and Jewish and he was raised Catholic. Between us both, traditional Judeo-Christian holidays were celebrated with an occasional trip to church for Easter and Christmas. Even though we were married in a church by my childhood pastor, we were not living out our faith. Yet, God was drawing me to Him, though I couldn't see it at the time.

One of the advantages of a Mary Kay business is that you can do it from anywhere. Once we got settled in California, the first thing I did was to find a local chapter so that I could stay on pace with my team. At one of the very first meetings I attended, I saw an invitation postcard on the desk that said, "Are you struggling and know there is more to life?" I grabbed a few and threw them into my bag, thinking they were new marketing materials for Mary Kay. A few days later I actually looked at the postcard, front and back, and realized it had nothing to do with Mary Kay at all. It was an invitation to a local community church, Crossroads.

Later that night over dinner the conversation sounded something like this.

"You know a bunch of the Mary Kay ladies invited us to a church service. They say it's really laid back. They meet in a movie theater, serve coffee, and the pastor wears jeans and a 49er jersey."

My husband, a die-hard Dallas Cowboy fan, looked at me and said, "Well, Sunday is football day, and this weekend we are going away to celebrate our first wedding anniversary. If that's something you want to do later, go for it, but I'm not going to listen to someone in a 49er jersey."

That weekend, just as planned, we celebrated our first wedding anniversary. We enjoyed a hot air balloon ride over the Wine Country, natural spa remedies, and a trip to see the great Redwoods in our open Jeep Wrangler. The beauty and majesty of it all were breathless. There is something magical when you drive your Jeep through a giant redwood, literally, through the middle of it. Being in nature like that and feeling the sun on my face provided some comfort and helped me be less angry about the move and more open to making the best of the situation. Little did I know, God was speaking to my husband during that trip. On the drive back that Sunday evening he looked at me and said, "Do you still have that postcard? We can check it out next weekend if you want." I smiled and agreed, not sure what was happening, but I went along with it.

Sitting in movie theater seats, sipping coffee and trying to wrap our heads around a church having a full band with drums and electric guitars, we waited for the pastor to begin, curious if he would be wearing a jersey. The message for that day was titled "God in Nature" We sat and listened. Halfway through the message, the pastor was making his point about God's fingerprints everywhere in creation. He asked the congregation, "Have you ever seen the Redwoods? Have you ever gone up North with the big ones, ever driven through one?" My husband turned to me, eyes wide open, and said, "You set me up!" I replied, "I swear I did not, I have never met this man!"

That was it. That was all it took. From that day forward, we could not get enough of God's word and His people. We went on picnics and hikes and celebrated birthdays together with the pastor and his wife. We learned what it meant to live in a Christian community like the first church in Acts 2. I made amazing female friends and we grew in our faith together. My heart was beginning to soften and heal when in March of 1998, both my husband and I participated in believers' baptism and made our declarations of Jesus as our Lord and Savior.

Every holiday or family birthday still reminded me of the loss and sacrifice that was made. I was conflicted between my newfound faith and spiritual family, and my longing to return home to Florida to be with my natural family. There was a constant battle in my heart. I was afraid to fully embrace this new life in California. I was afraid that just like before, a major change would happen to take it all away. I resisted making California home.

When I found out I was pregnant with our first child Brandon in the Spring of '99, I experienced a mix of emotions. Joy at the idea of building a family. Sadness of knowing my family was not nearby. My husband and I had a long deep conversation about my desire to go back to Florida. I wanted to raise our family near cousins and grandparents. He agreed, but the company did not have a position for him to return. It would mean paying the cost to move back across the country ourselves and starting all over in a new job. A job he hadn't even begun to look for. We agreed to pray about it and see where God would have us go.

As I became more and more pregnant, the desire to move lessened. The thought of packing and moving while being sick and large did not seem fun. In addition to this, my husband's company offered him a huge raise and a bonus to use towards a down payment on a house. They wanted to ensure he was going to stay and run the Bay Area facility so they made leaving very difficult. We looked at this like God was saying, "I want you to plant roots here." We called our realtor friend and said, what are the first steps at getting approved. My journey into calling California home was beginning to take shape. I was imagining a future here.

The California market was crazy. We were living in the middle of the Dot Com Boom. Here we were putting in offers on a house, praying and asking God if this was the house where we were meant to raise a family, imagining the landscaping and decor, only to find out we'd been outbid. It was heartbreaking, frustrating, and demoralizing. Maybe we should pack it all up and go back to Florida after all.

One of the last houses we looked at was in an old neighborhood that had become known as the "Ghetto of Fremont." The schools were not great. Some of the houses were known as drug houses. It definitely wasn't our first choice, but it was in our budget and we were so tired of always being outbid. We put in an offer. Just like all the others, we were outbid. The selling family had learned that we were Christians with a new baby. They too were Christians and prayed for a buyer that would enjoy raising a family in the home just as they did. They chose us, even though the other bid was higher. Oh My Goodness! We were homeowners! We were actually homeowners! California is where we were supposed to be. Every morning I would sit in our backyard, coffee in hand, sun on my face, and praise and thank God for his favor. I felt safe, calm, and happy. I was feeling like this could be home.

A few years later, we had our second son, Zachary, and I was in full swing of being a Stay-At-Home Mom and Housewife. The first two years of raising Brandon ignited a desire in me that I didn't know I had. I nursed for almost 2 years. We co-slept. I was a firm believer in attachment parenting. My days of pink lipsticks and winning cars were a distant, faint aspiration. "How could I have ever imagined trying to juggle a career and motherhood? Being a Mom was what I was called to do!"

Of course, there were changes in my life. Having children always brings changes, but it was different this time. My trust in God and my faith carried me through. Things may have seemed chaotic, but I had peace about me. I was finally understanding who I was truly meant to be. My new identity of motherhood had taken over and it was what I needed to heal completely. Past trauma, hurts, abandonments, and pain were all seen as learning experiences to help me be the absolute best mother I could be. I knew exactly the type of life I wanted my boys to have and was going to do everything I could to ensure it happened. They would never know the pain of divorce. They were allowed to express themselves and have opinions. They were raised as a collective "we," instead of being shunned. Life was amazing. I was living out my heart's desire. There was no greater feeling than being a mom to these two amazing little boys.

As they grew, I noticed that both boys had struggles in their own way. Brandon wasn't grasping the concepts of letter sounds like his peers and he hated to hold a pencil and write. One day while dropping him off for preschool, he had a complete meltdown. He was begging me not to leave him. When I spoke to the teacher about what was going on, she shared that he hated to write his name on his artwork and could barely make the letter B. As he progressed into Kindergarten, I began to notice more and more his difficulty with writing and reading He was falling farther and farther behind in literacy, yet in math and science, he was 2 grades ahead. By 2nd grade, we started a full battery of testing. It was an arduous one, but I dove in head first knowing I had to be the best advocate for my child. I was fully open to considering any diagnosis so that from there I could learn how to best equip Brandon to be successful in life. Brandon was diagnosed with a Learning Processing Disorder, Dyslexia, and Dysgraphia; and also ADHD.

While this was going on with Brandon, Zachary was having his own issues. He was extremely particular about things, especially his toys, and by age 2, he still was not talking with full words but rather pointing and grunting for things. By the time he entered preschool, he would have complete meltdowns and frustration if the colored blocks were not put away in a very specific order. At home, he would display soothing behaviors like humming and waving his hands. Our journey of testing and diagnosing Zach began. We started with audiology because his vocabulary only had about 50 words and he had impeded speech. His results came back perfect. He could hear just fine. Next, we went into Autism testing. Zachary was diagnosed to have Asperger's (before the name was changed). This means that he did not read social cues very well and had a tendency for things to be very specific.

I realized I had two special needs children. Their life and educational journeys were not going to look like everyone else's. This was a big change. But unlike times before, anxiety did not take charge, but instead, determination and resilience did. I was navigating the world of IEPs and 504s and doing my best to create a successful environment for our kids. Again, I took on the challenge and committed myself to learning all I could about how to equip our boys for success. We focused on teaching the boys how to navigate and live in a world that is not set up for their convenience. We embraced the mindset that "you can accomplish anything with hard work and dedication. You are not owed anything. Your future is in your hands. Let's figure out what works for you and then excel at it." My husband is an immigrant to this country, and I was a second-generation immigrant, so we raised them through the lens of owning your life and not letting it own you.

Zach was excelling in academics but not socially. Brandon was killing it socially but not academically. We explored homeschooling as an option. Every year we prayed about what to do, and every year the Lord was clear. Brandon was to be homeschooled, but Zachary was not.

So, there I was fully diving in and learning how to best educate Brandon in the way his brain works and how to best parent Zachary in the way his brain works. Flexibility and creative ideas worked for Brandon. Rules and structure worked for Zachary. On a typical weekday evening, you could see the dining room table covered in art supplies for Brandon's history project, while Zachary was crying, extremely upset, and on the verge of a meltdown because said art supplies were on 'his' side of the table and he can't sit and eat dinner. I am trying calmly to help Brandon understand that he needs to honor Zach's space and not create a mess on his side of the table while simultaneously working with Zach to understand this is not an intended malicious violation of space. (If you are a parent of an ASD child, you totally get this.)

The cost of Zachary's school and private tutoring for Brandon was a decent-sized monthly bill. Yet, against the odds, we were managing to be homeowners and surviving in the Bay Area with one income. Our faith grew and solidified year after year as we witnessed God meet every need and provide.

California had fully felt like home. Our Spiritual family was growing. Our life was made up of sports, scouts, homeschooling, marching band, church activities, Bible studies, and the list goes on. We settled into a lifestyle that worked well for the four of us and the Lord had showered blessing upon blessing. Finances were always covered, trips and activities for the kids were never an issue, and my passion and calling became clearer and clearer as the years went on. I proudly embraced the honored title: Mother.

When Brandon graduated high school, he attended the State University and was accepted to the Mechanical Engineering Program. Three years later, just like his brother, Zach graduated high school, and he too was off to become a Mechanical Engineer.

That summer, with both boys home I had such a swelled sense of pride as a mother who had done her job well. Both our children were going to college for Mechanical Engineering degrees, and becoming the masters of their future while leaning on and loving God through it all. This is what I had hoped and prayed for all those years ago. From the middle of the night feedings all the way through the weeklong church camps, I had only ever wanted to be the best mom I could to my Neuro-Divergent children and set them up to be successful adults in life.

When they left for college again that fall, the house became empty, and I – an amazing homeschooling Stay-At-Home Mom – realized I had no idea what I was supposed to do with the rest of my life. If I'm not volunteering on a committee, driving a group of kids somewhere, or doing a ton of laundry, then who am I? What am I supposed to do with my life? The reflection in the mirror that stared back at me was a stranger. Who is this woman? This was a huge change and I was not able to make it better with sunshine and nature walks. I was having a full-blown identity crisis.

Memories of the early days came flooding into my mind. Should I go back to work? Should I go back to school? Should I volunteer? I wrestled with my identity and purpose for months on end. I was filled with doubts and insecurity. Who would hire a 50-year-old woman who hasn't worked in over 20 years? What experience can I bring to the table in a corporate setting? A depression came over me and I was faced with having to rediscover who I was and what I offered the world. Those long-gone feelings of abandonment started to resurface.

I needed a purpose again, something to help me believe in myself, and create some consistency. After some research and discussion with my husband, I enrolled to earn my Master's degree in Psychology and Life Coaching.

After earning my Master's degree I began an entrepreneurial journey into Life Coaching, writing, and speaking. People wanted, no, they needed to hear and learn from my story. There are mothers who experience this every Fall. The house becomes empty, the bedrooms are quiet, and who they were and all they thought they were called to do has come to a pause.

I had to face this change. I had to embrace this challenge and see it as an opportunity to rely fully on God and what he was going to do. He knew my time of being a Stay-at-Home mom was going to end. He knew I still had the later years of my life to live a new calling and purpose. I had to surrender everything to him while I waited to learn what I was supposed to do next. Like my childhood, once again, I was discovering who I was and what was being expected of me. The difference this time was I knew my creator and I knew He was in control. I knew I could always find peace and comfort in Him.

My typical morning now starts with a cup of coffee outside while I sit on my patio and enjoy the warm California sun. Its purpose is not to give me a sense of calm and hope as in years past, but instead, it reminds me of God's faithfulness. I have had to face changes, and know more will come, but I now know the author of change and see it for what it is: provision, guidance, redirection. What used to be seen in my life as scary and painful, is now seen as necessary and attainable. I am able to embrace the changes as they come and know I will overcome the challenge. I know who I am and who God has made me to be. My titles may change, but my identity has not. I am Roberta Quimson. I am an overcomer. I am a Child of God.

Samantha Sheppard

Founder and CEO of Samantha Sheppard Consulting

https://www.linkedin.com/in/samanthaksheppard/
https://www.facebook.com/samantha.lehmansheppard
https://www.instagram.com/ssheppard.consulting/
http://www.samanthasheppardconsulting.com/

Samantha Sheppard is the owner and founder of Samantha Sheppard Consulting. She is from Pennsylvania and lives out each day with faith, passion and enormous amounts of coffee! With a degree in marketing and over 20 years experience in the field, she is focused on helping other women in business reach their goals through teaching the art of marketing by providing training and consultation services. Whether you're just getting started and need help putting together a marketing plan for your new business OR you are a seasoned entrepreneur and are looking for some fresh and new ideas, she is here to help. She believes that each day should be spent on progress over perfection!

Bloom Where You Are Planted:
A Woman's Guide to Faith and Resilience

By Samantha Sheppard

Hello, lovely ladies! As we begin on this short written journey together, I feel led to dive into the timeless wisdom of blooming where you're planted. Picture yourself as a beautiful flower, thriving in the soil of your life, no matter where you find yourself. We'll draw inspiration from scripture, share personal stories, and sprinkle in some humor along the way.

In the Bible, we're reminded that our faith is meant to shine bright, no matter the circumstances (Matthew 5:16). Just like flowers bloom in different environments, we're called to let our light shine wherever life takes us. Whether you're a busy mom, a career woman, or both, your faith can be a beacon of hope and light for those around you.

Let me share a bit about my own journey. As a mom of 2 teenagers, a wife of almost 20 years, and a seasoned business owner for over 2 decades, life has thrown its fair share of curveballs. My husband and I have weathered storms in both our personal and professional lives, but through it all, our faith has kept us grounded. We have learned to bloom where we are planted, trusting that God has a plan for each twist and turn.

But don't get me wrong, this does not mean that we loved every place we found ourselves planted. There were definitely some situations where we had to purposefully seek God's wisdom because, to our human eyes, it just did not make any sense.

Have you ever found yourself in a place where you could not seem to grasp God's plan at that moment? Perhaps you stumbled around confused (like us) at times in your life and just couldn't seem to see the forest between the trees. However, no matter where you have been in life, or may currently may find yourself, just know this - you are not alone! This happens to all of us and the most important thing to do is this - seek God's wisdom and insight before we throw in the towel!

So what does this look like in real life? No matter where you are in life right now, perhaps you are sitting in your living room under a comfy blanket sipping a warm cup of coffee while reading this chapter... Or maybe you're in the office trying to squeeze in a few minutes to yourself between business calls and zoom meeting - sit tight, my friend. This chapter was written from the bottom of my heart to help you embrace where you are in this moment and have faith that God always has a plan.

So buckle up - let's dive right in! Here are some ideas to help you bloom no matter where you are or what circumstances you find yourself in:

1. Embrace Your Environment: Just like flowers adapt to their surroundings, embrace the unique circumstances of your life. Whether you're in the hustle and bustle of city life or the tranquility of suburbia, know that God has placed you exactly where you need to be. The hardest part of this is that your current environment might not be what you expected, or ever wanted, it to be. But remember this - there is always a purpose in our life. There is always a silver lining. Whether you find yourself living out your current dream life or perhaps a place completely unexpected, seek God in every situation and he will show you how to bloom.

I can relate to this in so many ways, especially when I found myself in a very scary health situation in 2018. I was dealing with a pretty bad health crisis and was finally diagnosed with severe chronic Lyme disease late that year. The doctor told me that I had one of the worst cases of Lyme disease that he had seen in 20 years and that my organs were shutting down. Time was of the essence if I wanted to live and lead a thriving life. This diagnosis led me to a clinic in Scottsdale, Arizona, in January 2019.

The clinic staff and physicians were amazing. God truly led me there for a bigger purpose, even though the circumstances were not any that I would have chosen for myself. Although I knew that I was there to receive life-saving treatment (which worked by the way - I'm completely healthy today!) I kept finding myself questioning, "Why me?" (Have you ever been in that situation?)

To be honest, I felt pangs of guilt even feeling that way because I was sitting next to stage 4 cancer patients each and every day who were even in worse health than I was. The first 2 weeks were the worst both physically and mentally. I kept asking God why He would put me in this situation. Why was I so sick, why did I have to move across the country with my family for 3 months and go through this horrific experience? I tithed, I was faithful, and I loved the Lord with all my heart. So, why would I be put in this situation?!

It was all about perspective. Originally, I did not know why I was planted in this situation. How was I supposed to bloom here? Then it hit me - I had to change my perspective. If I had not been so sick, I never would have been at that clinic and I never would have been able to be an encourager to those other patients. As soon as I changed MY perspective, God changed everything.

Every single day I had the chance to witness God's love and encouragement to other patients who were not saved yet. I was able to support those who did not have family members with them. I saw my own faith grow to immeasurable levels that I had never experienced before. It is in times of deep sorrow and pain that our faith grows the MOST. Those are the times we lean into God and His word the deepest.

An even bigger bonus of being planted in this exact place in time was the amount of growth I saw my daughters experience. They were only 6 and 9 years old when we moved to Arizona. We were homeschooling at the time and they too had to leave the comfort of their own home, as well as their family and friends. They quickly became a beacon of hope and light to every single patient and staff member of this clinic. They were a light in the darkness! Watching them bloom in this situation was one of the highlights of what was originally a deeply scary situation.

So no matter where you find yourself, remember to take notice of your personal perspective and evaluate if it needs to be changed in order to see the opportunity to truly bloom where you are planted today!

2. Nurture Your Faith: Your faith is like a garden that requires tending. Set aside time each day to water your soul through prayer, meditation, and reading scripture. As you nurture your faith, watch it grow and flourish in unexpected ways. Trust me, I know how daunting it might feel sometimes when you are looking at your daily calendar and endless to-do list. However, we must first nurture and fill up our own cups if we want to help others. You will find it difficult to stay positive and encouraging to others if you are stressed out and struggling yourself. Taking even 10 minutes a day to dive into God's word and pray will have a huge impact on your overall outlook and ability to share your faith.

My best tip would be to find things that truly interest you and grab your attention. My oldest daughter LOVES to read. She would totally be content if she was locked in a library or bookstore for a week! However, I am not that way (even though I secretly want to love reading!). I am a slow reader and have a hard time sitting and focusing for long period of time (can I get an amen!) So for me, I find devotionals with short chapters or lessons pique my interest. I also love podcasts and audios. Perhaps you thrive in social settings and want to join an online community where you can share lessons, encouragement, and prayers with one another. These are great because it does not require driving anywhere and you can log into the group at any time of the day. Whatever it is - make sure that your TAG (time alone with God) time every day is something you look forward to!

3. Share Your Light: Don't hide your faith under a bushel! Whether it's through a kind word, a helping hand, or a simple act of love, share your faith boldly and authentically. You never know whose life you might touch with your light. Even a simple smile or hello to a stranger can have even the most profound effect. Don't underestimate the impact you can have on others. You don't have to quote scriptures and pray in tongues to share your faith with others. Living a life of love, courage, and kindness speaks volumes to those you encounter on a daily basis.

In today's world, social media is a great way to share your faith! I am not saying you have to blast it all day, every day. But social platforms are where millions of people are going daily for insights, encouragement, information, and more! Yes, I know that social media is the "highlight reel" of most lives, but imagine if you shared a favorite bible verse or word of encouragement one day and it impacted someone going through a really tough time. Life is impacted one word at a time. Don't be afraid to share your faith and God's love online. Trust me, in the society we live in today, people are seeking this!!

4. Find Joy in the Journey: Life is a roller-coaster ride full of ups and downs. Instead of waiting for the perfect moment to bloom, find joy in the journey itself. Celebrate the small victories, laugh in the face of adversity, and trust that God is weaving a beautiful tapestry of your life. This is especially true on days that feel like a total hot mess! Oftentimes, it is the days that are the most frustrating that we need to seek out the silver linings the most. What you choose to focus on is what will grow. Choose to focus on finding joy in every circumstance - it is there!!

Earlier in this chapter I shared about my health journey where I almost passed away from Lyme disease and how God planted me in a clinic in Arizona for several months. After I shifted my perspective, I actually began to see the joy in my daily treatments instead of focusing on the hell of it all. The biggest surprises came from my daughters.

My oldest daughter had dabbled in the kitchen up to that point, mostly baking with me. But in our small condo in Scottsdale, I saw her truly grow her culinary skills. Truth be told, she is now a much better cook than me! Watching her try new recipes, make her own grocery list, and light up when we tried her new creations - it brought so much joy to a stressful situation! My youngest daughter still laughs about the time they almost lost me rolling down a hill at a cactus farm (I was in a wheelchair at the time)! Luckily they caught me in time before it got bad!

There is JOY everywhere - we have to seek it out, no matter where we are. Make it a goal to share joy with one person every single day. It's hard to stay in a negative or worrisome frame of mind if we are focused on sharing JOY!

5. Lean on Community: Surround yourself with a supportive community of fellow believers who can uplift and encourage you. Whether it's through a women's Bible study, a church group, or a close-knit circle of friends, journey together in faith, supporting one another along the way.

You know the saying, "It takes a village"? Well, that does not just apply to raising children. Women need a village too. Life is meant to be shared with others so make sure to seek out other women who can lift you up, encourage you daily, and even speak the truth with courage and love when it is needed. There is strength in numbers and when life gets tough, you will want your village to surround you!

My dear sisters, you are fearfully and wonderfully made (Psalm 139:14). No matter what life throws your way, you have the strength, resilience, and faith to bloom right where you are. So stand tall, spread your wings, and let your light shine bright. Together, let's journey onward, rooted in faith and blooming in grace.

As we wrap up our time together, remember that your faith is a gift meant to be shared with the world. So, go forth with confidence, knowing that you are never alone on this journey. Bloom boldly, my friends, and may your light shine brightly wherever life takes you.

Stacey Dori Garel

CEO of Gifted Administrative Services

https://www.linkedin.com/in/staceygarel
https://www.facebook.com/stacey2qute
https://www.instagram.com/Iamstaceydori
https://www.yourspiritualgoddess.com/
https://www.giftedadministrativeservices.com/

Stacey Garel is an Bestselling published author & natural born Prophetess. Stacey is originally from Atlanta, GA, a certified Event Planner professional & writer. Stacey has been a dedicated expert of events for over 15 years working as a Director of Events & Tradeshows for CORT Tradeshow & Events Furnishings. Having worked on National conferences, trade shows, and events such as the 2012 DNC for former President Barack Obama & the 2013 & 2019 Super Bowl. In 2023 Stacey was nominated for a RICE Award as Founder's Rising Star. In 2023 she received and Outstanding Citizen Award from her home state of Georgia. Stacey is an active motional speaker & leader in her community. Her ultimate goal is to always be an inspiration to all she encounters.

Necessary tools for your destiny

By Stacey Dori Garel

Introduction

In a world filled with challenges and obstacles, it is essential for women to develop unwavering faith that empowers them to navigate through life's ups and downs. Becoming an unstoppable woman in faith is not only about strengthening your belief in a higher power but also about developing a deep sense of self-worth, resilience, and purpose. This chapter will explore the key principles and practices that can help you cultivate a powerful and unshakeable faith, enabling you to rise above any circumstances and become the unstoppable woman you were meant to be. Start by accessing the necessary tools for your destiny.

Embracing Your Identity

To start activating your faith, it is crucial to recognize and fully embrace your identity as a cherished creation of God. By understanding that you are uniquely designed with inherent worth and purpose. God said in Jeremiah 1:5, "Before I formed you in the womb I knew you, before you were born, I set you apart; I appointed you as a prophet to the nations." With this passage God wants you to embrace your strengths, talents, and passions, and align them with your faith journey. Remember that your identity is not defined by the world's standards but by the divine love and grace that surrounds you.

My Identity

In my journey to uncover my identity, I had to realize the unique capabilities & connections I had with God. For many years of my life, I was silenced and hid my abilities to tap into something so beautiful and amazing. It was my true calling, my destiny, and my gift to others. To hear God's voice so clearly and to share pure communications to form spiritual conversations for confirmation is truly an amazing gift. Once I discovered my ability to hear God's voice so clearly, I learned in that moment how much I needed to strengthen my connection with Him. In order to walk with God, one has to listen, but obedience is key to receiving God's promises. Being obedient to God meant following His commands, teachings, and guidance with humility and reverence.

For me, it involved aligning my actions, thoughts, and attitudes with His will and seeking to live in accordance with His principles. Obedience to God requires faith, trust, and a willingness to surrender your own desires and submit to His authority. Obedience is a lifelong journey of seeking His wisdom, seeking forgiveness when we fall short, and striving to live a life that honors and pleases Him. In my journey, so many times, I felt as if I was falling short of my obedience. So many times, I heard God telling me to stay on course and trust his way. However, many times I diverted the course and did things my way. I was sure I had all the right answers only to end up regretting my choices and asking for forgiveness. Each and every time I failed, God never failed me. His love for me was unmatched, unwavering, and unconditional. Our bond was unbreakable. I can remember the first time God had his hand on me so strongly. I was at a low point in my life where I had experienced a traumatic incident where my innocence and dignity were taken. I was so broken and felt all alone in this space. Who was I going to tell, and who was going to protect me? I remember driving home feeling so lost, going upstairs, and sitting in the shower as the water ran down my body. Sitting in a pool of my blood and tears. I was crying out to God to please take me as I no longer wanted to do this thing called life. I was done and wanted to leave. The next day I got in my mom's car and went to the doctor for assistance only for that doctor to tell me at that moment that what happened to me was common and a result of my own fault by being female. I was shocked and confused all at the same time.

How was I being SA'd my fault? He refused to treat me and told me my life didn't matter. I quickly grabbed my stuff and ran out of the office in tears. I got in the car and began to drive. As I was driving, I felt myself slipping in and out of consciousness. I literally felt as if I had escaped my body. I then drifted the car off into oncoming traffic as I wanted to end everything at that moment. I can recall talking to God and asking Him to please take me. In that very moment, I felt something overtake the steering wheel right before I was struck by a car. All I can remember seeing was headlights and the sound of a roaring horn. The force was so strong that the car veered off into a ditch. I was so scared and shocked by what just happened. The car had stopped. I remember trying to start it only for the car not to start as many times as I tried. I then began to sit there and cry. I felt an embrace over me that was so strong and a great sense of comfort. I heard a voice so strongly saying, I am with you and sending you help. Not even a moment later did I receive a call from my mom. She said, "I just had a bad feeling. Are you ok?" I told her no and to come get me. Once she showed up, she looked at me and hugged me. She told me things would be ok, and that she would help me get through it. She got in the car, and it started right up. Again, I was in shock, and I knew that God had intervened. He had saved me from harming myself and had given me another chance at life to live out my purpose. Know that when God has a calling over your life, he will always show up for you in times of need or understanding. Each and every one of you has a place on this earth to make a mark. A chance to stand out and do great things. Never let anyone or any event overtake your dreams or silence your voice. Know that you are individually unique and have a special gift that is needed in this world. Great things will happen to you, but greater things will always come to you once you believe, and let God in.

In Conclusion

Through the many challenges and trials I have faced in my life, I can confidently say that God has played a significant role in saving me. His divine intervention and unwavering love have guided me through the darkest moments and provided me with hope and strength when I needed it most. In times of despair, I have turned to prayer and found solace in knowing that God is always listening. His presence has brought me comfort and reassurance, reminding me that I am never alone. Through His guidance, I have been able to navigate difficult situations and make the right decisions. God's saving grace has been evident in the moments when I felt lost, broken, and without direction. He has shown me the path to take and has given me the courage to persevere. His divine intervention has protected me from harm and guided me towards a brighter future. Furthermore, God's saving power has extended beyond the physical realm. He has saved me from the darkness of despair, filling my heart with joy and peace. His love has healed my wounds and restored my faith, allowing me to experience true happiness and fulfillment. In conclusion, I am forever grateful for God's saving presence in my life. His divine intervention, love, and guidance have transformed my life and saved me from countless hardships. I will continue to trust in His plan and rely on His strength as I navigate the journey ahead.

My Power

Reclaiming Your Power with Faith

In life, we often encounter challenges and obstacles that can make us feel powerless and defeated. However, it is important to remember that we have the power within us to overcome these challenges and reclaim our strength. One powerful tool that has helped me in this journey is faith. Faith allowed me to tap into my higher power and find the strength and courage to face any hardship. My understanding of Faith was more than just a belief in something greater than ourselves. It is a deep trust and confidence in God. He provided me with a sense of hope, resilience, and confidence that helped me navigate through the darkest times of my life.

In times when I was dealing with grief, health attacks, financial hardships, or misconnections with love or friendships that I thought were genuine, God's love for me was all that I needed. God gave me the discernment to see when to let go. Not only when to let go but who to let go of. In my walk with God and my elevation to become exactly who God has designed me to be, I had to understand that my purpose depended on me staying strong in this walk with him alone. Sometimes in life, you must block out the noise to encounter the essence of God's favor. Learning that you are in a transformation season where God is working on you to place you in a position to be the best version of yourself. So that you can share your insight with others. This is definitely my thankful season where I thank God for every blessing, every day, and all the lessons I've learned along the way.

In this process, you must let go of fear and doubt. Fear and doubt can be major obstacles in reclaiming your power. They can paralyze us and prevent us from taking necessary actions in life. However, with faith, we can learn to let go of these negative emotions. By trusting in God and believing in ourselves, we can overcome fear and doubt and step into our power. Trusting that everything happens for a reason and God's love allows us to let go of control and embrace Him. It is through trust and surrender that we can find the strength to face challenges head-on and reclaim our power. When we trust God, we understand that our actions and experiences have a greater purpose, even if we can't see it immediately. Just know that you are never alone in this process as God is always there guiding us throughout all that we encounter.

In Conclusion

Reclaiming your power with faith is a transformative journey that allows us to overcome challenges, let go of fear and doubt, find meaning and purpose, and connect with God. By embracing God, we tap into a love that guides and supports us, giving us the strength and courage to reclaim our power and live a fulfilling life. Embrace God, reclaim your power, and unlock your true potential. Know that you are powerful! As it all belongs to you!

Tips to Building a solid foundation with God.

1. Cultivating a Strong Foundation:

Building a strong foundation for your faith requires intentional effort and dedication. Begin by immersing yourself in the teachings of your faith and seeking a deeper understanding of its principles. Engage in regular prayer, meditation, and reflection to connect with your spiritual essence. Surround yourself with a community of like-minded individuals who can support and uplift you on your journey. Take time to study scripture, attend religious services, and participate in meaningful rituals that strengthen your bond with the divine.

2. Developing Resilience:

Life is full of unexpected challenges and setbacks. To become an unstoppable woman in faith, it is essential to develop resilience and the ability to bounce back from adversity. Embrace difficulties as opportunities for growth and trust that your faith will guide you through the darkest times. Lean on your spiritual practices and seek solace in prayer during moments of doubt or despair. Remember that setbacks do not define you but rather provide valuable lessons that shape your character and deepen your faith.

3. Embracing Fearlessness:

Fear can often hinder our progress and prevent us from fully embracing our faith. To become unstoppable, cultivate fearlessness in the face of uncertainty and doubt. Trust in the divine plan and surrender control over outcomes. Step outside of your comfort zone and take bold steps in alignment with your faith. Embrace challenges as opportunities for personal and spiritual growth. Remember that with faith, there is no room for fear.

4. Serving Others:

An unstoppable woman in faith understands the importance of serving others and making a positive impact in the world. Look for opportunities to extend kindness, compassion, and love to those around you. By embodying the principles of your faith and serving others selflessly, you not only strengthen your own faith but also inspire and uplift those in need. Remember that your faith is not just a personal journey but a call to make a difference in the lives of others.

My top 10 Bible verses for Strength.

1. "I can do all things through Christ who strengthens me." - Philippians 4:13
2. "The Lord is my strength and my shield; my heart trusts in him, and he helps me." - Psalm 28:7
3. "Fear not, for I am with you; be not dismayed, for I am your God; I will strengthen you, I will help you, I will uphold you with my righteous right hand." - Isaiah 41:10
4. "But those who hope in the Lord will renew their strength. They will soar on wings like eagles; they will run and not grow weary, they will walk and not be faint." - Isaiah 40:31
5. "Be strong and courageous. Do not be afraid or terrified because of them, for the Lord your God goes with you; he will never leave you nor forsake you." - Deuteronomy 31:6

6. "The Lord is my strength and my song; he has become my salvation." - Exodus 15:2
7. "God is our refuge and strength, an ever-present help in trouble." - Psalm 46:1
8. "He gives strength to the weary and increases the power of the weak." - Isaiah 40:29
9. "The name of the Lord is a fortified tower; the righteous run to it and are safe." - Proverbs 18:10
10. "My flesh and my heart may fail, but God is the strength of my heart and my portion forever." - Psalm 73:26

What does being unstoppable encompass?

Becoming an unstoppable woman in faith is a lifelong journey that requires dedication, self-reflection, and a deep connection with the divine. By embracing your identity, cultivating a strong foundation, developing resilience, embracing fearlessness, and serving others, you can unlock the power of faith within you. Remember that faith is not just a belief; it is a transformative force that can propel you towards your purpose and help you overcome any obstacles that come your way. Embrace your faith, trust in the divine, and become the unstoppable woman you were destined to be.

Becoming an unstoppable woman of faith is a journey that requires dedication, perseverance, and a deep connection with God. It is about cultivating a strong and unshakeable belief in His power, love, and guidance, and allowing that faith to shape every aspect of your life. Here are some key principles to help you become an unstoppable woman of faith:

1. Seek a Personal Relationship with God:

Developing a personal relationship with God is the foundation of a strong faith. Dedicate time each day to connect with Him through prayer, meditation, and reading His Word. Seek His guidance, wisdom, and comfort in all areas of your life. The more you cultivate this relationship, the stronger your faith will become.

2. Embrace God's Promises:

God's promises are a source of strength and hope. Study and meditate on His promises found in the Bible, such as His love, provision, protection, and guidance. Trust in His faithfulness and believe that He will fulfill His promises in your life. Embracing these promises will help you overcome doubts and fears, and strengthen your faith.

3. Surround Yourself with a Supportive Community:

Being part of a supportive community of believers is essential for your spiritual growth. Seek out a church or fellowship where you can connect with like-minded individuals who can encourage, support, and mentor you on your faith journey. Share your struggles, victories, and doubts with them, and let them walk alongside you as you grow in your faith.

4. Develop a Spirit of Gratitude:

Gratitude is a powerful attitude that strengthens your faith. Cultivate a spirit of gratitude by recognizing and appreciating God's blessings, both big and small, in your life. Express your gratitude through prayer, thanksgiving, and acts of kindness. As you focus on the goodness of God, your faith will grow, and you will become unstoppable in your pursuit of His will.

5. Step Out in Faith:

An unstoppable woman of faith is not afraid to step out of her comfort zone and take risks for God's kingdom. Trust in His plan for your life and be willing to follow His leading, even when it seems uncertain or challenging. Step out in faith, knowing that God will equip and empower you to fulfill His purposes.

6. Persevere in the Face of Challenges:

Challenges and trials are inevitable in life, but as an unstoppable woman of faith, you can persevere through them. Lean on God's strength and rely on His promises during difficult times. Allow your faith to be a source of resilience and hope, knowing that God is with you every step of the way.

7. Be a Light to Others:

As an unstoppable woman of faith, your life can be a testimony to God's love and grace. Let your faith shine through your words, actions, and interactions with others. Show compassion, kindness, and forgiveness to those around you, and share the hope and joy that comes from knowing Jesus Christ. Be a light that draws others closer to God.

In conclusion, becoming an unstoppable woman of faith is a lifelong journey that requires a deep and unwavering belief in God. By seeking a personal relationship with Him, embracing His promises, surrounding yourself with a supportive community, cultivating gratitude, stepping out in faith, persevering through challenges, and being a light to others, you can become an unstoppable force for God's kingdom. Trust in His guidance, rely on His strength, and let your faith lead you to a life of purpose, impact, and fulfillment.

Suzanne E Minshew

Zannie Goods
Entrepreneur

https://www.facebook.com/sminshew/writer
https://www.instagram.com/zannie_minshew

Suzanne has a BA from Hiram College in Ohio and has had a successful career in hotel management, recruiting, career coaching and Healthcare. She is now a small business owner with years of volunteer work focused on fundraising. Throughout her career, she has been afforded the opportunity to do extensive amounts of writing from standard orders of procedures and company policies to employee hero stories, fundraising letters and press releases. In her personal life, she has written poetry and short stories for pure pleasure since childhood. She has spent her short life loving the Lord and is now eager to begin sharing her story as well as her personal journey of faith and healing.

Relentless Pursuit

By Suzanne E Minshew

Add 1 cup of sugar, 1 stick of butter, a whole lot of God. Mix, stir, blend, and boom! You have life perfected and reached the goal of being a whole woman of faith. I wish I could say to you that that is the perfect recipe for becoming an unstoppable woman of faith. Sadly, it isn't that simple. While most of life tastes better with sugar and butter added, becoming who I believe is an unstoppable woman of faith begins with me, and in your story, it begins with you. Each of us, individually, reaching out for God's hand to guide us. I can't say that I have the answers for you, but I can share my story and perhaps you might glean a little something to help you on your path with our loving Father.

Hindsight is 20/20 and today I see how the Lord made himself known and protected me throughout the years. When I was a small child, growing up in NE Ohio, I knew Jesus was with me and that God loved me. I don't believe I really understood the impact of that great love and companionship, I just knew what I knew and for my little self, I guess that was enough. As I grew, I went to church and camp and had Christian friends, who kept me on the straight and narrow. I got good grades, was involved in many school activities, and did my best to stay busy and away from what I now know was an unhealthy home life. My mom was a single mom and a closet alcoholic. She worked hard and provided for us beautifully, but being an elementary school teacher, she was exhausted by the time she got home and had little left for me. Much of my childhood was being shuffled, from one family member to another, from one activity to another, or alone. I have very few memories of my mom in my childhood, but I do remember the young gal who played the guitar and sang in our church. I remember summer vacation, Bible school, and the teacher I loved. I remember Grandma Loeffel, my babysitter during the week and at church on the weekends.

I remember Pastor Craig, who was gentle and kind, his wife, and his daughter, who was about my age and became my good friend. I remember feeling loved and feeling the love of Jesus through them.

In middle school, I went to a church not too far from my home. I walked to church, usually alone, but people knew me there and believed that I was well-liked. I didn't always stay past Sunday school, but at least, I was there. Truth was, I hated sitting alone. It was sad, awkward, and lonely. I wasn't mature enough at the time to accept that God was all I needed. During these formative years, God blessed me with the right friends in middle school, and each year, He solidified my friend group, adding and subtracting, but the core was solid, and each friend and their family provided a safety net for the gaps I had in me and insight to the inner workings of a family. They were God's angels for me.

My junior year in high school was when a fire for the Lord truly ignited in me. I was introduced to Youth for Christ in our town and the leader was so kind and so relatable that

I began to see my relationship with the Lord in a different way. A spring break trip to Florida with the group became the first time in my life that I truly felt alive. The way of worshiping the Lord was so foreign to me, but so beautifully comfortable. Who knew you could sing songs that weren't from a hymnal? Who knew that you could dance in the aisles and raise your hands to show Him how much you love Him? The experience changed my life. I knew Him, like never before. He was mine and I was His. I was still broken and flawed, but the Father had me.

In college, I was a fish out of water and never really found my groove or my place with God. I had put Him in the back seat and became desperate to fill the holes in me that only God could fill. I became an over-drinking, filled with shame, looking for love in all the wrong places, a square peg in a round hole environment. I was an out-of-control disaster and made many bad choices, resulting in experiences of trauma, death, loss, and even abuse. This 5 year period was very dark and I can see clearly how Satan had crept into my thoughts, causing me to believe lies about myself and of other people. Thankfully, I made it out, and have some great stories to tell because college was not all terrible. I was afforded many wonderful experiences and have some cherished memories, which gleaned lifelong friends.

What brought me back to God was hitting rock bottom. My choices had brought me to a point of either I lived or died, and I was too afraid to die, so I gave up trying. During this time in my life, God was with me, every step of the way. And while things got bad, they could have been so much worse. He knew my heart and while I could not see it, He protected and saved me repeatedly. Once I gave up the fight and surrendered everything, God took that broken lost child and put her back together so much more beautifully than I could have ever imagined. Intensive therapy, 12-step programs, praying, reading, and taking one baby step after another, God worked. He put strong, gentle, persistent women into my life to help me heal. I cried and screamed and cried some more until the angry wolf within my soul began to quiet. I was exhausted. My black-and-white world, not beautiful Ansel Adams' black and white, but ugly, jarring, startling, almost offensive to the senses black and white, began to soften around the edges, and hues of colors began to hint at emerging. I read my Bible, 12-step daily devotions, books on codependency, self-love, God's love, and others to heal my brokenness and correct my wrong thinking. I worked. I lived. I grew. Until, one day, my art-loving hippie therapist, whom I adored, said that it was time for her to quit the business and I was ready to do life on my own with God. I was sad, but I was not broken. I miss her today and wish I would have stayed in touch. She helped to save my life. Janet Faye Clark, if you're out there, THANK YOU!

Life continued with a relocation to Southern California for a wonderful job opportunity, my 18-month-old son in tow. Yes, I became a single mom in all that darkness. Next to God, my blue-eyed, tow-headed little boy, was my love, my life, and my purpose to move forward. In California, God presented an opportunity to rent a room from another single mom, with a child about the same age. The 6-ft-tall, red-headed, passionate about the Lord, roommate of mine also happened to lead a single moms group at the church around the corner. I was immediately plugged in and embraced. What an amazing gift! This time of my life was a bit of a reawakening, but also of growing up. Psychology tells us that the human brain doesn't stop forming until age 25 and if an individual experiences trauma, they can get emotionally stuck at that developmental stage, if they don't get the help needed to move past the trauma. I certainly experienced trauma over my life, though I can't pinpoint at what age or stage I became stuck. I stopped and started, made lots of mistakes, burnt bridges, hurt people and myself, so perhaps I got stuck at many different points, but just kept moving forward. God is good like that, offering grace and mercy and providing His people to help us along the way. Over the next year, the ladies in my single moms group became my confidants and cherished supports. They prayed for me, over me, and spoke truth and life into me. We went through a book called *Search for Significance* by Robert S. McGee. I don't remember specifically all that I learned, but I do remember being left with a new awareness that my significance was not in anything worldly, but only in God, the one who loves me perfectly and sees me as perfect. What a relief that I no longer had to "perform" and "people please" my way through life. I loved my church family, fell in love with the Lord in a new way, and recommitted myself in February of 1996. With my family and extended family present, I was baptized by full immersion. I truly felt my sin washed away that day and a new life began for me. I was still myself, with all the issues and baggage, but I was free and now more able to let God carry them for me.

I would love to say that once all of these things happened life was beautiful and perfect. It wasn't, but my path was gold and I was Dorothy dancing my way down the yellow brick road towards heaven. Along the way, on a cool evening night on the beach in Huntington Beach, at a church single's event, I met a very handsome, very tan young man with luscious dark hair and sparkling blue eyes that seemed to bore right through to my soul. His smile was so sweet and temperament gentle and kind. We talked for quite some time and I was TERRIFIED. Insert much laughter. After being so broken for so long and unable to maintain decent relationships with pretty much anyone, especially men, I was afraid that I would revert to old behaviors and ruin what might be something good and what God wanted for me. So, I trusted God and didn't get too excited, at least for the first five minutes. I will spare you the details of our courtship and marriage. It was wonderful and exciting. I was growing. God was there and He was smiling, likely laughing at how ridiculous I was! Yes, I married that handsome fellow and have been married for over 27 years.

God has been the one constant in my life and I certainly have done a lot of growing, but find that the greatest growth seems to have been in the roughest of times. I wish it weren't so, but that seems to be the trend, with me, anyway. The first year of marriage was an adjustment. Learning to trust this relationship to God's hands and continue to grow individually, as a couple, and as a family of 3 was a challenging and fulfilling balancing act. Pregnancy with baby #2 came along and contrary to my first child, I was very ill. Pregnancy exacerbated an issue I was already having with my gallbladder. Physically ill and turning shades of yellow, I had emergency surgery when the baby was 14 weeks gestational age. Surgery any earlier left little hope of the baby's survival, any later, it would have put the baby at a greater risk for injury as he would have been too big. My husband and I felt helpless and were forced to surrender it all to God. Sometimes many times in a day.

When all was said and done, the doctors marveled at how lucky I was. Our precious baby went full term and was born healthy with all fingers and toes intact. I say luck had nothing to do with it, it was all God. Holding that precious one in my arms and knowing that God held and kissed him before he became ours, solidified this and grew me more.

Life continued. I worked full-time, had 2 kids, a job transfer, and a thousand-mile relocation for graduate school for my husband. We had a full and busy life and we were happy. Going to church and raising our babies. Being good humans and trusting the Lord with all of it. It wasn't perfect, but it was our life and we loved it. We became pregnant unexpectedly a couple of years later and lost our little one, Anna, and were brokenhearted. This wasn't something I had experienced before nor was I prepared. I felt this loss so deeply. I grieved hard and God was with us. He held me and comforted me through the ache of losing our daughter, continuing His good work as He spoke through our pastor's prayers for us. "For you formed my inward parts, you knitted me together in my mother's womb." Psalm 139 with a heartfelt prayer to again fill my womb with another child, were it His will. From this, I felt a peace that transcends all understanding. My Anna was in the arms of Jesus along with my father, my husband's mother, and others we love in heaven. I healed over time and I grew. Having become accustomed to the idea of another child, we decided to try for another, and 9 months later, we welcomed our 3rd son.

Years went by, one child was diagnosed with Asperger's Syndrome; my husband was in the final stretch of graduate school; another child was molested by a friend; and I was exhausted from the load that I carried. I wish I could say that I surrendered it all to God and allowed myself to live fully. Sadly, that is not true. I battled depression and was attacked by Satan daily. It was at this point, my breaking point, that my husband went to work full-time while going to school, and I left my job to find healing for myself and my children. I was a dutiful, busy every minute of the day wife and mother, and while I was still connected with God and went to church, I felt lost and disconnected and alone. I had no tribe, no support. For me, my workplace was my tribe, and I didn't have that any longer. This was a realization that perhaps I had not established a balance in my life with God and the world. Either that or I did a huge backslide into the old people-pleasing behaviors I once lived by. Likely it was a combination of both. It truly is amazing to me how easily a backslide can happen and it took hitting rock bottom again, in order for me to allow God back into my heart to build me up again. Fortunately, it was not as low as before, so the transition was smoother, at least that is how I remember it. And so it began, again.

We all entered into therapy and the healing started in each of us. Our middle and oldest were removed from traditional school and we homeschooled. I began to connect with God in new ways. While I had grown up in church, I realized I had a very casual view of what my relationship with God should be, and that it should change, especially for our children. I read everything I could consume on all of our issues and how best to deal with each as a family and as a guide for each child, as well as how to deepen my relationship with God. I learned so much about being a better child of God, a better wife, a better mom, and simply, a better human being. Perhaps I shouldn't use the word "better" because, through the blood of Christ, God loves us and sees us as spotless and blameless. Maybe I just worked to be different. I was one way and because of Him, I am different. I worked hard on being different. I worked on forgiveness for myself and for those in my life who had hurt me. I worked to help my children and my husband with their issues separately and those we shared as a family, and I worked on me. God blessed me with a small tribe through the homeschool community and I am so grateful for their presence in my life. It was the support I desperately needed. There were no miracles during this time period, that I can recall, but there was a process of healing that occurred, treasured connectedness with my children, and much groundwork that was laid for the path before me and our family.

Years of boring normalcy passed and our middle son, age 14, alerted us to feeling sad and depressed, so we addressed it quickly as there was a predisposition to depression in our family. Long conversations turned into finding him help. I wish I could say that this was the answer to all of his issues, our issues, and that we lived happily ever after, but it wasn't. It felt like the beginning of a very long and painful battle of good vs evil for the souls of our children and the stability of our family. Satan had infiltrated our family and was attacking us one by one. He got a hold of our eldest son for a time, who had chosen drugs and bad choices. I cried buckets of tears, not knowing what to do, crying out to God for answers. So many prayed for that wayward son, and thankfully, God saved him. Today, our beautiful blue-eyed, tow-headed boy is in his 30s. He is in a successful career, happily married with 2 beautiful boys. Thank you, Jesus!

Navigating a full-time job and trying to keep our home healthy and happy for our family was not an easy task, but I did it. I can't say that I was successful, but I sure tried hard. Our middle son battled depression and went through years of counseling, medications and adjustments, side effects, biofeedback, suicidal ideation, attempts, and more. Anxiety and fear became my norm. Trips to the ER, hospitalizations, doctors and psychiatrists, it was never-ending The tenor of our home ebbed and flowed based on his condition. He was finally connected with our county mental health services, which was a blessing. I had become a case manager without even knowing it. He then developed anorexia/bulimia, went to inpatient treatment in WA, then to OR for outpatient treatment, and then home. He finished high school, began college, and was the chief caregiver for my elderly mother, who came to visit several years prior and became too ill to return home to Ohio. She passed away on March 12, 2018. This was a sad day for our family and a joy-filled one for her! She had lived a good life. One week later, unexpectedly, our middle son would decide that he no longer wished to live and made an attempt on his own life. For 5 days our little family watched as God and Satan battled for our boy and on March 27, 2018, he took his last breath and was in the arms of Jesus. He was 20. Our family of 5 was all together for the last time, and each of us broke in our own way as we left OHSU, Portland, OR, and him behind.

After our son died, our youngest boy, age 15 at the time of his brother's death, turned to drugs and alcohol to ease the pain of years of trauma, experiencing the constant stress and tension that dealing with someone with a mental illness can cause. He became a chronic runaway, disappearing for months at a time. The non-emergency number for the local police department was on speed dial. He was listed as a missing person multiple times, and I prayed. I couldn't grasp what he was going through, watching his brother go through years of mental illness and then losing his grandma and brother within two weeks. It's just too much for a person to handle, especially at such a young age. Zero coping skills, but feeling grown up enough to try to deal with it alone. Buckets of tears, cries of desperation, I couldn't imagine losing another child, but God. He was with me and with our boy. He eventually brought that boy home. Today he is 21, loves the Lord, is clean and sober, and works very hard at his dream job of being a mechanic. God is good!

Since our middle son passed, the Lord has done a tremendous amount of work in me. The traumatic events took me to a place I had never experienced before. The sights, sounds, and smells played over and over through my mind and senses. I immediately sought help through an EMDR therapist to soften those experiences so that I wasn't constantly feeling the rush of emotions that went along with those experiences.

After all was said and done with the memorial services for both my mom and my son, I sat for days, maybe weeks, staring out the back windows of our house watching the winds blow through the cottonwood trees. Tears were a constant stream down my face and neck. Life continued on, but for me, I felt like it had stopped. Breathing didn't come easily. Talking was scarce. Singing or humming was absent. I attempted prayer, but couldn't form the words. I know that God understood. He was with me, holding me, carrying me, so that I didn't fall into the abyss of despair. That was not, is not His plan for me. Jeremiah 29:11, "For I know the plans I have for you, plans to prosper you and not to harm you, plans to give you hope and a future, declares the Lord." I found many online groups that were grief and loss related, but kept myself down to a few, adding and deleting as my needs were refined or redefined. I met a beautiful soul in one group, Amy, who lost her son one week prior to mine. We made an instant connection and took it quickly to texting. We messaged several times daily and were it not for her, I can't imagine getting through all that I did. We have met once and talked a few times, but now do monthly check-ins. We have laughed and cried, prayed and grieved, cheered, and shared our mother's hearts. God truly blessed me when he gave me her.

I also read Psalms and Proverbs concurrently, starting at the beginning of Psalms and the end of Proverbs and reading my way to the middle. What a gift this task was for me. I had an assignment that I could check off my list every day, which in turn spoke to my grieving heart. Psalm 34:18, "The Lord is near to the brokenhearted and saves the crushed in spirit." It became a comforting verse that God tucked in my heart and I visited often. Oh, how I needed it then and can pull it out at any time to provide the comfort that I sometimes still need.

I was urgent to find healing, to find clarity in the chaos of emotion that I was experiencing, desperate to heal myself so I could help my family, so I attended as many support groups as I could. Survivors of Suicide, While We're Waiting, and Compassionate Friends. They are all wonderful groups, but early on, I felt the most connected and understood by those who had experienced suicide. The stories were similar, yet unique to each individual, and the emotions were so relatable. There was no illness or freak accident. This was intentional. The person was desperate to be out of pain, they made a choice, and we are the ones left behind. I believe that God placed, in those meetings, the right people with the right stories and feelings that began a beautiful healing in me. A healing of my relationship with God, as I may have blamed Him for a minute, with myself and from the greatest loss of my life. Life was hard, but God provided. The bills were paid and we were all physically healthy. People entered and left our lives. We were saddened by the seeming abandonment of our church family, but we moved on and so did they.

Attending church virtually can certainly be a wonderful thing, which we did when COVID hit and the world shut down. We were able to listen to pastors from all over, some of whom we still listen to, but I quickly learned that they cannot be the only way that one gets fed the word of God. Growth can certainly occur when listening to the word of God, but if you truly want to grow, get connected. Seriously, join a Bible study, a prayer group, or something. The church is filled with broken imperfect people, but when brought together truly seeking the will of God and growing in Him, it can be powerful. Several years ago, we moved from the neighborhood that we had lived in for almost 10 years, into a small rural community. After moving I received a sweet and gentle invitation to attend a Christian ladies' luncheon. I went and encountered the most welcoming, loving, giving, accepting, and encouraging women I have ever met. I can be transparent and authentic without fear of rejection or judgment. They truly have become my mentors, my friends, and my sisters. We study God's word and share our burdens, our blessings, and our lives. We pray with a fierceness that would frighten Satan and his demons. Best of all, we laugh together, cry together, and love each other dearly. From the time I was a little girl, this was the family I always wanted, but didn't know that I needed. God's goodness, once again.

Like I said in the beginning, there truly is no simple recipe to becoming an unstoppable woman of faith. This is my story and the simplest way to summarize it is that through every person I have met and every experience I have had, I have learned something and grown. I have learned to be grateful, even when life appears dismal. I have learned to forgive quickly because life is short. I have learned to love, to laugh, and to trust Him above all people and things. I have grown to love the Lord with every ounce of my being and hold my relationship with Him as the highest in my life. He is my Father and my friend. I strive to be **relentless** in my daily pursuit of developing a more intimate relationship with Him. And as each day passes, I seek to become a mightier force against evil and to love and serve people, as Jesus did and still does.

Dear one, I pray that you know our heavenly Father, just as I do, or even better. If you don't know Him, I pray that you will find your way into His arms. He is the way, the truth, and the light. Without Him, I would be nothing. With Him, I am whole!

> *"For God so loved that world that He gave his only son,*
> *that whosoever believes in Him shall have everlasting life"*
> *John 3:16.*

Theresa Savanah Dion

Spiritual Coach and Author

https://www.linkedin.com/in/theresa-savanah-d-9b18093a/
https://www.facebook.com/soulfullfilledconnect
https://www.instagram.com/soulfullfilledconnect
https://www.coachingsurmesure.com/

Theresa Savanah D. is an author and spiritual life coach and currently working on her third book. Grief coaching will also be offered in the near future. For the past 20years she has supported beautiful souls from all walks of life on their journey and her interest in well being stems from a young age, bringing with it many transitions that life put on her path. Having lived in Europe for seven years gave her a profound understanding of what it means to go through a transitional experience. She brings in her work a deep understanding of the spiritual component that comes when going through a life transition. In addition to the spiritual coaching, she has a passion for ancient philosophy, meditations and relaxation/self care techniques. Her passion and life mission is helping others being empowered, walk with self-confidence so they can flourish in their authentic self.

Faith, Soul, and Empowerment

By Theresa Savanah Dion

Faith. A five-letter word that has baffled me the better part of my life. After all, how can I live with it and yet live without it? Having lost my mother at a young age and becoming a single mother in my twenties, I needed faith. Even if consciously, I was not always aware of it. I grew up in a catholic family, my mother was deeply ingrained in her faith. I remember her sharing some of her beliefs during our afternoon resting period while my sisters were in school. Some of her faith I connected with, but some I did not.

At the time I was unsure if life was really molded that way for me. And yet, I believed in a Creator, some Higher Power. After all, who has the power to create this world? To create my soul?

My mother was very sick for most of my childhood. I guess her faith gave her strength to deal the best way she could with her illness. I don't recall much of her since I was ten years old when she passed. But what I do remember is that we went to funerals yearly until her passing. They seemed to stop thereafter or was it simply because my soul no longer needed that experience? To this day, into my sixties, I have been to more funerals in my life than weddings. So, I suppose faith has been, in a way, showing me a different angle to life. The art of letting go…

Going to church every Sunday while growing up was part of bonding with my mother. A strange concept perhaps but since her illness dominated our family life, I got glimpses of what it means to have no control over what faith may be. Growing up in a French-Canadian family, our perception of what life is supposed to be was very different. But that is another subject altogether.

In my early twenties, I became a mom, and it was during those years, I would say that I began soul-searching and describing what living with faith meant to me. Being a single parent early on taught me how living with faith was going to be the propeller for the rest of my life while remaining in the present moment. But first I had to define what faith was for me. What it meant. I had to define it so I could interact with it. So, I could identify with it.

I think you will agree that faith is no different than an illusion. It cannot be touched; it cannot be seen but it certainly can be felt. It gives us self-confidence and helps to take away the burdens that the mind likes at times to create for us. Engaging in life with faith helps us to see its challenges and obstacles with a different view. It helps us to make choices and decisions with an alternate sense of belonging. Somehow, we know deep within that we are not alone. That when we are aligned with faith, our soul knows the route to take. It has a blueprint to follow. And by doing so, we can feel more serenity and align with its Divine source, its Creator.

I've had several challenges throughout my life. From severe back issues and being deformed as a teenager, to learning to walk the path of self-love in my early forties. There is no way I could have made it without having a clear definition of what faith meant to me. During that time, it was then that I became inspired to learn how to live with faith. To walk alongside it. To allow its guidance to take form. After all, we cannot touch faith, but we can have glimpses of it.

What I've come to know for myself is that faith is directly tied to my soul. It is like my soul lives within it and faith lives within my soul and from there, it connects with the Divine essence. Faith for me is not a religious thing, it is a spiritual thing. It is to trust enough in life, so faith can lead the way. It's like it helps to detangle what no longer serves and opens the door to what is meant to be.

One of many examples of when I had to let faith take the lead was when I left my twenty-year relationship in my mid-forties. The relationship had become emotionally stagnant. I supposed our soul contract of being together was no longer beneficial for its evolution. There were a lot of uncertainties because I had not built a solid foundation for myself. All the choices I had made were predominantly based on what the need to be a couple was. I was emotionally attached to the relationship and was not faced with reinventing myself. Needless to say; it took me months to untangle what my soul had to experience and the teachings that stemmed from being together. I had no option but to depend on my faith that all was going to be fine. No matter what.

During the relationship transition, I no longer could *figure it out* from a logical perspective because it became counterintuitive. The transition of having to reinvent and reconnect with myself was challenging enough. I did not need intrusion from the fear that this transition was bringing. And since faith cannot be seen or touched, the only option I gravitated towards was to soul connect because I knew that my soul lived with my faith. And from there, guidance was able to take form.

Living with faith is not easy because we often want to control the outcome, to keep some kind of reassurance that we can see the end of the road clearly. However, from my personal experience and the challenges that were put on my path over my sixty years, all the outcomes came because of having faith. And they were more of a blessing than I could have anticipated.

Imagine if we knew everything in advance, there are many choices we would not make. Decisions we would abstain from, which would be very counterintuitive.

There is also another side to faith. It needs to be integrated within. As much as it is not something we can see nor touch, it is important to integrate it within and not see us separate from its essence. It is easy for us to say that *faith will take care of it* as if it is a separate thing. But what

I came to realize is that it is part of me, part of my soul so it must be integrated into my daily life. Integrating it means changing my perception of how something should be; it is to trust that things will turn out exactly as it is intended at a soul level. It is to allow my intuition to guide me with clarity when I am called to decide and pass into action; to know that when I choose to be aligned with my faith, I feel and walk with more self-confidence because I know deep within that behind every occurings, there is a blessing. A wink from the Creator.

So, it means that each decision, each choice that life brings to me daily, by tuning into my soul and having faith, that all is aligned as Divinely intended.

I've had to make unconventional choices over the course of my life. Choices that got me outside of my comfort zone. Some of them were challenging, others felt like a breeze. However, the most important thing I have learned is that, when choices are made from faith, no matter how challenging and unconventional they are, the end is always as it is meant to be. Even if I had to walk through the darker side of my soul which entailed doing deeper inner work.

I also realized that sometimes we are called to make choices for the sole benefit of another. By that I mean, at times we need to lead the way for another person to live in their faith. At least for that person to begin walking in faith.

I've always known that I am not a *conventional* type of mother, however, I will say this. For about one year, I lived with my son and during that transitional phase of my life, I learned a valuable lesson. An adult child cannot be parented. It was one of the most challenging experiences, more likely for both of us, but since faith had put me in that situation, it was also what was needed for both of us. My soul needed to show me a different way of being and I am sure it opened the door for my son as well even though I cannot speak for his soul experience. You see, if I had tried to fight against my being at his place for that year, it would not have served what I needed to experience at a soul level. And yet I lived out of faith to move through this transitional phase. Often, we do not know the end result, but we certainly can feel the blessings that emerge from the occurrence. The main takeaway from this experience for me was that I cannot parent an adult child. No matter how much I try or feel guilty of not doing so.

Living in faith is like a trigger for something bigger to take the reins at different times in our lives. It is up to us to go with it or against it. To try to control and remain in our comfort zone or choose to take the leap. It can be viewed as a sacrifice or a blessing. The beauty is it is up to us, in how we perceive it. But one thing for sure is that it is difficult to live without it.

Being outside of our comfort zone is not pleasant because we often like to keep control of the *what-ifs*. When we are aligned in faith, however, we tend to find some kind of comfort when propelled outside of familiarity.

The mind, what I like to call like the Buddhist do, the monkey mind, likes to keep tabs on me. Especially, in my thoughts and beliefs. When I look back, I can objectively see that often, I have found myself outside of my comfort zone. These were times when extra faith was needed. Times when I had to let my soul take the lead and be graced by the power of living in faith.

We often like to determine what we are willing to experience and what we are not willing to. We may think or believe that something is not for us. What is fascinating to me is how we think we can have control over our lives through the choices we make. But what I also have observed for myself and in others is that we often make unconscious decisions because we are not in the present moment, which is when we can feel faith in action.

You see, faith that is part of our soul has no timeline when it comes to the present moment. Let me explain what I mean by that.

An example is when I was preparing to return to Canada after living and working in Europe for seven years. The work contract I had ended in the summer of 2016 and I had decided to stay in Europe and look for something else, even though I was not fully convinced I was going to remain in Europe. I had an inner dilemma that needed to be worked through, and that needed clarification on my part. Simultaneously, after my work contract ended, I had to leave the place I was at. So, along with the practicality of work, I now needed a place to stay.

During my time in Europe, I trained to follow my passion and become a life coach. I met a woman who became what I call my physical angel because she helped me to the best of her abilities during this time. She was without a doubt put on my path by faith. Or perhaps it was faith that led me to take the training so I could meet her...

I had no idea if I was going to find a place or not. With no work and on a different continent, it was not so easy, to say the least. Time was running out and there was no place in sight for me to have this checked off my to-do list.

So, one morning, I got in my car and began driving. It felt like the best thing to do. Whenever I feel I need to align with faith and connect with my soul, I drive. It is like meditation for me. In simple terms, I needed to let go of the fear and control of the conditions put on by my monkey mind and the fear of *what-ifs*.

Anyways, low and behold, this same physical angel friend gave me a call later that day, saying that she knew of a room that was going to be available for 300.00 Euros. I was shocked. The condition for me having the room was that I had to say yes right away, without even seeing it.

YES, of course! I shouted and took the room. That part was resolved.

Well, it turned out the room was in an old residence for nuns that was now rented to ladies only and my friend heard about it because her office was located on the first floor. There were still a couple of nuns living on site, and business offices on the first floor.

Choosing to let go of the fear and worry and going instead for a drive allowed me to align with faith; to see this experience as a way to connect with my soul resulting in providing exactly what I needed. It was perfect and effortless. What was needed was to get out of control, merge with synchronicity of life, and align with faith. Connect with my soul and have faith that the solution was already present. Driving kept me in the present moment which is what I needed to focus on. The solution was already within. The dots were connected. I just needed to get out of my own way, of the inner limiting beliefs I held of potentially not finding a place.

There are many examples I can write about. But what matters is how I allowed faith to guide me, after all, it lies within my soul. And if my soul has my life's blueprint and by believing, it will unfold no matter what. The solution of having the room came in like a breeze. From there, I was able to determine if remaining in Europe and working was for my highest good, which turned out not to be. So, after a few months, I returned home.

- And you, how do you see or feel the presence of faith in your life?
- How does its presence support you daily?
- Do you live your life based on faith or is it some abstract concept?

Throughout my twenties, I intuitively knew how important it would be for me to define what faith means. I came to understand that faith is made up of different backgrounds and cultures and may even be social conditionings for some. And for others, it is a natural thing. We certainly hold an intention when we align in faith. It's like we feel that something is beyond our human capacities. It is to surrender to what we cannot see but feel its presence.

For some, faith may be part of a philosophical concept. I suppose in a way it can be categorized like that. We can easily get in the way of faith and not let it unfold as it should. And yet, I'm not sure we can control its purpose. It catches up sooner rather than later. We may feel we embark on some kind of terrain that is not paved but becomes once we step onto it.

It's an internal process where seeing the outcome can take time as we blaze through the trials and tribulations. One thing I know for myself is that the outcome has always carried a blessing and worked out for my highest good often in hindsight.

Aligning with faith helps us to move out of linear thinking because there is no precision or time frame given. It is like we interact with this illusion that becomes driven with intention. This ethereal intense essence that resides within each one of us.

Whether we call it trust or faith, it reflects in many aspects of our lives. Which is interesting. We have faith or trust in the undertaking of a business concept we want to develop. We trust or have faith that we will find the right position when it comes to work. We can also put our faith in someone. And most importantly, we have faith in ourselves; at least, we should first and foremost.

My foundation and philosophy in life is to ask why I need to trust. Why do I need to have faith and hold the intention that the solutions and what is needed are already there? For me, it is the essence of having faith, of trusting.

I also know we can lose faith; I sure have in times of desperation. One example is during a period of financial setbacks. No matter what I tried, no matter how I had worked on my belief around money during my thirties, there was a period where I lost faith that I was going to be financially okay. Life has taught me a challenging lesson. As you know, I grew up with the illness of my mother. My father, whom I think had enough worries with my mother, was emotionally distant. In fact, I did not learn proper skills from my father throughout my childhood. Skills such as healthy management of money. So, when I left my twenty-year relationship, I was facing a wall because all my faith was financially in the man I was with. Now being on my own, I had no alternative but to learn about money.

I always believed money is an energy, a vibration, however, how do you align with this energy? One mentality my father held, bless his soul, is scarcity mentality and how money does not grow on trees. Sounds familiar? That was a big one to detach from. In my healing process, I realized that this scarcity mentality had been part of a deeply ingrained belief in me and how it affected all aspects of my life. After all, I didn't really need to think too much about money because I had faith in the man I was with. He was taking care of it. However, when I left the relationship, the first thing that went with it was me losing my faith because I was not with him anymore. I lost faith that I would be okay, that my needs were going to be met no matter what. I went through a phase of losing faith that there was a deeper reason I needed to leave the relationship, even though I was not able to see it yet. And yet, I trusted the fact that I needed to take action.

The point I am making here is that when I realized that I had all my financial faith in this one person, when that part of my life collapsed, my faith went with it because I was still holding on to this ingrained belief from my dad. So, I was faced with doing my inner work around that belief and transforming it by first having faith in my soul, in life, and in myself that I would find a way out and feel more at ease with the energy of money. I am making a long story short by sharing this but I think you get the idea of how we can put too much trust or faith in something or someone outside of ourselves without checking in ourselves first.

There are many other experiences I could share here with you where faith was taking over. Where faith was leading the way simply because I had no choice but to live in faith.

I suppose it can also be counterproductive to just let fate take its hold. You see, for me the solution to any transition I have been through presented itself after I am not only decided on something that life put on my path, but also to take action when the solution was there.

It is a fine line, I get that. We can easily misunderstand the meaning of faith. We can also view it as a coincidence. A coincidence that this person was there so why not? A coincidence that a particular meeting simply took place.

It is definitely a question of how we individually perceive faith to be. What role it plays or our belief of what it is. We may think it is something that happens out of our control to which I would agree. For me, faith is something I need to hold in my intention, in my belief, and from there, options and circumstances will arise for me to align with faith by taking action. You see, I also think for faith to guide us on our spiritual path, we need to first make a decision and then act on that decision.

There was a solution that presented itself to me when I left my twenty-year relationship. What I needed to do was make the decision, do self-care and be intuitively aware of the opportunities put on my path. All the while aligning with faith. At a soul level, I had to leave because our soul contract was no longer fulfilling its purpose. On a faith level, doors were opening.

It is the same for the room to show up and not end up being homeless on a different continent, like countless times in my life where blessings took place as a result of having faith.

In any of the transitions and challenges life has put on my path, it propelled me to deepen my faith by meditating, self-reflecting, journal writing, speaking with my mentor or a close friend, and doing a whole lot of self-care. And as a result, what seemed at first to be scary and challenging came without effort. I had to get out of my own way and allow myself to see the Creator's blink.

In conclusion, there is no guarantee in life that is for sure. but when we allow our perception of what it should be to be what it is, it sure helps with moving forward with self-confidence, faith, and being soul-empowered.

As an author and spiritual life coach, my work entails empowering ladies in their fifties and beyond to be the best version of themselves at all levels. Spiritually by being soul-empowered while living in faith, walk with self-confidence that they are on the right path which will affect all aspects of one's life. May it relate to business, work, relationship, and life purpose.

Living with faith helps us make decisions with intuitive clarity, with soul-driven purpose. It helps us be authentic in who we are and how we respond to life in general.

I love this saying by Tony Robbins: "Life happens for us, not to us."

Whether we believe faith to be a religious or spiritual part of life, it nevertheless remains an integral part of life. After all, what would we be without it?

Here are some questions to assist you in defining what faith means for you:

- Is faith a belief I hold that is interchangeable depending on the circumstances that take place in my life? Or is holding my intention in having faith whenever I feel guided to come naturally?

- Is faith an abstract concept or is it something I know truly exists because I have felt its gracefulness at different times?
- Describe a time when you knew faith was on your side. Where you felt soul-empowered and had intuitive clarity to make a decision and take action. What was the result? What were the steps you felt inspired to take?

Food for thought...

In the Old Testament, Abraham is regarded as the head of the covenant line, which is personified in the house of Israel. He is often called the "father of the faithful." Abraham reflected this, and he is known as the "father of the faithful" (Romans 4:16).

By faith Abraham, when he was called to go out into a place, which he should after receive for an inheritance, obeyed; and he went out, not knowing whither he went. By faith he sojourned in the land of promise, as in a strange country, dwelling in tabernacles with Isaac and Jacob, the heirs with him of the same promise: For he looked for a city which hath foundations, whose builder and maker is God. (https://www.focusongod.com/change.htm) - (Hebrews 11:8-10)

Toks Omowunmi Olunloyo

Purple Patch Cereals
Mom Coach | Food Business Mentor | Speaker

https://www.linkedin.com/in/toks-omowunmi-olunloyo-58363110
https://www.facebook.com/OmowunmiOlunloyo/
https://www.instagram.com/omowunmi_toks/
https://purplepatchcereals.co.uk/
https://linktr.ee/toksolunloyo

Omowunmi Olunloyo, known as Toks, is a multifaceted professional with over a decade of experience as a busy working mother coach, food technologist, bestselling author, film producer, and speaker. She has graced the airwaves of Reconcilers Radio, Hope FM, and Premier Christian Radio and received prestigious accolades like the Courageous Award. As the Owner of Purple Patch Cereals, an award-winning breakfast cereal brand, she fulfils her dream of providing healthy food for health-conscious families. Toks also heads Peacock Omowunmi Production, releasing her debut movie "Hustle" to acclaim on Amazon Prime. Her journey from personal struggles to empowerment drives her mission to help women especially mothers find purpose and fulfilment, highlighted in her international bestselling books, The Purpose Driven Lady magazine, and Motherhood Aid CIC. Respected for her loyalty and inspiration, Toks empowers busy working mothers to thrive in every aspect of life.

Empowered by Grace:
The Journey to Becoming a Woman of Faith

By Toks Omowunmi Olunloyo

Introduction

In a world that constantly challenges our beliefs and values, standing firm in faith can be an overwhelming endeavor. Yet, it is in these very challenges that our faith is tried and tested, and our character is strengthened. "Becoming An Unstoppable Woman in Faith" is a journey of discovering and embracing the divine power within us, empowering us to overcome obstacles, encourage others, and inspire change.

Embracing My Identity in Christ

As a woman of faith, my journey began with understanding and embracing my identity in Christ. Knowing who we are in Him lays the foundation for a life of purpose and power.

The Bible tells us, "But you are a chosen race, a royal priesthood, a holy nation, a people for his own possession, that you may proclaim the excellencies of him who called you out of darkness into his marvelous light" (1 Peter 2:9, ESV). This scripture reminds us that we are chosen and set apart for a divine purpose.

When we grasp who we truly are in Him, we unlock the potential to live out our God-given purpose with confidence and authority. Our identity in Christ is more than a title; it is the essence of who we are as believers. The Apostle Paul writes, "Therefore, if anyone is in Christ, the new creation has come: The old has gone, the new is here!" (2 Corinthians 5:17, NIV). This verse encapsulates the transformative power of accepting Christ into our lives. We are not defined by our past mistakes, our failures, or even our successes. Instead, we are defined by the love and grace of Jesus Christ.

In Christ, we are

- Loved: "For we are God's masterpiece. He has created us anew in Christ Jesus, so we can do the good things he planned for us long ago" (Ephesians 2:10, NLT). Understanding that we are God's masterpieces helps us see our worth through His eyes.
- Forgiven: "In him we have redemption through his blood, the forgiveness of sins, in accordance with the riches of God's grace" (Ephesians 1:7, NIV). Our past sins are forgiven, and we are given a fresh start.
- Chosen: "But you are a chosen people, a royal priesthood, a holy nation, God's special possession, that you may declare the praises of him who called you out of darkness into his wonderful light" (1 Peter 2:9, NIV). We are chosen by God for a unique purpose.

Once I understood my identity in Christ, I began to live with purpose. God has a specific plan for each of our lives and discovering that purpose is a journey of faith. Jeremiah 29:11 (NIV) reassures us, "For I know the plans I have for you," declares the Lord, "plans to prosper you and not to harm you, plans to give you hope and a future." This verse is a promise that God has a good plan for our lives, one that is filled with hope and a future.

This is my understanding of what living with purpose means:

1. Seeking God's Guidance
2. Using My Gifts and Talents
3. Stepping Out in Faith

I began to walk in authority. As a child of God, we have been given authority in Christ to overcome challenges and impact the world around us. Jesus said, "I have given you authority to trample on snakes and scorpions and to overcome all the power of the enemy; nothing will harm you" (Luke 10:19, NIV). This authority is not of our own making; it is given to us by Jesus Christ.

This is my understanding of what walking in authority means:

1. Claiming God's Promises
2. Praying with Confidence
3. Living Boldly

Embracing my identity in Christ is not a one-time event but a daily walk of faith. It involved continuously renewing my mind and aligning my thoughts with God's word.

Steps to change

1. Daily Affirmations: I start each day by affirming who I am in Christ. I speak out scriptures that declare my identity and purpose.
2. Journaling: I keep a journal to document my day. I write down everything from revelations from God's Word, answered prayers, testimonies, and gratitude.
3. Accountability: I find a trusted friend to walk with me on this journey. I share my struggles and victories and we encourage each other to stay rooted in our identity in Christ.

Embracing my identity in Christ was the first step in becoming an unstoppable woman in faith. It laid the foundation for a life of purpose, power, and impact. As I grew in my understanding of who I am in Christ, I found the confidence and strength to face challenges and fulfill my God-given purpose.

Remember, you are loved, forgiven, and chosen by God. Walk boldly in your identity and let your life be a testament to His grace and power.

By embracing our identity in Christ, we position ourselves to live out our faith with unshakable confidence and divine authority. This foundational understanding empowers us to navigate life's challenges, serve others with our unique gifts, and step boldly into the purpose God has for us.

This will be a good place to share my journey with you, how I became this Unstoppable Woman in Faith.

The Beginning

In 2004, I arrived in the UK seeking greener pastures. I came with a passion to serve, a commitment to make a difference, and a vision to create lasting impact. However, the journey was anything but smooth. I faced valley moments where every aspect of her life was crumbling—from my career, family, finances, and love life. The challenges were immense, and I often felt lonely and insecure, although no one else knew it but me.

I did not know my worth, I did not love myself, I was anything but myself. Despite the psychological trauma, low self-esteem, and constant struggle to fit in, I had an assignment. I desired to help women, especially mothers, find their place, position, and purpose in life so they could live their best lives. However, with my own life in turmoil, I couldn't see how my vision could become a reality.

My faith empowerment story is the story of not appreciating myself, thinking I was not beautiful, and a people pleaser with low self-esteem. I struggled for over 20 years of my life, and I got to the place where I was just working and serving, trying to do everything to earn people's love and trust and have a reputation for myself. I even did a lot of training just to have qualifications so that I could be respected.

Turnaround

The change came when I attended a women's conference in Chicago; the theme was "The Supernatural Woman." It was at the conference that I had light-bulb moments, I realized for once in my life that I didn't have to be everything to everyone, that I was enough just the way I was. My life was complete and designed just for me.

I dropped everything I was doing when I came back from the conference and I went to church. I dropped most of the positions I occupied because I was on a mission to find myself again. I stopped driving to work; I got on the bus so I could read my Bible, reflect, and journal. It was during this time that I started loving myself again. I found my place, position, and purpose. That is my journey of discovery and the quality of my life improved.

I'm now a woman of purpose sharing my story of how God loves me more than anything in the whole wide world and that I can Be, Do, and Have. I am enjoying myself as much as I can and being the best version of myself, so, no more people pleasing.

I am a top UK Women Empowerment Coach, Speaker, and Mentor. Exemplifying the Proverbs 31 woman, skilfully leading in my roles as a woman, wife, and working mother. I utilized my skills and talents in various ways, including managing administration in children's church, joining the sign language ministry, acting, teaching, singing, dancing, and event management, to name a few.

Friends describe me as loyal, inspirational, and a woman whose words empower and motivate people, especially busy working mothers, to fulfill their destinies.

Overcoming Fear and Doubt

Now a reformed, intentional woman living on purpose, free from condemnation, lack, and low self-esteem, I use my own story to motivate, encourage, and empower other women. A plain-spoken, ever-bubbly lady, as I am often described, with a knack for simplifying circumstances, breaking them down into step-by-step formulas that are easy to follow, make sense, and can be applied instantly for immediate results. This is my reality now.

Right now, I do so many things, I can't even begin to count, the energy I have is unbelievable. I know it is the grace of God, from the moment I was able to accept me, love me, and accept the love of God, my life has not been the same again. I also forgave myself and others who I was holding hostage in my heart.

My life, honestly, has been transformed remarkably. I can't even begin to list the blessings that I have received afterwards from freedom in my heart: The weight being lifted from my shoulder, financial increase, amazing relationship, bigger exposure and connection, my business booming with opportunities to meet people, be a speaker at events, and do the things that I love to do.

I started organizing meetings to inspire women to live their desired lifestyles. The beginnings were humble, with just five attendees—all of whom were family members. However, as my reputation grew, so did my audience. My brand expanded because I dared to believe in my uniqueness and embraced being different. I am Enough.

In 2014, I hosted my first Women in Purpose conference, which was well-attended and gave birth to the "Find Your Place, Position & Purpose Blueprint." I show busy working mothers who feel stressed, overwhelmed, and out of control how to develop a road map that supports them, allowing them to regain control of all aspects of their lives. This leads to fulfillment, happiness, and better results.

I am a mom coach. I empower busy working mothers through my unique transformational program. These mothers, who feel like their search for fulfillment is heading nowhere or that their efforts are not yielding results, learn to reorganize their busy lifestyles. This allows them to prioritize what is truly important and achieve better results within 30 days or less. My message is simple: No more procrastination, no more excuses, no more reasons why—simply put, no more delays! This challenges women to take charge of their lives and become accountable.

Through my work, I help my clients fully embrace their true selves, uncover their purpose, identify roadblocks to that purpose, and create a road map to success.

I feel like a superstar, a headliner if you can imagine with me, just because I am in my place and that's really my faith story. So, from low self-esteem to this person who is now living a life of purpose, I am in the entertainment space; I have a movie on Amazon Prime called *Hustle*, it's Nollywood; I am a fashion model; a food business mentor; I own a food business, cereals to be specific, an award-winning brand—Purple Patch Cereals.

I was elected President of Day Star Acquisition Program Set 36 in 2022 where one of my major accomplishments was raising close to half a million naira for the organization.

I have written six books, of which four are anthologies; this is my seventh anthology. I am an international best-selling author. The recent launch of my growing online magazine in 2016, *The Purpose Driven Lady*, is gaining ground and becoming increasingly popular. It is on Issue 10 at the moment, written by women for women to spread the message of living a life of purpose.

I registered my Community Interest Company (CIC) in 2023, Motherhood Aid, which supports women, especially mothers, to thrive and enjoy the motherhood experience.

I was appointed Zonal Coordinator for APC Professional Women's Council in 2023, Diaspora Coordinator, and Head of Training & Development in 2024.

I host online summits/conferences, I do a lot of MCs/Red Carpet and moderation for events online and offline for book launches, birthdays, and weddings.

I have spoken on different platforms on topics supporting motherhood, childhood, and womanhood.

Since embarking on this path to empower, encourage, and educate others, I have appeared on Reconcilers Radio, Hope FM, Kids & Mum, and Premier Christian Radio and received prestigious accolades like the Courageous Award & Lift Effects Star Award and Meghan Award.

Nominated for Entrepreneur of the Year and Mentor of the Year at the Wholelife Activation Awards, and Positive Role Model Award in 2018. Featured in digital publications such as Women Empowering Women Magazine, Bounce Back In Style, and The Purpose Driven Lady Magazine.

I am married with three boys and my youngest is three.

Doors are open to me because I dared to believe that just maybe I am that special, unique, and different, and that is absolutely fine. I simply believed that I could, and I did. I am now a minister of enjoyment. I rest and receive.

I keep saying it, I am the woman who God loves, and I am helped by God.

Closing words

My journey has not only been about personal growth but also about making a significant impact on others. My vision to help women especially mothers find their purpose and live their best lives has become a reality. I continue to inspire women to take charge of their lives and pursue their dreams with confidence and determination.

My message to women is clear: live with purpose, make conscious decisions to be the best version of yourself, and remember that you are not in competition with anyone. You are unique, special, and one of a kind. Life is for living, and you are here once; you might as well live your best life ever.

My life story is a testament to the power of faith, resilience, and the unwavering belief that even in the darkest times, there is hope and a way forward. I hope that my story is a source of inspiration for you reading this book.

As you embrace your journey of becoming an unstoppable woman in faith, remember that you are not alone, God is with you every step of the way empowering you, and remember the lessons from my story:

1. Embracing Your Identity in Christ: "Therefore, if anyone is in Christ, he is a new creation. The old has passed away; behold, the new has come." (2 Corinthians 5:17)
2. Cultivating Unshakable Faith: "Now faith is the assurance of things hoped for, the conviction of things not seen." (Hebrews 11:1)
3. Overcoming Fear and Doubt: "For God gave us a spirit not of fear but of power and love and self-control." (2 Timothy 1:7)
4. Harnessing the Power of Prayer: "Do not be anxious about anything, but in everything by prayer and supplication with thanksgiving let your requests be made known to God." (Philippians 4:6)
5. Living a Life of Worship: "But the hour is coming, and is now here, when the true worshipers will worship the Father in spirit and truth, for the Father is seeking such people to worship him." (John 4:23)
6. Building Godly Relationships: "Iron sharpens iron, and one man sharpens another." (Proverbs 27:17)

7. Embracing Your Unique Calling: "For we are his workmanship, created in Christ Jesus for good works, which God prepared beforehand, that we should walk in them." (Ephesians 2:10)

8. Persevering Through Trials: "Count it all joy, my brothers, when you meet trials of various kinds, for you know that the testing of your faith produces steadfastness." (James 1:2-3)

9. Leading with Love: "A new commandment I give to you, that you love one another: just as I have loved you, you also are to love one another." (John 13:34)

10. Living with Boldness and Courage: "Be strong and courageous. Do not be frightened, and do not be dismayed, for the Lord your God is with you wherever you go." (Joshua 1:9)

Reflection

Think of a bold step of faith you can take this week. Write down any fears that are holding you back and pray for the courage to overcome them.

I am so grateful to all of you for your passion, sense of purpose, and your dedication. And I can think of no better way to end my story than celebrating you for taking the bold step to become an unstoppable woman in faith. So, I want to close by saying thank you. Thank you for believing in yourself enough to invest in your faith, personal development, and growth. Being a co-author in the *Becoming An Unstoppable Woman In Faith* series is one of the greatest honors of my life, and I hope I have inspired you and shined a torch of light and hope on you.

JOIN THE MOVEMENT!
#BAUW

Becoming An Unstoppable Woman
With She Rises Studios

She Rises Studios was founded by Hanna Olivas and Adriana Luna Carlos, the mother-daughter duo, in mid-2020 as they saw a need to help empower women worldwide. They are the podcast hosts of the *She Rises Studios Podcast* and Amazon best-selling authors and motivational speakers who travel the world. Hanna and Adriana are the movement creators of #BAUW - Becoming An Unstoppable Woman: The movement has been created to universally impact women of all ages, at whatever stage of life, to overcome insecurities, and adversities, and develop an unstoppable mindset. She Rises Studios educates, celebrates, and empowers women globally.

Looking to Join Us in our Next Anthology or Publish YOUR Own?

She Rises Studios Publishing offers full-service publishing, marketing, book tour, and campaign services. For more information, contact info@sherisesstudios.com

We are always looking for women who want to share their stories and expertise and feature their businesses on our podcasts, in our books, and in our magazines.

SEE WHAT WE DO

OUR PODCAST   **OUR BOOKS**   **OUR SERVICES**

Be featured in the Becoming An Unstoppable Woman magazine, published in 13 countries and sold in all major retailers. Get the visibility you need to LEVEL UP in your business!

Have your own TV show streamed across major platforms like Roku TV, Amazon Fire Stick, Apple TV and more!

Learn to leverage your expertise. Build your online presence and grow your audience with FENIX TV.
https://fenixtv.sherisesstudios.com/

Visit www.SheRisesStudios.com to see how YOU can join the #BAUW movement and help your community to achieve the UNSTOPPABLE mindset.

Have you checked out the *She Rises Studios Podcast?*

Find us on all MAJOR platforms: Spotify, IHeartRadio, Apple Podcasts, Google Podcasts, etc.

Looking to become a sponsor or build a partnership?

Email us at info@sherisesstudios.com

SHE RISES
STUDIOS